BIG IDEAS
MATH.
Modeling Real Life

Grade 4

Volume 2

Ron Larson
Laurie Boswell

BIG IDEAS
LEARNING.

Erie, Pennsylvania
BigIdeasLearning.com

Big Ideas Learning, LLC
1762 Norcross Road
Erie, PA 16510-3838
USA

For product information and customer support, contact Big Ideas Learning
at 1-877-552-7766 or visit us at BigIdeasLearning.com.

Cover Image
Valdis Torms, Brazhnykov Andriy/Shutterstock.com

Copyright © 2019 by Big Ideas Learning, LLC. All rights reserved.

No part of this work may be reproduced or transmitted in any form or by any means,
electronic or mechanical, including, but not limited to, photocopying and recording, or
by any information storage or retrieval system, without prior written permission of
Big Ideas Learning, LLC, unless such copying is expressly permitted by copyright law.
Address inquiries to Permissions, Big Ideas Learning, LLC, 1762 Norcross Road,
Erie, PA 16510.

Big Ideas Learning and Big Ideas Math are registered trademarks of Larson Texts, Inc.

Printed in the U.S.A.

ISBN 13: 978-1-63598-890-1

5 6 7 8 9 10—22 21

About the Authors

Ron Larson

Ron Larson, Ph.D., is well known as the lead author of a comprehensive program for mathematics that spans school mathematics and college courses. He holds the distinction of Professor Emeritus from Penn State Erie, The Behrend College, where he taught for nearly 40 years. He received his Ph.D. in mathematics from the University of Colorado. Dr. Larson's numerous professional activities keep him actively involved in the mathematics education community and allow him to fully understand the needs of students, teachers, supervisors, and administrators.

Ron Larson

Laurie Boswell

Laurie Boswell, Ed.D., is the former Head of School at Riverside School in Lyndonville, Vermont. In addition to textbook authoring, she provides mathematics consulting and embedded coaching sessions. Dr. Boswell received her Ed.D. from the University of Vermont in 2010. She is a recipient of the Presidential Award for Excellence in Mathematics Teaching and is a Tandy Technology Scholar. Laurie has taught math to students at all levels, elementary through college. In addition, Laurie has served on the NCTM Board of Directors and as a Regional Director for NCSM. Along with Ron, Laurie has co-authored numerous math programs and has become a popular national speaker.

Laurie Boswell
Laurie Boswell

Dr. Ron Larson and Dr. Laurie Boswell began writing together in 1992. Since that time, they have authored over four dozen textbooks. This successful collaboration allows for one voice from Kindergarten through Algebra 2.

Contributors, Reviewers, and Research

Big Ideas Learning would like to express our gratitude to the mathematics education and instruction experts who served as our advisory panel, contributing specialists, and reviewers during the writing of *Big Ideas Math: Modeling Real Life*. Their input was an invaluable asset during the development of this program.

Contributing Specialists and Reviewers

- **Sophie Murphy**, Ph.D. Candidate, Melbourne School of Education, Melbourne, Australia
  Learning Targets and Success Criteria Specialist and Visible Learning Reviewer

- **Linda Hall**, Mathematics Educational Consultant, Edmond, OK
  Advisory Panel

- **Michael McDowell**, Ed.D., Superintendent, Ross, CA
  Project-Based Learning Specialist

- **Kelly Byrne**, Math Supervisor and Coordinator of Data Analysis, Downingtown, PA
  Advisory Panel

- **Jean Carwin**, Math Specialist/TOSA, Snohomish, WA
  Advisory Panel

- **Nancy Siddens**, Independent Language Teaching Consultant, Las Cruces, NM
  English Language Learner Specialist

- **Kristen Karbon**, Curriculum and Assessment Coordinator, Troy, MI
  Advisory Panel

- **Kery Obradovich**, K–8 Math/Science Coordinator, Northbrook, IL
  Advisory Panel

- **Jennifer Rollins**, Math Curriculum Content Specialist, Golden, CO
  Advisory Panel

- **Becky Walker**, Ph.D., School Improvement Services Director, Green Bay, WI
  Advisory Panel and Content Reviewer

- **Deborah Donovan**, Mathematics Consultant, Lexington, SC
  Content Reviewer

- **Tom Muchlinski**, Ph.D., Mathematics Consultant, Plymouth, MN
  Content Reviewer and Teaching Edition Contributor

- **Mary Goetz**, Elementary School Teacher, Troy, MI
  Content Reviewer

- **Nanci N. Smith**, Ph.D., International Curriculum and Instruction Consultant, Peoria, AZ
  Teaching Edition Contributor

- **Robyn Seifert-Decker**, Mathematics Consultant, Grand Haven, MI
  Teaching Edition Contributor

- **Bonnie Spence**, Mathematics Education Specialist, Missoula, MT
  Teaching Edition Contributor

- **Suzy Gagnon**, Adjunct Instructor, University of New Hampshire, Portsmouth, NH
  Teaching Edition Contributor

- **Art Johnson**, Ed.D., Professor of Mathematics Education, Warwick, RI
  Teaching Edition Contributor

- **Anthony Smith**, Ph.D., Associate Professor, Associate Dean, University of Washington Bothell, Seattle, WA
  Reading and Writing Reviewer

- **Brianna Raygor**, Music Teacher, Fridley, MN
  Music Reviewer

- **Nicole Dimich Vagle**, Educator, Author, and Consultant, Hopkins, MN
  Assessment Reviewer

- **Janet Graham**, District Math Specialist, Manassas, VA
  Response to Intervention and Differentiated Instruction Reviewer

- **Sharon Huber**, Director of Elementary Mathematics, Chesapeake, VA
  Universal Design for Learning Reviewer

Student Reviewers

- T.J. Morin
- Alayna Morin
- Ethan Bauer
- Emery Bauer
- Emma Gaeta
- Ryan Gaeta

- Benjamin SanFrotello
- Bailey SanFrotello
- Samantha Grygier
- Robert Grygier IV
- Jacob Grygier
- Jessica Urso

- Ike Patton
- Jake Lobaugh
- Adam Fried
- Caroline Naser
- Charlotte Naser

Research

Ron Larson and Laurie Boswell used the latest in educational research, along with the body of knowledge collected from expert mathematics instructors, to develop the *Modeling Real Life* series. The pedagogical approach used in this program follows the best practices outlined in the most prominent and widely accepted educational research, including:

- *Visible Learning*
  John Hattie © 2009
- *Visible Learning for Teachers*
  John Hattie © 2012
- *Visible Learning for Mathematics*
  John Hattie © 2017
- *Principles to Actions: Ensuring Mathematical Success for All*
  NCTM © 2014
- *Adding It Up: Helping Children Learn Mathematics*
  National Research Council © 2001
- *Mathematical Mindsets: Unleashing Students' Potential through Creative Math, Inspiring Messages and Innovative Teaching*
  Jo Boaler © 2015
- *What Works in Schools: Translating Research into Action*
  Robert Marzano © 2003
- *Classroom Instruction That Works: Research-Based Strategies for Increasing Student Achievement*
  Marzano, Pickering, and Pollock © 2001
- *Principles and Standards for School Mathematics*
  NCTM © 2000
- *Rigorous PBL by Design: Three Shifts for Developing Confident and Competent Learners*
  Michael McDowell © 2017

- *Universal Design for Learning Guidelines*
  CAST © 2011
- Rigor/Relevance Framework®
  International Center for Leadership in Education
- *Understanding by Design*
  Grant Wiggins and Jay McTighe © 2005
- Achieve, ACT, and The College Board
- *Elementary and Middle School Mathematics: Teaching Developmentally*
  John A. Van de Walle and Karen S. Karp © 2015
- *Evaluating the Quality of Learning: The SOLO Taxonomy*
  John B. Biggs & Kevin F. Collis © 1982
- *Unlocking Formative Assessment: Practical Strategies for Enhancing Students' Learning in the Primary and Intermediate Classroom*
  Shirley Clarke, Helen Timperley, and John Hattie © 2004
- *Formative Assessment in the Secondary Classroom*
  Shirley Clarke © 2005
- *Improving Student Achievement: A Practical Guide to Assessment for Learning*
  Toni Glasson © 2009

Mathematical Processes and Proficiencies

Big Ideas Math: Modeling Real Life reinforces the Process Standards from NCTM and the Five Strands of Mathematical Proficiency endorsed by the National Research Council. With *Big Ideas Math*, students get the practice they need to become well-rounded, mathematically proficient learners.

Problem Solving/Strategic Competence

- *Think & Grow: Modeling Real Life* examples use problem-solving strategies, such as drawing a picture, circling knowns, and underlining unknowns. They also use a formal problem-solving plan: understand the problem, make a plan, and solve and check.
- Real-life problems are provided to help students learn to apply the mathematics that they are learning to everyday life.
- Real-life problems help students use the structure of mathematics to break down and solve more difficult problems.

Reasoning and Proof/Adaptive Reasoning

- *Explore & Grows* allow students to investigate math and make conjectures.
- Questions ask students to explain and justify their reasoning.

Communication

- Cooperative learning opportunities support precise communication.
- Exercises, such as *You Be The Teacher* and *Which One Doesn't Belong?*, provide students the opportunity to critique the reasoning of others.
- *Apply and Grow: Practice* exercises allow students to demonstrate their understanding of the lesson up to that point.
- *ELL Support* notes provide insights into how to support English learners.

Connections

- Prior knowledge is continually brought back and tied in with current learning.
- Performance Tasks tie the topics of a chapter together into one extended task.
- Real-life problems incorporate other disciplines to help students see that math is used across content areas.

Representations/Productive Disposition

- Real-life problems are translated into pictures, diagrams, tables, equations, and graphs to help students analyze relations and to draw conclusions.
- Visual problem-solving models help students create a coherent representation of the problem.
- Multiple representations are presented to help students move from concrete to representative and into abstract thinking.
- *Learning Targets* and *Success Criteria* at the start of each chapter and lesson help students understand what they are going to learn.
- Real-life problems incorporate other disciplines to help students see that math is used across content areas.

Conceptual Understanding

- *Explore & Grows* allow students to investigate math to understand the reasoning behind the rules.

Procedural Fluency

- Skill exercises are provided to continually practice fundamental skills.
- Prior knowledge is continually brought back and tied in with current learning.

Meeting Proficiency and Major Topics

Meeting Proficiency

As standards shift to prepare students for college and careers, the importance of focus, coherence, and rigor continues to grow.

FOCUS — *Big Ideas Math: Modeling Real Life* emphasizes a narrower and deeper curriculum, ensuring students spend their time on the major topics of each grade.

COHERENCE — The program was developed around coherent progressions from Kindergarten through eighth grade, guaranteeing students develop and progress their foundational skills through the grades while maintaining a strong focus on the major topics.

RIGOR — *Big Ideas Math: Modeling Real Life* uses a balance of procedural fluency, conceptual understanding, and real-life applications. Students develop conceptual understanding in every *Explore and Grow*, continue that development through the lesson while gaining procedural fluency during the *Think and Grow*, and then tie it all together with *Think and Grow: Modeling Real Life*. Every set of practice problems reflects this balance, giving students the rigorous practice they need to be college- and career-ready.

Major Topics in Grade 4

Operations and Algebraic Thinking
- Use the four operations with whole numbers to solve problems.

Number and Operations in Base Ten
- Generalize place value understanding for multi-digit whole numbers.
- Use place value understanding and properties of operations to perform multi-digit arithmetic.

Number and Operations—Fractions
- Extend understanding of fraction equivalence and ordering.
- Build fractions from unit fractions by applying and extending previous understandings of operations on whole numbers.
- Understand decimal notation for fractions, and compare decimal fractions.

Use the color-coded Table of Contents to determine where the major topics, supporting topics, and additional topics occur throughout the curriculum.

- ◼ Major Topic
- ◼ Supporting Topic
- ◼ Additional Topic

Place Value Concepts

Add and Subtract Multi-Digit Numbers

■ Major Topic
■ Supporting Topic
■ Additional Topic

③ Multiply by One-Digit Numbers

Multiplication Quest

Directions:

1. Players take turns rolling a die. Players solve problems on their boards to race the knights to their castles.
2. On your turn, solve the next multiplication problem in the row of your roll.
3. The first player to get a knight to a castle wins!

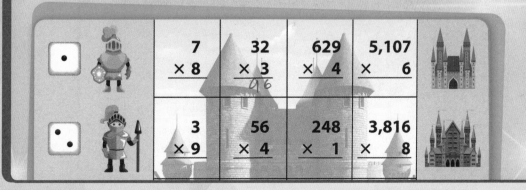

4 Multiply by Two-Digit Numbers

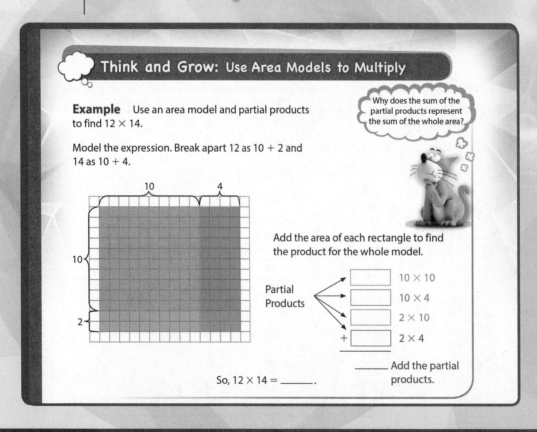

Think and Grow: Use Area Models to Multiply

Example Use an area model and partial products to find 12×14.

Model the expression. Break apart 12 as $10 + 2$ and 14 as $10 + 4$.

Why does the sum of the partial products represent the sum of the whole area?

Add the area of each rectangle to find the product for the whole model.

Partial Products

10×10
10×4
2×10
$+ \quad 2 \times 4$

_____ Add the partial products.

So, $12 \times 14 = $ _____.

Divide Multi-Digit Numbers by One-Digit Numbers

Factors, Multiples, and Patterns

■ Major Topic
■ Supporting Topic
■ Additional Topic

Understand Fraction Equivalence and Comparison

Add and Subtract Fractions

■ Major Topic
■ Supporting Topic
■ Additional Topic

Multiply Whole Numbers and Fractions

Relate Fractions and Decimals

Let's learn how to relate fractions and decimals!

Understand Measurement Equivalence

Use Perimeter and Area Formulas

■ Major Topic
■ Supporting Topic
■ Additional Topic

Identify and Draw Lines and Angles

Identify Symmetry and Two-Dimensional Shapes

Let's learn how to identify symmetry!

Descartes

8 Add and Subtract Fractions

- Do you know someone who plays an instrument? Have you ever seen sheet music?

- How can fractions help a musician keep time when reading sheet music?

Chapter Learning Target:
Understand adding and subtracting fractions.

Chapter Success Criteria:
- [ ] I can use a number line to add fractions.
- [ ] I can write a fraction as a sum of unit fractions.
- [ ] I can solve a problem using fractions.
- [ ] I can model different types of fractions.

© Big Ideas Learning, LLC

345

8 Vocabulary

Review Words

eighths
fourths
halves
sixths

Organize It

Use the review words to complete the graphic organizer.

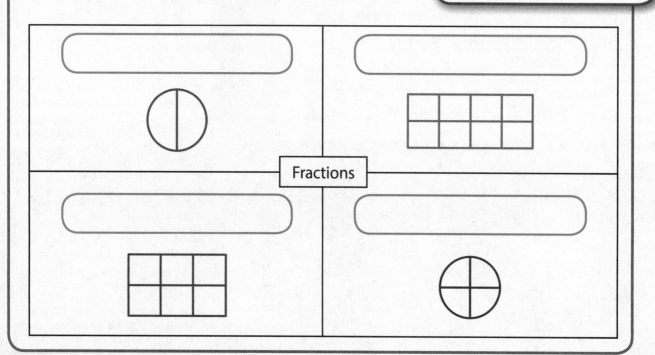

Fractions

Define It

Use your vocabulary cards to complete each definition.

1. mixed number: Represents the _____ of a _____ number

    and a _____ less than _____

2. unit fraction: Represents one _____ part of a _____

Chapter 8 Vocabulary Cards

mixed
number

unit fraction

Represents one equal part of a whole

Examples:

$\dfrac{1}{2}$

$\dfrac{1}{5}$

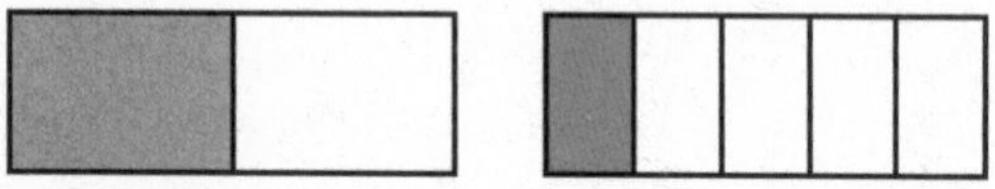

Represents the sum of a whole number and a fraction less than 1

Examples: $2\dfrac{1}{3}$, $1\dfrac{4}{5}$, $5\dfrac{3}{10}$

Name _____

Learning Target: Use area models and number lines to add fractions.

Success Criteria:
- I can use an area model to add fractions.
- I can use a number line to add fractions.
- I can explain what it means to add fractions.

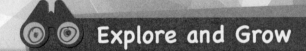 **Explore and Grow**

Draw models to show $\frac{2}{8}$ and $\frac{5}{8}$.

Use your models to find $\frac{2}{8} + \frac{5}{8}$. Explain your method.

 Repeated Reasoning Write two fractions that have a sum of $\frac{6}{8}$. Explain your reasoning.

Think and Grow: Use Models to Add Fractions

You can add fractions by joining parts that refer to the same whole.

Example   Use a model to find $\frac{1}{5} + \frac{3}{5}$.

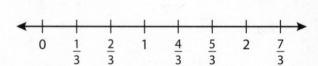

Each part is $\frac{1}{5}$ of the whole. Combine 1 part and 3 parts.

| $\frac{1}{5}$ | $\frac{1}{5}$ | $\frac{1}{5}$ | $\frac{1}{5}$ | $\frac{1}{5}$ |

$+$

| $\frac{1}{5}$ | $\frac{1}{5}$ | $\frac{1}{5}$ | $\frac{1}{5}$ | $\frac{1}{5}$ |

$=$

| $\frac{1}{5}$ | $\frac{1}{5}$ | $\frac{1}{5}$ | $\frac{1}{5}$ | $\frac{1}{5}$ |

$\frac{1}{5}$ $\frac{3}{5}$ $\frac{\square}{\square}$

So, $\frac{1}{5} + \frac{3}{5} = \frac{4}{5}$.

Example   Use a number line to find $\frac{5}{4} + \frac{2}{4}$.

Join lengths of $\frac{5}{4}$ and $\frac{2}{4}$.

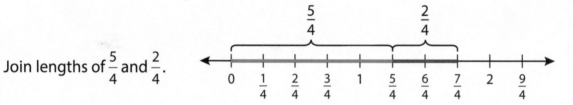

So, $\frac{5}{4} + \frac{2}{4} = \frac{\square}{\square}$.

Show and Grow   I can do it!

Find the sum. Explain how you used the model to add.

1. $\frac{3}{10} + \frac{4}{10} = \frac{7}{10}$

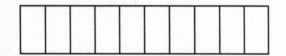

2. $\frac{2}{3} + \frac{4}{3} = $ _____

0   $\frac{1}{3}$ $\frac{2}{3}$ 1 $\frac{4}{3}$ $\frac{5}{3}$ 2 $\frac{7}{3}$

Name _____

Find the sum. Use a model or a number line to help.

3. $\frac{1}{2} + \frac{7}{2} =$ ___4___

4

4. $\frac{5}{12} + \frac{4}{12} =$ ___$\frac{9}{12}$___

5. $\frac{8}{5} + \frac{4}{5} =$ ___$\frac{12}{5}$___

$\frac{2}{5}$

6. $\frac{3}{3} + \frac{2}{3} =$ ___$\frac{5}{3}$___

7. $1 + \frac{2}{6} =$ ___$1\frac{2}{6}$___

8. $5 + \frac{6}{8} =$ _____

9. $\frac{1}{4} + \frac{1}{4} + \frac{1}{4} =$ ___$\frac{3}{4}$___

10. $\frac{5}{10} + \frac{2}{10} + \frac{1}{10} =$ ___$\frac{6}{10}$___

11. $\frac{20}{100} + \frac{15}{100} =$ ___$\frac{35}{100}$___

12. (MP) **Structure** Write the addition equation represented by the models.

 +  =

Wow

13. **Open-Ended** Write three fractions with different numerators that have a sum of 1.

14. **Writing** Explain why $\frac{1}{8} + \frac{4}{8}$ does *not* equal $\frac{5}{16}$.

Think and Grow: Modeling Real Life

Example You need $\frac{2}{3}$ cup of hot water and $\frac{4}{3}$ cups of cold water for a science experiment. How many cups of water do you need in all?

Because each fraction represents a part of the same whole you can join the parts.

Use a model to find $\frac{2}{3} + \frac{4}{3}$.

$$\begin{array}{c} \boxed{\frac{1}{3}}\,\boxed{\frac{1}{3}}\,\boxed{\frac{1}{3}} \\[4pt] \frac{2}{3} \end{array} \quad + \quad \begin{array}{c} \boxed{\frac{1}{3}}\,\boxed{\frac{1}{3}}\,\boxed{\frac{1}{3}} \\[2pt] \boxed{\frac{1}{3}}\,\boxed{\frac{1}{3}}\,\boxed{\frac{1}{3}} \\[4pt] \frac{4}{3} \end{array} \quad = \quad \begin{array}{c} \boxed{\frac{1}{3}}\,\boxed{\frac{1}{3}}\,\boxed{\frac{1}{3}} \\[2pt] \boxed{\frac{1}{3}}\,\boxed{\frac{1}{3}}\,\boxed{\frac{1}{3}} \\[4pt] \frac{\square}{\square} = \text{\_\_\_\_} \end{array}$$

So, you need _____ cups of water in all.

Show and Grow I can think deeper!

15. You cut a foam noodle for a craft. You use $\frac{2}{4}$ of the noodle for one part of the craft and $\frac{1}{4}$ of the noodle for another part. What fraction of the foam noodle do you use altogether?

16. You make a fruit drink using $\frac{4}{8}$ gallon of orange juice, $\frac{2}{8}$ gallon of mango juice, and $\frac{4}{8}$ gallon of pineapple juice. How much juice do you use in all?

17. **DIG DEEPER!** A community plants cucumbers in $\frac{5}{12}$ of a garden, broccoli in $\frac{3}{12}$ of the garden, and carrots in $\frac{4}{12}$ of the garden. What fraction of the garden is planted with green vegetables?

Name _____

 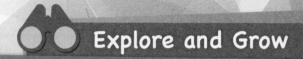
Learning Target: Write a fraction as a sum of fractions.
Success Criteria:
• I can write a fraction as a sum of unit fractions.
• I can write a fraction as a sum of two fractions.
• I can write a fraction as a sum of fractions in more than one way.

Explore and Grow

Use a model to find $\dfrac{1}{10} + \dfrac{1}{10} + \dfrac{1}{10} + \dfrac{1}{10} + \dfrac{1}{10}$.

How can you write $\dfrac{7}{10}$ as a sum of unit fractions? Explain your reasoning.

 Structure Explain how you can write $\dfrac{7}{10}$ as a sum of two fractions. Draw a model to support your answer.

A **unit fraction** represents one equal part of a whole.
You can write a fraction as a sum of unit fractions.

Example Write $\frac{3}{4}$ as a sum of unit fractions.

The fraction $\frac{3}{4}$ represents 3 parts
that are each $\frac{1}{4}$ of the whole.

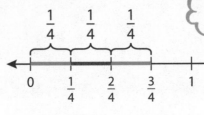

The numerator of a unit fraction is 1.

So, $\frac{3}{4} = \dfrac{\square}{\square} + \dfrac{\square}{\square} + \dfrac{\square}{\square}$.

....

Example Write $\frac{5}{12}$ as a sum of fractions.

One Way: Write $\frac{5}{12}$ as a sum of unit fractions.

The fraction $\frac{5}{12}$ represents 5 parts that are each $\frac{1}{12}$ of the whole.

So, $\frac{5}{12} = \dfrac{\square}{\square} + \dfrac{\square}{\square} + \dfrac{\square}{\square} + \dfrac{\square}{\square} + \dfrac{\square}{\square}$.

Another Way: Write $\frac{5}{12}$ as a sum of two fractions.

Break apart 5 parts of $\frac{1}{12}$ into 2 parts of $\frac{1}{12}$ and 3 parts of $\frac{1}{12}$.

So, $\frac{5}{12} = \dfrac{\square}{\square} + \dfrac{\square}{\square}$.

Think: Is there another way to write the sum?

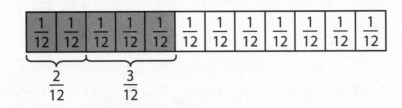

Show and Grow I can do it!

1. Write $\frac{4}{5}$ as a sum of unit fractions.

2. Write $\frac{5}{6}$ as a sum of fractions in two different ways.

Name _____

 Apply and Grow: Practice

Write the fraction as a sum of fractions in two different ways.

3. $\frac{4}{7}$

4. $\frac{7}{8}$

5. $\frac{3}{10}$

6. $\frac{10}{100}$

7. $\frac{6}{2}$

8. $\frac{9}{4}$

9. $\frac{8}{12}$

10. $\frac{5}{3}$

11. **Writing** You write $\frac{4}{6}$ as a sum of unit fractions. Explain how the numerator of $\frac{4}{6}$ is related to the number of addends.

12. **DIG DEEPER!** Why is it important to be able to write a fraction as a sum of fractions in different ways?

13. **MP Precision** Match each fraction with an equivalent expression.

$\frac{5}{12}$ $\frac{3}{12} + \frac{3}{12} + \frac{3}{12}$

$\frac{9}{12}$ $\frac{5}{12} + \frac{2}{12} + \frac{3}{12}$

$\frac{10}{12}$ $\frac{5}{12} + \frac{2}{12} + \frac{1}{12}$

$\frac{8}{12}$ $\frac{1}{12} + \frac{1}{12} + \frac{1}{12} + \frac{1}{12} + \frac{1}{12}$

© Big Ideas Learning, LLC

Think and Grow: Modeling Real Life

Example A chef has $\frac{8}{10}$ liter of soup. How can the chef pour all of the soup into 2 bowls?

Break apart $\frac{8}{10}$ into any two fractions that have a sum of $\frac{8}{10}$.

One Way: Break apart 8 parts of $\frac{1}{10}$ into 4 parts of $\frac{1}{10}$ and _____ parts of $\frac{1}{10}$.

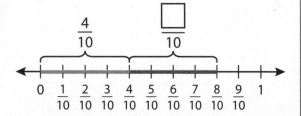

So, the chef can pour _____ liter

of soup into one bowl and _____ liter of soup into the other bowl.

Another Way: Break apart 8 parts of $\frac{1}{10}$ into 5 parts of $\frac{1}{10}$ and _____ parts of $\frac{1}{10}$.

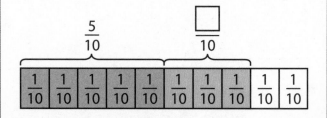

So, the chef can pour _____ liter

of soup into one bowl and _____ liter of soup into the other bowl.

Show and Grow   *I can think deeper!*

14. You have $\frac{7}{3}$ pounds of almonds. What are two different ways you can put all of the almonds into 2 bags?

15. A 3-person painting crew has $\frac{10}{12}$ of a fence left to paint. What is one way the crew can finish painting the fence when each person paints a fraction of the fence?

16. **DIG DEEPER!** Three teammates have to run a total of $\frac{6}{4}$ miles for a relay race. Can each team member run the same fraction of a mile, in fourths, to complete the race? Explain.

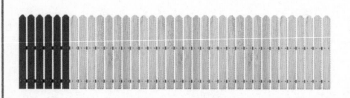

Name _____

 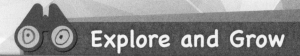

Learning Target: Add fractions with like denominators.
Success Criteria:
- I can use models to add fractions.
- I can use a rule to add fractions.
- I can explain how to add fractions with like denominators.

Explore and Grow

Write each fraction as a sum of unit fractions. Use models to help.

$\dfrac{3}{6}$	$\dfrac{5}{6}$

How many unit fractions did you use in all to rewrite the fractions above?

How does this relate to the sum $\dfrac{3}{6} + \dfrac{5}{6}$?

 Construct Arguments How can you use the numerators and the denominators to add fractions with like denominators? Explain why your method makes sense.

Think and Grow: Add Fractions

To add fractions with like denominators, add the numerators. The denominator stays the same.

$$\frac{1}{5} + \frac{3}{5} = \frac{1+3}{5} = \frac{4}{5}$$

Example Find $\frac{3}{10} + \frac{4}{10}$.

$$\frac{3}{10} + \frac{4}{10} = \frac{\boxed{3} + \boxed{4}}{10}$$

$$= \frac{\boxed{7}}{10}$$

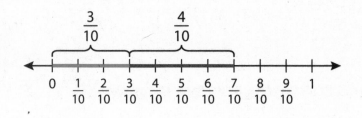

So, $\frac{3}{10} + \frac{4}{10} = \frac{\boxed{}}{10}$.

Example Find $\frac{5}{4} + \frac{3}{4}$.

$$\frac{5}{4} + \frac{3}{4} = \frac{\boxed{5} + \boxed{3}}{4}$$

$$= \frac{\boxed{8}}{4}$$

$$= \frac{8}{4}$$

So, $\frac{5}{4} + \frac{3}{4} = $ _____.

Show and Grow I can do it!

Add.

1. $\frac{1}{4} + \frac{2}{4} = \frac{\boxed{1} + \boxed{2}}{4}$

$$= \frac{\boxed{3}}{4}$$

2. $\frac{6}{5} + \frac{2}{5} = \frac{8}{5}$

3. $\frac{4}{8} + \frac{4}{8} = 1$

Name _____

Add.

4. $\frac{3}{6} + \frac{2}{6} = \frac{5}{6}$

5. $\frac{8}{2} + \frac{4}{2} = \frac{12}{2}$

6. $\frac{4}{5} + \frac{1}{5} = 1$
   9

7. $\frac{60}{100} + \frac{35}{100} = \frac{95}{100}$

8. $2 + \frac{5}{3} = \frac{25}{3}$

9. $6 + \frac{1}{12} = 6\frac{1}{12}$

10. $\frac{3}{4} + \frac{1}{4} + \frac{1}{4} = \frac{5}{4}$

11. $\frac{6}{8} + \frac{5}{8} + \frac{4}{8} = \frac{15}{8}$

12. $\frac{43}{100} + \frac{16}{100} + \frac{10}{100} = \frac{69}{100}$

13. You eat $\frac{2}{10}$ of a vegetable pizza. Your friend eats $\frac{3}{10}$ of the pizza.
    What fraction of the pizza do you and your friend eat together?

    $\frac{2}{10} + \frac{3}{10} = \frac{5}{10}$

14. 🔵 **Number Sense** A sum has
    5 addends. Each addend is a unit
    fraction. The sum is 1. What are the
    addends?

    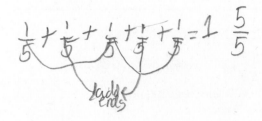

15. **Writing** Explain how to add $\frac{3}{4}$ and $\frac{1}{4}$.
    Use a model to support your answer.

    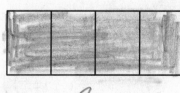

    $\frac{3}{4} + \frac{1}{4}$

Think and Grow: Modeling Real Life

Example The table shows the natural hazards studied by 100 students for a science project. What fraction of the students studied a weather-based natural hazard?

Science Project Topic		
Earthquake (Earth-based)	🌢🌢	12
Hurricane (weather-based)	🌢🌢🌢	20
Tornado (weather-based)	🌢🌢🌢	24
Tsunami (Earth-based)	🌢🌢	16
Volcano (Earth-based)	🌢🌢🌢🌢	28

Interpret the picture graph.

Hurricane: 2 🌢s = 2 × 8 = 16   1 ◖ = 4
    16 + 4 = 20 students

Tornado: 3 🌢s = 3 × 8 = 24 students

Each 🌢 = 8 students.

Write the fraction of students who studied each weather-based hazard.

$$\frac{\text{number of students}}{\text{total number of students surveyed}}$$

Hurricane: $\frac{20}{100}$ Tornado: $\frac{24}{100}$

Add the fractions.

$$\frac{20}{100} + \frac{24}{100} = \frac{\boxed{} + \boxed{}}{100}$$

$$= \frac{\boxed{}}{100}$$

So, _____ of the students studied a weather-based natural hazard.

Show and Grow   I can think deeper!

16. Use the graph above to find what fraction of the students studied an Earth-based natural hazard.

2 12
20
24
16
+ 28
110

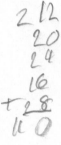

17. **DIG DEEPER!** A caterer needs at least 2 pounds of lunch meat to make a sandwich platter. She has $\frac{6}{4}$ pounds of turkey and $\frac{3}{4}$ pound of ham. Does the caterer have enough lunch meat to make a sandwich platter? Explain.

Learning Target: Use area models and number lines to subtract fractions.

Success Criteria:
- I can use an area model to subtract fractions.
- I can use a number line to subtract fractions.
- I can explain what it means to subtract fractions.

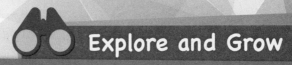 Explore and Grow

Draw a model to show $\frac{9}{12}$.

Use your model to find $\frac{9}{12} - \frac{5}{12}$. Explain your method.

MP **Repeated Reasoning** Write two fractions that have a difference of $\frac{7}{12}$. Explain your reasoning.

Think and Grow: Use Models to Subtract Fractions

You can subtract fractions by taking away parts that refer to the same whole.

Example Use a model to find $\frac{5}{6} - \frac{2}{6}$.

Taking $\frac{2}{6}$ away from $\frac{5}{6}$ leaves $\frac{3}{6}$.

Model $\frac{5}{6}$. Then take away $\frac{2}{6}$.

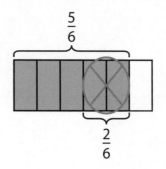

$$\text{So, } \frac{5}{6} - \frac{2}{6} = \frac{\square}{\square}.$$

Example Use a number line to find $\frac{7}{3} - \frac{5}{3}$.

Take away a length of $\frac{5}{3}$ from a length of $\frac{7}{3}$.

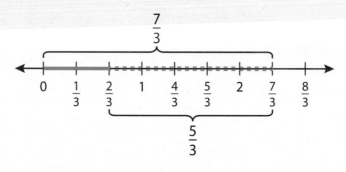

$$\text{So, } \frac{7}{3} - \frac{5}{3} = \frac{\square}{\square}.$$

Show and Grow   *I can do it!*

Find the difference. Explain how you used the model to subtract.

1. $\frac{9}{10} - \frac{4}{10} = \frac{5}{10}$

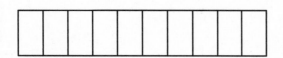

2. $\frac{6}{4} - \frac{2}{4} =$ _____

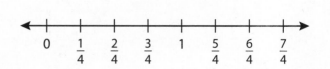

366

© Big Ideas Learning, LLC

Name _____

Apply and Grow: Practice

Find the difference. Use a model or a number line to help.

3. $\dfrac{8}{8} - \dfrac{4}{8} =$ _____

4. $\dfrac{10}{12} - \dfrac{2}{12} =$ _____

5. $\dfrac{4}{5} - \dfrac{1}{5} =$ _____

6. $\dfrac{9}{2} - \dfrac{3}{2} =$ _____

7. $\dfrac{15}{6} - \dfrac{5}{6} =$ _____

8. $\dfrac{76}{100} - \dfrac{50}{100} =$ _____

9. You need to walk $\dfrac{3}{4}$ mile for your physical education class. So far, you have walked $\dfrac{2}{4}$ mile. How much farther do you need to walk?

10. **MP Number Sense** Which expressions have a difference of $\dfrac{4}{5}$?

$\dfrac{5}{5} - \dfrac{1}{5}$

$\dfrac{10}{5} - \dfrac{6}{5}$

$\dfrac{6}{5} - \dfrac{3}{5}$

$\dfrac{9}{5} - \dfrac{5}{5}$

11. **MP Structure** Write the subtraction equation represented by the model.

12. **Writing** Explain why the numerator changes when you subtract fractions with like denominators, but the denominator stays the same.

Think and Grow: Modeling Real Life

Example A lizard's tail is $\frac{10}{12}$ foot long. It sheds a $\frac{7}{12}$ foot long part of its tail to escape a predator. How long is the remaining part of the lizard's tail?

Because each fraction represents a part of the same whole, you can take away a part.

Use a model to find $\frac{10}{12} - \frac{7}{12}$.

Model $\frac{10}{12}$. Then take away $\frac{7}{12}$.

$$\frac{10}{2} - \frac{7}{12} = \frac{\square}{\square}$$

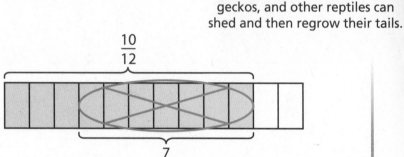

When in danger, some lizards, geckos, and other reptiles can shed and then regrow their tails.

So, the remaining part of the lizard's tail is $\frac{\square}{\square}$ foot long.

Show and Grow   I can think deeper!

13. You have $\frac{9}{8}$ cups of raisins. You eat $\frac{2}{8}$ cup. What fraction of a cup of raisins do you have left?

14. A large bottle has $\frac{7}{4}$ quarts of liquid soap. A small bottle has $\frac{3}{4}$ quart of liquid soap. How much more soap is in the large bottle than in the small bottle?

15. **DIG DEEPER!** You need 2 cups of milk for a recipe. You have $\frac{1}{3}$ cup of milk. How much more milk do you need? Explain.

368

© Big Ideas Learning, LLC

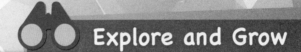

Learning Target: Subtract fractions with like denominators.

Success Criteria:
- I can use models to subtract fractions.
- I can use a rule to subtract fractions.
- I can explain how to subtract fractions with like denominators.

Explore and Grow

Write each fraction as a sum of unit fractions. Use models to help.

$\frac{4}{5}$	$\frac{3}{5}$

How many more unit fractions did you use to rewrite $\frac{4}{5}$ than $\frac{3}{5}$?

How does this relate to the difference $\frac{4}{5} - \frac{3}{5}$?

 Construct Arguments How can you use the numerators and the denominators to subtract fractions with like denominators? Explain why your method makes sense.

Think and Grow: Subtract Fractions

To subtract fractions with like denominators, subtract the numerators. The denominator stays the same.

$$\frac{3}{5} - \frac{1}{5} = \frac{3-1}{5} = \frac{2}{5}$$

Example Find $\frac{7}{8} - \frac{3}{8}$.

$\frac{7}{8} - \frac{3}{8} = \dfrac{\boxed{} - \boxed{}}{8}$

$\qquad = \dfrac{\boxed{}}{8}$

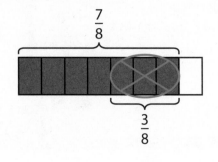

$\frac{7}{8}$

$\frac{3}{8}$

So, $\frac{7}{8} - \frac{3}{8} = \dfrac{\boxed{}}{8}$.

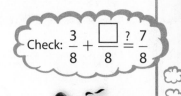

Check: $\frac{3}{8} + \dfrac{\boxed{}}{8} \overset{?}{=} \frac{7}{8}$

Example Find $1 - \frac{3}{5}$.

$1 - \frac{3}{5} = \frac{5}{5} - \frac{3}{5}$

$\qquad = \dfrac{\boxed{} - \boxed{}}{5}$

$\qquad = \dfrac{\boxed{}}{5}$

$1 = \frac{5}{5}$

0   $\frac{1}{5}$ $\frac{2}{5}$ $\frac{3}{5}$ $\frac{4}{5}$ 1 $\frac{6}{5}$ $\frac{7}{5}$ $\frac{8}{5}$

$\frac{3}{5}$

So, $1 - \frac{3}{5} = \dfrac{\boxed{}}{5}$.

Show and Grow I can do it!

Subtract.

1. $\frac{3}{2} - \frac{1}{2} = \dfrac{\boxed{3} - \boxed{1}}{2}$

$\qquad = \dfrac{\boxed{2}}{2}$

2. $1^{\frac{12}{12}} - \frac{8}{12} = \frac{4}{12}$

3. $\frac{50}{100} - \frac{30}{100} = \frac{20}{100}$

Name _____

Subtract.

4. $\frac{9}{3} - \frac{2}{3} =$ _$\frac{7}{3}$_

5. $\frac{8}{10} - \frac{6}{10} =$ _$\frac{2}{10}$_

6. $\frac{12}{6} - \frac{7}{6} =$ _$\frac{5}{6}$_

7. $\frac{4}{5} - \frac{3}{5} =$ _$\frac{1}{5}$_

8. $\frac{60}{100} - \frac{43}{100} =$ _$\frac{17}{100}$_

9. $\frac{10}{2} - \frac{2}{2} =$ _$\frac{8}{2}$_

10. $1 - \frac{7}{12} =$ _$\frac{5}{12}$_

11. $1 - \frac{5}{8} =$ _$\frac{3}{8}$_

12. $2 - \frac{1}{4} =$ _$\frac{7}{4}$_ wow

13. You have 1 gallon of paint. You use $\frac{2}{3}$ gallon to paint a wall. How much paint do you have left?

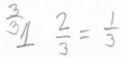 $1 \quad \frac{2}{3} = \frac{1}{3}$

14. **MP Reasoning** Why is it unreasonable to get a difference of $\frac{7}{8}$ when subtracting $\frac{1}{8}$ from $\frac{7}{8}$? Use a model to support your answer.

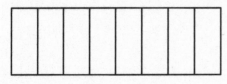

15. **DIG DEEPER!** Your friend says each difference is $\frac{3}{10}$. Is your friend correct? Explain.

$\frac{10}{10} - \frac{7}{10} = ?$

$\frac{100}{100} - \frac{70}{100} = ?$

© Big Ideas Learning, LLC

Think and Grow: Modeling Real Life

Example A flock of geese has completed $\frac{5}{12}$ of its total migration. What fraction of its migration does the flock of geese have left to complete?

Because the total migration is 1 whole, find $1 - \frac{5}{12}$.

$$1 - \frac{5}{12} = \frac{12}{12} - \frac{5}{12}$$

$$= \frac{\Box - \Box}{12}$$

$$= \frac{\Box}{12}$$

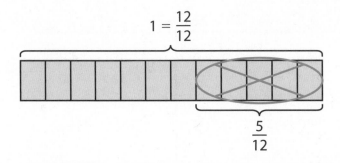

$$1 = \frac{12}{12}$$

$$\frac{5}{12}$$

So, the flock of geese has $\dfrac{\Box}{\Box}$ of its migration left to complete.

Show and Grow   *I can think deeper!*

16. A runner has completed $\frac{6}{10}$ of a race. What fraction of the race does the runner have left to complete?

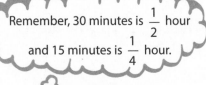

$\dfrac{4}{10}$

17. A pizza buffet serves pizzas of the same size with different toppings. There is $\frac{7}{8}$ of a vegetable pizza and $\frac{2}{8}$ of a pineapple pizza left. How much more vegetable pizza is left than pineapple pizza?

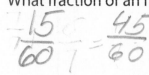

$\dfrac{7}{8}$ $\dfrac{5}{8}$

Remember, 30 minutes is $\frac{1}{2}$ hour and 15 minutes is $\frac{1}{4}$ hour.

18. **DIG DEEPER!** Baseball practice is 1 hour long. You stretch for 7 minutes and play catch for 8 minutes. What fraction of an hour do you have left to practice?

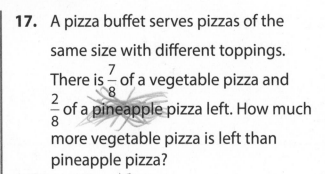

$\dfrac{15}{60}$ $= \dfrac{45}{60}$

374

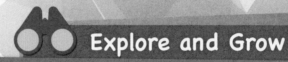

Model Fractions and Mixed Numbers 8.6

Learning Target: Write mixed numbers as fractions and fractions as mixed numbers.

Success Criteria:
- I can model a mixed number.
- I can write a mixed number as a fraction.
- I can write a fraction greater than 1 as a mixed number.

Explore and Grow

Draw a model to show $1 + 1 + \frac{2}{3}$.

Use your model to write the sum as a fraction.

MP **Repeated Reasoning** How can you write a fraction greater than 1 as the sum of a whole number and a fraction less than 1? Explain.

Think and Grow: Write Fractions and Mixed Numbers

A **mixed number** represents the sum of a whole number and a fraction less than 1.

$$3 + \frac{1}{2} = 3\frac{1}{2}$$

> A mixed number represents a sum, but it is written without the + sign.

Example Write $1\frac{5}{6}$ as a fraction.

Write the mixed number as a sum. Then write the sum as a fraction.

$$1\frac{5}{6} = 1 + \frac{5}{6}$$
$$= \frac{6}{6} + \frac{5}{6}$$
$$= \frac{6 + 5}{6}$$
$$= \frac{\square}{\square}$$

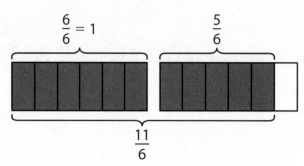

$$\frac{6}{6} = 1 \qquad \frac{5}{6}$$

$$\frac{11}{6}$$

So, $1\frac{5}{6} = \dfrac{\square}{\square}$.

Example Write $\frac{5}{2}$ as a mixed number.

Find how many wholes are in $\frac{5}{2}$ and how many halves are left over.

$$\frac{5}{2} = \frac{2}{2} + \frac{2}{2} + \frac{1}{2}$$
$$= 1 + 1 + \frac{1}{2}$$
$$= 2 + \frac{1}{2}$$
$$= \square\frac{\square}{\square}$$

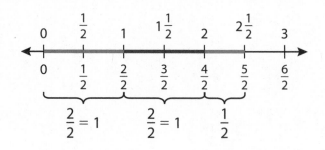

$$\frac{2}{2} = 1 \qquad \frac{2}{2} = 1 \qquad \frac{1}{2}$$

So, $\dfrac{5}{2} = \square\dfrac{\square}{\square}$.

Show and Grow   I can do it!

1. Write $3\frac{1}{4}$ as a fraction. Use a model or a number line to help.

2. Write $\frac{9}{6}$ as a mixed number. Use a model or a number line to help.

Name _____

Write the mixed number as a fraction.

3. $\frac{19}{4}$ $3\frac{4}{5}$ $\frac{19}{5}$

4. $2\frac{1}{3}$ $\frac{7}{3}$

5. $6\frac{7}{12}$ $\frac{79}{12}$

6. $1\frac{82}{100}$

7. $11\frac{3}{8}$

8. $9\frac{5}{10}$

Write the fraction as a mixed number or a whole number.

9. $\frac{9}{8}$

10. $\frac{19}{3}$

11. $\frac{38}{5}$

12. $\frac{22}{10}$

13. $\frac{460}{100}$

14. $\frac{20}{4}$

Compare.

15. $1\frac{1}{2}$ ◯ $\frac{3}{2}$

16. $3\frac{3}{12}$ ◯ $\frac{15}{12}$

17. $\frac{21}{6}$ ◯ 4

18. **Which One Doesn't Belong?** Which expression does *not* belong with the other three?

$3\frac{2}{3}$ $\qquad$ $\frac{9}{3}+\frac{3}{3}$ $\qquad$ $\frac{3}{3}+\frac{3}{3}+\frac{3}{3}+\frac{2}{3}$ $\qquad$ $\frac{11}{3}$

DIG DEEPER! Find the unknown number.

19. $1\frac{\square}{6}=\frac{8}{6}$

20. $8\frac{\square}{4}=\frac{35}{4}$

21. $\square\frac{9}{12}=\frac{129}{12}$

Example A construction worker needs nails that are $\frac{9}{4}$ inches long. Which size of nails should the worker use?

NAILS $1\frac{3}{4}$ inches NAILS $2\frac{1}{4}$ inches NAILS $2\frac{3}{4}$ inches

Write $\frac{9}{4}$ as a mixed number.

$$\frac{9}{4} = \frac{4}{4} + \frac{4}{4} + \frac{1}{4}$$

$$= 1 + 1 + \frac{1}{4}$$

$$= 2 + \frac{1}{4}$$

$$= \boxed{}\frac{\boxed{}}{\boxed{}}$$

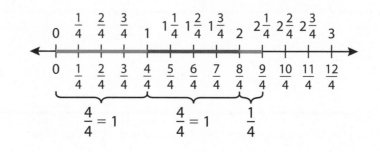

$\frac{4}{4} = 1 \qquad \frac{4}{4} = 1 \qquad \frac{1}{4}$

So, the construction worker should use the nails that are $\boxed{}\frac{\boxed{}}{\boxed{}}$ inches long.

Show and Grow *I can think deeper!*

22. You need screws that are $\frac{13}{8}$ inches long to build a birdhouse. Which size of screws should you use?

SCREWS $1\frac{1}{8}$ inches SCREWS $1\frac{3}{8}$ inches SCREWS $1\frac{5}{8}$ inches

23. You and your friend each measure the distance between two bean bag toss boards. You record the distance as $3\frac{3}{5}$ meters. Your friend records the distance as $\frac{18}{5}$ meters. Did you and your friend record the same distance? Explain.

24. **DIG DEEPER!** You use a $\frac{1}{3}$-cup scoop to measure $3\frac{1}{3}$ cups of rice. How many times do you fill the scoop?

25. **DIG DEEPER!** A sunflower plant is $\frac{127}{10}$ centimeters tall. A snapdragon plant is $8\frac{9}{10}$ centimeters tall. Which plant is taller? Explain.

Learning Target: Add mixed numbers with like denominators.
Success Criteria:
- I can add fractional parts and whole number parts of mixed numbers with like denominators.
- I can use equivalent fractions to add mixed numbers with like denominators.
- I can explain two ways to add mixed numbers with like denominators.

 Explore and Grow

Use a model to find $2\frac{3}{8} + 1\frac{1}{8}$.

 Construct Arguments How can you use the whole number parts and the fractional parts to add mixed numbers with like denominators? Explain why your method makes sense.

Think and Grow: Add Mixed Numbers

To add mixed numbers, add the fractional parts and add the whole number parts. Another way to add mixed numbers is to rewrite each number as a fraction, then add.

> Use the Commutative and the Associative Properties to change the order and the grouping of the addends.

Example Find $1\frac{1}{5} + 2\frac{2}{5}$.

$$1\frac{1}{5} + 2\frac{2}{5} = 1 + \frac{1}{5} + 2 + \frac{2}{5}$$

$$= (1 + 2) + \left(\frac{1}{5} + \frac{2}{5}\right)$$

$$= 3 + \frac{3}{5} = \Box\frac{\Box}{\Box}$$

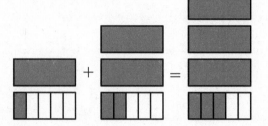

So, $1\frac{1}{5} + 2\frac{2}{5} = \Box\frac{\Box}{\Box}$.

Example Find $4\frac{2}{8} + 2\frac{7}{8}$.

One Way: Add the fractional parts and then add the whole number parts.

$$4\frac{2}{8}$$
$$+ 2\frac{7}{8}$$
$$\overline{\frac{9}{8}}$$

$$4\frac{2}{8}$$
$$+ 2\frac{7}{8}$$
$$\overline{6\frac{9}{8}}$$

Write $6\frac{9}{8}$ as a mixed number.

$$6\frac{9}{8} = 6 + \frac{8}{8} + \frac{1}{8} = \Box\frac{\Box}{\Box}$$

Another Way: Write each mixed number as a fraction, then add.

$$4\frac{2}{8} = 4 + \frac{2}{8} = \frac{32}{8} + \frac{2}{8} = \frac{34}{8}$$

$$2\frac{7}{8} = 2 + \frac{7}{8} = \frac{16}{8} + \frac{7}{8} = \frac{23}{8}$$

$$\frac{34}{8} + \frac{23}{8} = \frac{57}{8}$$

Write $\frac{57}{8}$ as a mixed number.

$$\frac{57}{8} = \frac{56}{8} + \frac{1}{8} = \Box\frac{\Box}{\Box}$$

So, $4\frac{2}{8} + 2\frac{7}{8} = \Box\frac{\Box}{\Box}$.

Show and Grow   I can do it!

Add.

1. $1\frac{2}{4} + 2\frac{1}{4} = $ _____

2. $5\frac{1}{10} + 2\frac{9}{10} = $ _____

384

Name _____

Add.

3. $5\frac{1}{3} + 3\frac{2}{3} =$ _____

$8 + 1 = 9$

$\frac{3}{1}$

4. $2\frac{8}{12} + 7\frac{5}{12} =$ _____

5. $4 + 1\frac{1}{2} =$ _____ $5\frac{1}{2}$

6.
$$3\frac{78}{100}$$
$$+\ \frac{124}{100}$$
_____
$3\frac{202}{100}$ $\frac{2}{100}$

$+\frac{3}{5}$

7.
$$8\frac{4}{8}$$
$$5\frac{3}{8}$$
$$+\ 2\frac{4}{8}$$
_____
$15\frac{11}{8}$
$16\frac{1}{8}$

8.
$$10\frac{4}{5}$$
$$9\frac{2}{5}$$
$$+\ 4\frac{1}{5}$$
_____
$24\frac{3}{5}$

9. **MP** **Number Sense** Explain how to use the addition properties to find $6\frac{3}{4} + 8\frac{2}{4} + 1\frac{1}{4}$ mentally. Then find the sum.

10. **DIG DEEPER!** When adding mixed numbers, is it always necessary to write the sum as a mixed number? Explain.

11. **DIG DEEPER!** Find the unknown number.

$$4\frac{5}{6} + \boxed{3\frac{4}{6}} = 8\frac{3}{6}$$

Think and Grow: Modeling Real Life

Example You pick $2\frac{3}{4}$ pounds of cherries. Your friend picks $1\frac{2}{4}$ pounds of cherries. How many pounds of cherries do you and your friend pick in all?

Add the amounts of cherries you and your friend each pick.

$$2\frac{3}{4} + 1\frac{2}{4} = 2 + \frac{3}{4} + 1 + \frac{2}{4}$$

$$= (2 + 1) + \left(\frac{3}{4} + \frac{2}{4}\right)$$

$$= 3 + \frac{5}{4}$$

$$= 3\frac{5}{4}$$

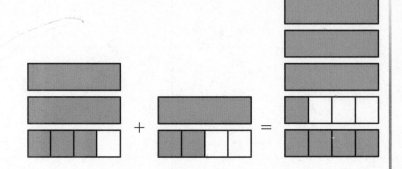

Write $3\frac{5}{4}$ as a mixed number.

$$3\frac{5}{4} = 3 + \frac{4}{4} + \frac{1}{4} = \boxed{}\frac{\boxed{}}{\boxed{}}$$

So, you and your friend pick $\boxed{}\frac{\boxed{}}{\boxed{}}$ pounds of cherries in all.

Show and Grow   *I can think deeper!*

12. Before noon, $2\frac{3}{8}$ inches of snow falls in a city. After noon, $4\frac{6}{8}$ inches of snow falls. How many inches of snow falls in the city that day?

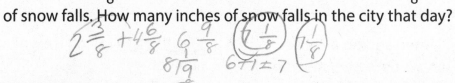

13. **DIG DEEPER!** A student driver must practice driving at night for a total of at least 10 hours. Has the student met the nighttime driving requirement yet?

Week	Driving Time (at Night)
1	$2\frac{1}{2}$ hours
2	$3\frac{1}{2}$ hours
3	$2\frac{1}{2}$ hours

Learning Target: Subtract mixed numbers with like denominators.

Success Criteria:
- I can subtract fractional parts and whole number parts of mixed numbers with like denominators.
- I can use equivalent fractions to subtract mixed numbers with like denominators.
- I can explain two ways to subtract mixed numbers with like denominators.

 Explore and Grow

Use a model to find $2\frac{3}{8} - 1\frac{1}{8}$.

 Construct Arguments How can you use the whole number parts and the fractional parts to subtract mixed numbers with like denominators? Explain why your method makes sense.

Think and Grow: Subtract Mixed Numbers

To subtract mixed numbers, subtract the fractional parts and subtract the whole number parts. Another way to subtract mixed numbers is to rewrite each number as a fraction, then subtract.

Example Find $5\frac{2}{3} - 2\frac{1}{3}$.

Subtract the fractional parts and subtract the whole number parts.

$$
\begin{array}{r}
5\frac{2}{3} \\
- 2\frac{1}{3} \\
\hline
3\frac{1}{3}
\end{array}
$$

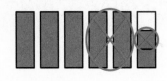

So, $5\frac{2}{3} - 2\frac{1}{3} = \boxed{}\dfrac{\boxed{}}{\boxed{}}$.

Use the relationship between addition and subtraction to check:

$2\frac{1}{3} + \boxed{} \dfrac{\boxed{}}{\boxed{}} \overset{?}{=} 5\frac{2}{3}$

Example Find $5\frac{3}{6} - 4\frac{5}{6}$.

One Way: Subtract the fractional parts and subtract the whole number parts.

$$
\begin{array}{r}
5\frac{3}{6} = 4\frac{9}{6} \\
- 4\frac{5}{6} = 4\frac{5}{6} \\
\hline
\dfrac{\boxed{}}{\boxed{}}
\end{array}
$$

← There are not enough sixths to subtract $\frac{5}{6}$ from $\frac{3}{6}$. So, rename $5\frac{3}{6}$.

$5 + \frac{3}{6} = 4 + \frac{6}{6} + \frac{3}{6} = 4\frac{9}{6}$

Another Way: Write each mixed number as a fraction, then subtract.

$5\frac{3}{6} = 5 + \frac{3}{6} = \frac{30}{6} + \frac{3}{6} = \frac{33}{6}$

$4\frac{5}{6} = 4 + \frac{5}{6} = \frac{24}{6} + \frac{5}{6} = \frac{29}{6}$

$\frac{33}{6} - \frac{29}{6} = \dfrac{\boxed{}}{\boxed{}}$

So, $5\frac{3}{6} - 4\frac{5}{6} = \dfrac{\boxed{}}{\boxed{}}$.

Show and Grow   I can do it!

Subtract.

1. $5\frac{4}{5} - 1\frac{2}{5} =$ _____

2. $7\frac{1}{3} - 2\frac{2}{3} =$ _____

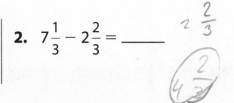

Name _____

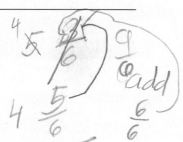

Subtract.

3. $15\frac{10}{12} - 4\frac{8}{12} =$ _____

$15\frac{10}{12}$
$- 4\frac{8}{12}$

$11\frac{2}{12}$ yay

$11\frac{2}{12}$

4. $6\frac{6}{8} - 3\frac{6}{8} =$ _____

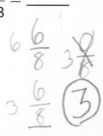

$6\frac{6}{8}$
$-3\frac{6}{8}$
3

5. $5\frac{7}{10} - 1\frac{9}{10} =$ _____

$\frac{4}{6}$

6. $11\frac{50}{100}$ $\frac{150}{100}$
$-\ 7\frac{85}{100}$

$3\frac{65}{100}$

7. 8
$-1\frac{3}{6}$

8. 10
$-\ 9\frac{3}{4}$

$\frac{1}{4}$

9. **YOU BE THE TEACHER** Your friend says the difference of 9 and $2\frac{3}{5}$ is $7\frac{3}{5}$. Is your friend correct? Explain.

10. **Writing** Explain how adding and subtracting mixed numbers are similar and different.

11. **DIG DEEPER!** Write two mixed numbers with like denominators that have a sum of $5\frac{2}{3}$ and a difference of 1.

Think and Grow: Modeling Real Life

Example   A replica of the Eiffel Tower is 6 inches tall. It is $2\frac{2}{5}$ inches taller than a replica of the Space Needle. How tall is the replica of the Space Needle?

Find the difference between the height of the Eiffel Tower replica, 6 inches, and $2\frac{2}{5}$ inches.

Write each measurement as a fraction.

$$6 = \frac{30}{5} \qquad 2\frac{2}{5} = \frac{10}{5} + \frac{2}{5} = \frac{12}{5}$$

Subtract $\frac{12}{5}$ from $\frac{30}{5}$.

$$\frac{30}{5} - \frac{12}{5} = \frac{18}{5}$$

Write $\frac{18}{5}$ as a mixed number.

$$\frac{18}{5} = \frac{15}{5} + \frac{3}{5} = \square\frac{\square}{\square}$$

So, the Space Needle replica is $\square\frac{\square}{\square}$ inches tall.

Show and Grow   I can think deeper!

12. A cook has a 5-pound bag of potatoes. He uses $2\frac{1}{3}$ pounds of potatoes to make a casserole. How many pounds of potatoes are left?

13. A half-marathon is $13\frac{1}{10}$ miles long. A competitor runs $9\frac{6}{10}$ miles. How many miles does the competitor have left to run?

14. **DIG DEEPER!** You want to mail a package that weighs $18\frac{2}{4}$ ounces. The weight limit is 13 ounces, so you remove $4\frac{3}{4}$ ounces of items from the package. Does the lighter package meet the weight requirement? If not, how much more weight do you need to remove?

Name _____

Problem Solving: Fractions **8.9**

Learning Target: Solve multi-step word problems involving fractions and mixed numbers.

Success Criteria:
- I can understand a problem.
- I can make a plan to solve.
- I can solve a problem using an equation.

 Explore and Grow

Make a plan to solve the problem.

The table shows the tusk lengths of two elephants. Which elephant's tusks have a greater total length? How much greater?

	Right Tusk	Left Tusk
Male Elephant	$4\frac{1}{12}$ ft	$4\frac{3}{12}$ ft
Female Elephant	4 ft	$3\frac{7}{12}$ ft

 Make Sense of Problems A $\frac{7}{12}$-foot long piece of one of the male elephant's tusks breaks off. Does this change your plan to solve the problem? Will this change the answer? Explain.

Think and Grow: Problem Solving: Fractions

COOLEST PLACE ON EARTH

Example A family spends $2\frac{2}{4}$ hours traveling to a theme park, $7\frac{1}{4}$ hours at the theme park, and $2\frac{3}{4}$ hours traveling home. How much more time does the family spend at the theme park than traveling?

Understand the Problem

What do you know?

- The family spends $2\frac{2}{4}$ hours traveling to the theme park, $7\frac{1}{4}$ hours at the theme park, and $2\frac{3}{4}$ hours traveling home.

What do you need to find?

- You need to find how much more time the family spends at the theme park than traveling.

Make a Plan

How will you solve?

- Add $2\frac{2}{4}$ and $2\frac{3}{4}$ to find how much time the family spends traveling.

- Then subtract the sum from $7\frac{1}{4}$ to find how much more time they spend at the theme park.

Solve

Step 1: $2\frac{2}{4} + 2\frac{3}{4} = c$

c is the unknown sum.

$$2\frac{2}{4}$$
$$+\ 2\frac{3}{4}$$
$$\overline{}$$
$$4\frac{5}{4} = 4 + \frac{4}{4} + \frac{1}{4} = \underline{}$$
$$c = \underline{}$$

Step 2: $7\frac{1}{4} - c = m$

m is the unknown difference.

$$7\frac{1}{4}$$
$$-\ \boxed{}$$
$$\overline{\boxed{}}$$
$$m = \underline{}$$

So, the family spends _____ more hours at the theme park than traveling.

Show and Grow   I can do it!

1. Explain how you can check your answer in each step of the example above.

Apply and Grow: Practice

Understand the problem. What do you know? What do you need to find? Explain.

2. You are making a sand art bottle. You fill $\frac{1}{6}$ of the bottle with pink sand, $\frac{3}{6}$ with red sand, and $\frac{2}{6}$ with white sand. How much of the bottle is filled?

3. Your friend has $\frac{1}{8}$ of a photo album filled with beach photographs and $\frac{4}{8}$ of the album filled with photos of friends. What fraction of the photo album is left?

Understand the problem. Then make a plan. How will you solve? Explain.

4. In Race A, an Olympic swimmer swims 100 meters in $62\frac{25}{100}$ seconds. In Race B, she cuts $2\frac{38}{100}$ seconds off her Race A time. How many seconds does she need to cut off her Race B time to swim 100 meters in $58\frac{45}{100}$ seconds?

5. A semi-truck has 2 fuel tanks that each hold the same amount of fuel. A truck driver fills up both tanks and uses $\frac{3}{4}$ tank of gasoline driving to his first stop. He uses $\frac{2}{4}$ tank of gasoline driving to his second stop. How much gasoline does he have left?

6. A bootlace worm holds the record as the longest animal at 180 feet long. How much longer is it than 2 blue whales combined?

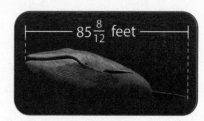

$85\frac{8}{12}$ feet

Blue Whale

Think and Grow: Modeling Real Life

Example You walk $\frac{1}{10}$ kilometer on Monday, $\frac{3}{10}$ kilometer on Tuesday, and $\frac{5}{10}$ kilometer on Wednesday. You continue the pattern on Thursday and Friday. How many kilometers do you walk in all?

Think: What do you know? What do you need to find? How will you solve?

Step 1: Identify the pattern.

Day of the Week	Mon	Tues	Wed	Thurs	Fri
Distance Walked (kilometers)	$\frac{1}{10}$	$\frac{3}{10}$	$\frac{5}{10}$		

$+\dfrac{\square}{10}$ $+\dfrac{\square}{10}$

Pattern:

Each day, you walk $\dfrac{\square}{10}$ kilometer more than the day before.

Step 2: Use the pattern to find the distances you walk on Thursday and Friday.

Wed   Thurs

$\dfrac{5}{10} + \dfrac{2}{10} = \dfrac{\square}{10}$

Thurs   Fri

$\dfrac{\square}{10} + \dfrac{2}{10} = \dfrac{\square}{10}$

Step 3: Add all of the distances.

$$\frac{1}{10} + \frac{3}{10} + \frac{5}{10} + \frac{7}{10} + \frac{9}{10} = \frac{1+3+5+7+9}{10}$$

$$= \frac{25}{10}$$

$$= \frac{20}{10} + \frac{5}{10}$$

$$= \square\dfrac{\square}{\square}$$

So, you walk $\square\dfrac{\square}{\square}$ kilometers in all.

Show and Grow   I can think deeper!

7. You save $\frac{1}{4}$ dollar the first week, $\frac{2}{4}$ dollar the next week, and $\frac{3}{4}$ dollar the following week. You continue the pattern for 3 more weeks. How much money do you save after 6 weeks?

Learning Target: Solve multi-step word problems involving fractions and mixed numbers.

Example   A baker buys a 5-pound bag of flour. He uses $1\frac{1}{4}$ pounds of flour for one recipe and $2\frac{3}{4}$ pounds for another recipe. How many pounds of flour does he have left?

Think: What do you know? What do you need to find? How will you solve?

Step 1: Find how many pounds of flour the baker uses.

$$1\frac{1}{4} + 2\frac{3}{4} = c$$

c is the unknown sum.

$$\begin{array}{r} 1\frac{1}{4} \\ + 2\frac{3}{4} \\ \hline 3\frac{4}{4} = \underline{\quad 4 \quad} \end{array}$$

$$c = \underline{\quad 4 \quad}$$

Step 2: Find how many pounds of flour the baker has left.

$$5 - c = k$$

k is the unknown difference.

$$5 - \underline{\quad 4 \quad} = \underline{\quad 1 \quad}$$

$$k = \underline{\quad 1 \quad}$$

So, the baker has __1__ pound of flour left.

Understand the problem. Then make a plan. How will you solve? Explain.

1. An older washing machine uses $170\frac{3}{10}$ liters of water per load. A new, high-efficiency, washing machine uses $75\frac{7}{10}$ fewer liters than the older washing machine. How many liters of water will the high-efficiency washing machine use for 2 loads of laundry?

2. A student jumps $40\frac{5}{12}$ inches for the high jump. On his second try, he jumps $1\frac{8}{12}$ inches higher. He can tie the school record if he raises the bar another $3\frac{10}{12}$ inches and successfully jumps over it. What is the school record for the high jump?

3. You are shipping three care packages. The first package weighs $10\frac{1}{10}$ pounds. The second weighs $5\frac{7}{10}$ pounds, and the third weighs $25\frac{8}{10}$ pounds. What is the total weight of the packages?

4. A person's arm span is approximately equal to the person's height. How tall is this fourth grader according to his arm span?

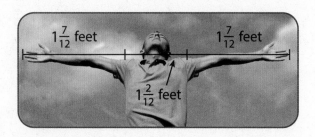

$1\frac{7}{12}$ feet $1\frac{7}{12}$ feet

$1\frac{2}{12}$ feet

5. **Writing** Write and solve a two-step word problem with mixed numbers that can be solved using addition or subtraction.

6. **Modeling Real Life** Your friend walks $\frac{2}{10}$ mile to school each day. She walks the same distance home. How many miles does she walk to and from school in one 5-day school week?

7. **DIG DEEPER!** A store sells cashews in $\frac{2}{3}$-pound bags. You buy some bags and repackage the cashews into 1-pound bags. What is the least number of bags you should buy so that you do not have any cashews left over?

Review & Refresh

Compare.

8. $\frac{8}{12} \bigcirc \frac{1}{6}$

9. $\frac{9}{10} \bigcirc \frac{14}{8}$

10. $\frac{3}{4} \bigcirc \frac{1}{2}$

Name _____

Performance Task 8

The notes on sheet music tell you what note to play and how long to hold each note. The table shows how long you hold some notes compared to the length of one whole note.

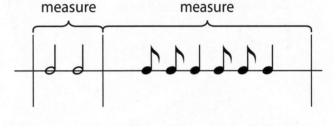

Whole note	$\frac{1}{2}$ note	$\frac{1}{4}$ note	$\frac{1}{8}$ note
$\frac{\Box}{8}$	$\frac{\Box}{8}$	$\frac{\Box}{8}$	$\frac{1}{8}$

1. **a.** Complete the table by writing equivalent fractions.

b. Each group of notes represents one measure. What is the sum of the values of the notes in each measure?

measure   measure

$$\frac{\Box}{\Box} + \frac{\Box}{\Box} = \frac{\Box}{\Box} + \frac{\Box}{\Box} + \frac{\Box}{\Box} + \frac{\Box}{\Box} + \frac{\Box}{\Box} + \frac{\Box}{\Box} = \underline{\quad}$$

c. Draw the missing note to complete each measure.

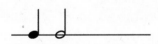

$$\frac{2}{8} + \frac{4}{8} + \frac{\Box}{\Box} = 1$$ $$\frac{\Box}{\Box} + \frac{\Box}{\Box} + \frac{\Box}{\Box} + \frac{\Box}{\Box} = 1$$

d. Draw one measure of notes where the sum of the values is 1. Show your work.

_____

e. Write the fraction represented by the sum of the notes. Then write the fraction as a sum of fractions in two different ways.

© Big Ideas Learning, LLC

Three In a Row: Fraction Add or Subtract

Directions:

1. Players take turns.
2. On your turn, spin both spinners. Choose whether to add or subtract.
3. Add or subtract the mixed number and fraction. Cover the sum or difference.
4. If the sum or difference is already covered, you lose your turn.
5. The first player to get three in a row wins!

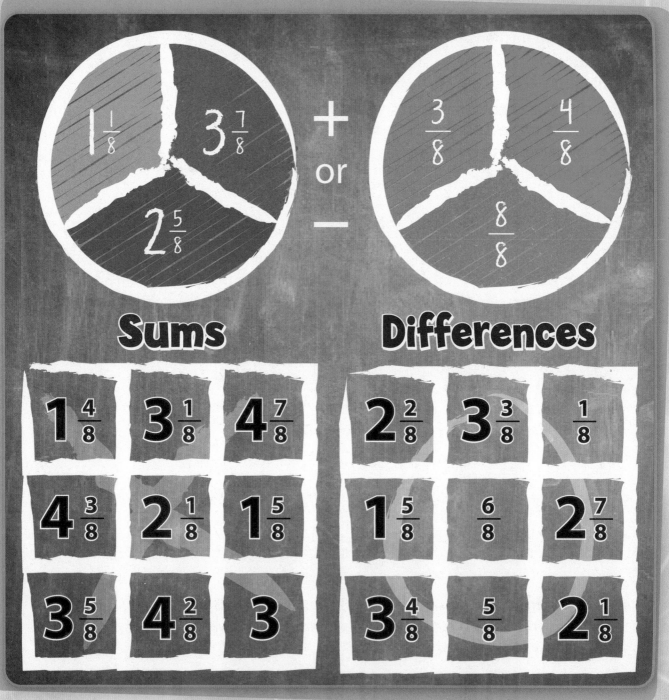

9

Multiply Whole Numbers and Fractions

- Dolphins use echolocation to communicate with other dolphins, to determine their location, and to find food. What other animals use echolocation?

- A dolphin is hunting prey that is $\frac{1}{4}$ mile away. How can you use multiplication to find how long it will take the dolphin to catch its prey?

Chapter Learning Target:
Understand multiplying whole numbers and fractions.

Chapter Success Criteria:
- I can identify a fraction as a sum of unit fractions.
- I can write a fraction as a sum of unit fractions.
- I can find the product of a whole number and a fraction.
- I can solve a problem using fractions.

©Big Ideas Learning, LLC

Name _____

Organize It

Use a review word to complete the graphic organizer.

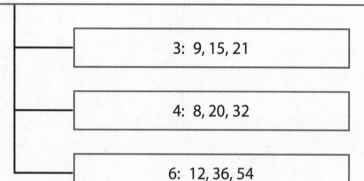

_____ : The product of a number and any other counting number

3: 9, 15, 21

4: 8, 20, 32

6: 12, 36, 54

Review Words
Associative Property of Multiplication
Distributive Property
multiple
Multiplication Property of One

Define It

Match each review word to an equation.

1. Associative Property of Multiplication

2. Distributive Property

3. Multiplication Property of One

$3 \times (5 + 2) = (3 \times 5) + (3 \times 2)$

$5 \times 1 = 5$

$2 \times (3 \times 4) = (2 \times 3) \times 4$

Learning Target: Write fractions as multiples of unit fractions.

Success Criteria:
• I can write a fraction as a sum of unit fractions.
• I can use multiplication to rewrite a sum of unit fractions.
• I can write a fraction as a multiple of a unit fraction.

 Explore and Grow

Draw a model of any fraction using unit fractions. Then write an addition equation to represent your model.

 Reasoning How can you rewrite the equation using multiplication? Explain.

Think and Grow: Multiples of Unit Fractions

Any fraction can be written as a multiple of a unit fraction with a like denominator.

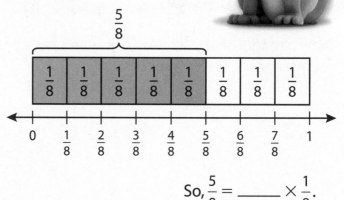

Think: $\frac{5}{8}$ is a multiple of $\frac{1}{8}$.

Example Write $\frac{5}{8}$ as a multiple of a unit fraction.

The fraction $\frac{5}{8}$ represents 5 parts that are each $\frac{1}{8}$ of the whole.

$\frac{5}{8} = \frac{\square}{\square} + \frac{\square}{\square} + \frac{\square}{\square} + \frac{\square}{\square} + \frac{\square}{\square}$

$= \underline{\hspace{1cm}} \times \frac{1}{8}$

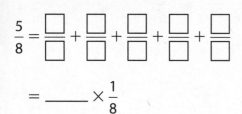

So, $\frac{5}{8} = \underline{\hspace{1cm}} \times \frac{1}{8}$.

Show and Grow   I can do it!

Write the fraction as a multiple of a unit fraction.

1. $\frac{2}{3} = \frac{\square}{\square} + \frac{\square}{\square}$

$= \underline{\hspace{1cm}} \times \frac{1}{3}$

2. $\frac{4}{8} = \frac{\square}{\square} + \frac{\square}{\square} + \frac{\square}{\square} + \frac{\square}{\square}$

$= \underline{\hspace{1cm}} \times \frac{1}{8}$

3. $\frac{6}{5}$

4. $\frac{7}{100}$

410

Name _____

 Apply and Grow: Practice

Write the fraction as a multiple of a unit fraction.

5. $\dfrac{2}{6}$

6. $\dfrac{6}{8}$

7. $\dfrac{5}{4}$

8. $\dfrac{3}{12}$

9. $\dfrac{8}{100}$

10. $\dfrac{7}{10}$

11. **MP Structure** When a fraction is written as a multiple of a unit fraction, what is the relationship between the numerator of the fraction and the number that is multiplied by the unit fraction?

DIG DEEPER! Write the mixed number as a multiple of a unit fraction.

12. $1\dfrac{1}{8}$

13. $3\dfrac{4}{5}$

Think and Grow: Modeling Real Life

Example   A juice stand worker uses $\frac{1}{12}$ of an orange to garnish each drink. The worker has $\frac{7}{12}$ of an orange left. How many more drinks can the worker garnish?

Write the fraction of orange left as a multiple of $\frac{1}{12}$.

$$\frac{7}{12} = \frac{\square}{\square} + \frac{\square}{\square} + \frac{\square}{\square} + \frac{\square}{\square} + \frac{\square}{\square} + \frac{\square}{\square} + \frac{\square}{\square}$$

$$= \underline{\hspace{1cm}} \times \frac{1}{12}$$ So, the worker can garnish _____ more drinks.

Show and Grow   *I can think deeper!*

14. A piece of rope is $\frac{8}{5}$ meters long. You cut the rope into $\frac{1}{5}$-meter long pieces. How many pieces do you cut?

15. A restaurant serves $\frac{4}{10}$ of a meatloaf to 4 customers. Each customer receives the same amount of meatloaf. What fraction of the meatloaf does each customer receive?

16. You use $3\frac{3}{4}$ pounds of trail mix to make treat bags. You put $\frac{1}{4}$ pound of trail mix into each bag. How many treat bags do you make?

17. **DIG DEEPER!** You walk from home to school and then back home again each day for 5 days. Altogether, you walk $\frac{10}{8}$ miles. What is the distance from your home to school? Explain.

© Big Ideas Learning, LLC

412

Learning Target: Write fractions as multiples of unit fractions.

Example Write $\frac{3}{4}$ as a multiple of a unit fraction.

The fraction $\frac{3}{4}$ represents 3 parts

that are each $\frac{1}{4}$ of the whole.

$\frac{3}{4} = \boxed{\dfrac{1}{4}} + \boxed{\dfrac{1}{4}} + \boxed{\dfrac{1}{4}}$

$= \underline{\quad 3 \quad} \times \dfrac{1}{4}$

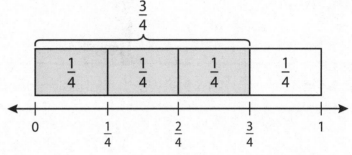

So, $\dfrac{3}{4} = \underline{\quad 3 \quad} \times \dfrac{1}{4}$.

Write the fraction as a multiple of a unit fraction.

1. $\dfrac{2}{12} = \dfrac{\Box}{\Box} + \dfrac{\Box}{\Box}$

$= \underline{\quad\quad} \times \dfrac{1}{12}$

2. $\dfrac{5}{100} = \dfrac{\Box}{\Box} + \dfrac{\Box}{\Box} + \dfrac{\Box}{\Box} + \dfrac{\Box}{\Box} + \dfrac{\Box}{\Box}$

$= \underline{\quad\quad} \times \dfrac{1}{100}$

3. $\dfrac{3}{6}$

4. $\dfrac{7}{10}$

5. $\dfrac{4}{5}$

6. $\dfrac{9}{2}$

7. $\dfrac{8}{8}$

8. $\dfrac{6}{3}$

9. **Logic** What is Newton's fraction? Write the fraction as a multiple of a unit fraction.

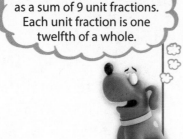

My fraction can be written as a sum of 9 unit fractions. Each unit fraction is one twelfth of a whole.

10. **Structure** Write a multiplication equation that represents the grapefruit halves.

11. **Which One Doesn't Belong?** Which expression does *not* belong with the other three?

$$5 \times \frac{1}{4} \qquad \frac{1}{4} + \frac{1}{4} + \frac{1}{4} + \frac{1}{4} + \frac{1}{4} \qquad \frac{5}{4} \qquad 4 \times \frac{1}{5}$$

12. **Modeling Real Life** You are making blueberry pancakes. You have $\frac{6}{8}$ cup of blueberries. You put $\frac{1}{8}$ cup of blueberries in each pancake. How many pancakes do you make?

13. **DIG DEEPER!** You cut a loaf of zucchini bread into 20 equal slices. You and your friends eat $\frac{3}{10}$ of the slices. You want to put each leftover slice into its own bag. How many bags do you need?

Review & Refresh

14. Is 46 a multiple of 5?

15. Is 3 a factor of 75?

Learning Target: Write multiples of fractions as multiples of unit fractions.

Success Criteria:
• I can write a fraction as a multiple of a unit fraction.
• I can write a multiple of a fraction as a multiple of a unit fraction.
• I can find the product of a whole number and a unit fraction.

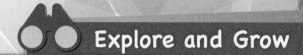

Explore and Grow

Draw a model for each expression. Then write a multiplication expression to represent each model.

$$\frac{2}{6} + \frac{2}{6} + \frac{2}{6} + \frac{2}{6}$$

$$\frac{1}{6} + \frac{1}{6} + \frac{1}{6} + \frac{1}{6} + \frac{1}{6} + \frac{1}{6} + \frac{1}{6} + \frac{1}{6}$$

 Structure Compare your expressions. How are they the same? How are they different?

A multiple of any fraction can be written as a multiple of a unit fraction with a like denominator.

Example Write $2 \times \dfrac{3}{5}$ as a multiple of a unit fraction. Then find the product.

$2 \times \dfrac{3}{5} = 2 \times \left(\underline{\hspace{1cm}} \times \dfrac{1}{5} \right)$

Think: $\dfrac{6}{5}$ is a multiple of $\dfrac{3}{5}$.

$= \left(2 \times \underline{\hspace{1cm}} \right) \times \dfrac{1}{5}$ Associative Property of Multiplication

$= \underline{\hspace{1cm}} \times \dfrac{1}{5}$

$\dfrac{1}{5}$	$\dfrac{1}{5}$	$\dfrac{1}{5}$	$\dfrac{1}{5}$	$\dfrac{1}{5}$
$\dfrac{1}{5}$	$\dfrac{1}{5}$	$\dfrac{1}{5}$	$\dfrac{1}{5}$	$\dfrac{1}{5}$

$\Big\} 2 \times \dfrac{3}{5}$

$\dfrac{6}{5}$

$= \dfrac{\square}{\square}$

So, $2 \times \dfrac{3}{5} = \underline{\hspace{1cm}} \times \underline{\hspace{1cm}} = \underline{\hspace{1cm}}$.

Show and Grow   I can do it!

Write the product as a multiple of a unit fraction. Then find the product.

1. $2 \times \dfrac{4}{5}$

2. $3 \times \dfrac{2}{10}$

3. $4 \times \dfrac{3}{2}$

Name _____

Apply and Grow: Practice

Write the product as a multiple of a unit fraction. Then find the product.

4. $5 \times \dfrac{2}{3}$

5. $6 \times \dfrac{5}{8}$

6. $9 \times \dfrac{7}{4}$

7. $7 \times \dfrac{4}{12}$

8. $\dfrac{9}{6} \times 8$

9. $10 \times \dfrac{20}{100}$

MP Number Sense Find the unknown number.

10. $\square \times \dfrac{8}{10} = \dfrac{16}{10}$

11. $4 \times \dfrac{\square}{2} = \dfrac{20}{2}$

12. $3 \times \dfrac{9}{\square} = \dfrac{27}{100}$

13. **MP Reasoning** Without calculating, would you plot the product of 5 and $\dfrac{3}{6}$ to the left or to the right of 5 on a number line? Explain.

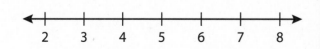

14. **MP Patterns** Describe and complete the pattern.

Expression	Product
$3 \times \dfrac{1}{5}$	$\dfrac{3}{5}$
$3 \times \dfrac{2}{5}$	
$3 \times \dfrac{3}{5}$	
$3 \times \dfrac{4}{5}$	
$3 \times \dfrac{5}{5}$	

Think and Grow: Modeling Real Life

Example A bird keeper uses a $\frac{1}{3}$-cup scoop to feed 3 birds. He feeds each bird $\frac{2}{3}$ cup of birdseed. How many times does he fill the scoop?

Three birds each need $\frac{2}{3}$ cup of birdseed, so find $3 \times \frac{2}{3}$.

$$3 \times \frac{2}{3} = 3 \times \left(\underline{\hspace{1cm}} \times \frac{1}{3} \right)$$

$$= \left(3 \times \underline{\hspace{1cm}} \right) \times \frac{1}{3} \qquad \text{Associative Property of Multiplication}$$

$$= \underline{\hspace{1cm}} \times \frac{1}{3}$$

So, the bird keeper fills the scoop _____ times.

Show and Grow   *I can think deeper!*

15. A chef makes 4 servings of honey oatmeal. She uses a $\frac{1}{2}$-tablespoon measuring spoon to measure $\frac{3}{2}$ tablespoons of honey for each serving. How many times does she fill the measuring spoon?

16. You have 7 magnetic blocks that are each $\frac{9}{100}$ meter long. You connect the ends of the blocks to make a snake. What fraction of a meter is the block snake?

17. Your friend roller-skates $\frac{15}{10}$ miles each day for 5 days. How many miles does your friend roller-skate in all?

Name _____

Name _____

Learning Target: Write multiples of fractions as multiples of unit fractions.

Example Write $3 \times \dfrac{5}{6}$ as a multiple of a unit fraction. Then find the product.

$$3 \times \frac{5}{6} = 3 \times \left(\underline{} 5 \times \frac{1}{6} \right)$$

$$= (3 \times \underline{} 5) \times \frac{1}{6}$$

$$= \underline{} 15 \times \frac{1}{6}$$

$$= \boxed{\frac{15}{6}}$$

$\frac{1}{6}$	$\frac{1}{6}$	$\frac{1}{6}$	$\frac{1}{6}$	$\frac{1}{6}$	$\frac{1}{6}$
$\frac{1}{6}$	$\frac{1}{6}$	$\frac{1}{6}$	$\frac{1}{6}$	$\frac{1}{6}$	$\frac{1}{6}$
$\frac{1}{6}$	$\frac{1}{6}$	$\frac{1}{6}$	$\frac{1}{6}$	$\frac{1}{6}$	$\frac{1}{6}$

$3 \times \dfrac{5}{6}$

$\dfrac{15}{6}$

So, $3 \times \dfrac{5}{6} = \underline{} 15 \times \underline{\phantom{\frac{1}{6}}} \dfrac{1}{6} = \underline{\phantom{\frac{15}{6}}} \dfrac{15}{6}$.

Write the product as a multiple of a unit fraction. Then find the product.

1. $2 \times \dfrac{2}{3}$

2. $3 \times \dfrac{5}{8}$

3. $4 \times \dfrac{8}{2}$

4. $5 \times \dfrac{9}{10}$

5. $8 \times \dfrac{6}{5}$

6. $\dfrac{2}{4} \times 10$

7. **MP Number Sense** Which expressions are equivalent to $4 \times \frac{7}{8}$?

$(4 \times 7) \times \frac{1}{8}$ $\frac{28}{8}$ 4×7 $\frac{32}{7}$ $\frac{7}{8} + \frac{7}{8} + \frac{7}{8} + \frac{7}{8}$

8. **MP Number Sense** Which is greater, $6 \times \frac{6}{2}$ or $5 \times \frac{7}{2}$? Explain.

9. **MP Structure** Your friend fills a $\frac{3}{4}$-cup measuring cup with rice 2 times. Write an equation to show how much rice she uses.

10. **Modeling Real Life** You are making a tornado in each of 2 bottles. Each bottle needs to contain $\frac{20}{4}$ cups of water. You only have a $\frac{1}{4}$-cup measuring cup. How many times do you need to fill the measuring cup?

11. **DIG DEEPER!** You and your friend are each selling 12 coupon books. So far, you have sold $\frac{2}{6}$ of your books. Your friend has sold 3 times as many as you. What fraction of your friend's coupon books has she sold?

Review & Refresh

Find the product.

12. $12 \times 47 =$ _____

13. $35 \times 31 =$ _____

14. $58 \times 49 =$ _____

Name _____

Learning Target: Multiply whole numbers and fractions.

Success Criteria:
• I can write a multiple of a fraction as a multiple of a unit fraction.
• I can use a rule to find the product of a whole number and a fraction.
• I can explain why the rule used to multiply a whole number and a fraction makes sense.

 Explore and Grow

Use models to help you complete the table. What do you notice about each expression and its product?

Expression	Product
$3 \times \dfrac{1}{12}$	☐/☐
$4 \times \dfrac{2}{10}$	☐/☐
$5 \times \dfrac{3}{6}$	☐/☐
$2 \times \dfrac{5}{4}$	☐/☐

 Construct Arguments Explain how to find the product of a whole number and a fraction without using models.

You can find the product of a whole number and a fraction by multiplying the numerator by the whole number. The denominator stays the same.

Example   Find $4 \times \dfrac{2}{3}$.

One Way: Multiply the numerator by the whole number.

$$4 \times \frac{2}{3} = \frac{\Box \times \Box}{3}$$

$$= \frac{\Box}{\Box}$$

$\frac{1}{3}$	$\frac{1}{3}$	$\frac{1}{3}$
$\frac{1}{3}$	$\frac{1}{3}$	$\frac{1}{3}$
$\frac{1}{3}$	$\frac{1}{3}$	$\frac{1}{3}$
$\frac{1}{3}$	$\frac{1}{3}$	$\frac{1}{3}$

$\left.\right\} 4 \times \dfrac{2}{3}$

$\dfrac{8}{3}$

Another Way: Rewrite the expression as a multiple of a unit fraction.

$$4 \times \frac{2}{3} = 4 \times \left(\underline{\quad} \times \frac{1}{3}\right)$$

$$= (4 \times \underline{\quad}) \times \frac{1}{3} \qquad \text{Associative Property of Multiplication}$$

$$= \underline{\quad} \times \frac{1}{3}$$

$$= \frac{\Box}{\Box}$$

So, $4 \times \dfrac{2}{3} = \underline{\quad}$.

Show and Grow   *I can do it!*

Multiply.

1. $4 \times \dfrac{1}{6} = \underline{\quad}$

2. $3 \times \dfrac{2}{4} = \underline{\quad}$

3. $7 \times \dfrac{3}{2} = \underline{\quad}$

Name _____

 Apply and Grow: Practice

Multiply.

4. $2 \times \dfrac{1}{5} = $ _____

5. $5 \times \dfrac{3}{10} = $ _____

6. $6 \times \dfrac{7}{8} = $ _____

7. $8 \times \dfrac{9}{10} = $ _____

8. $3 \times \dfrac{60}{100} = $ _____

9. $\dfrac{4}{2} \times 10 = $ _____

Compare.

10. $7 \times \dfrac{2}{4} \bigcirc 5 \times \dfrac{3}{4}$

11. $4 \times \dfrac{1}{8} \bigcirc 4 \times \dfrac{1}{10}$

12. $\dfrac{4}{3} \times 9 \bigcirc 6 \times \dfrac{6}{3}$

13. **YOU BE THE TEACHER** Your friend says the product of 6 and $\dfrac{5}{8}$ is $\dfrac{5}{48}$. Is your friend correct? Explain.

14. **Open-Ended** The product of a whole number and a fraction is $\dfrac{24}{10}$. What could the two factors be?

Think and Grow: Modeling Real Life

Example A short roller-coaster track is $\frac{3}{10}$ mile long.

A longer roller-coaster track is about 4 times as long as the short track. About how long is the longer roller-coaster track?

Multiply the shorter roller-coaster track length by 4.

$$4 \times \frac{3}{10} = \frac{\boxed{} \times \boxed{}}{10}$$

$$= \frac{\boxed{}}{\boxed{}}$$

So, the longer roller-coaster track is about _____ miles long.

Show and Grow   I can think deeper!

15. The Renaissance Tower in Dallas, Texas is $\frac{27}{100}$ kilometer

tall. The Burj Khalifa is about 3 times as tall as the Renaissance Tower. About how tall is the Burj Khalifa?

The Burj Khalifa is located in Dubai, and it is the tallest building in the world.

16. You water 6 plants using $\frac{3}{5}$ liter of water for each. How many liters of water do you use? Between which two whole numbers does your answer lie?

17. **DIG DEEPER!** You have 6 cups of strawberries. You want to make 4 strawberry-banana smoothies and 4 strawberry-kiwi smoothies.

Each smoothie needs $\frac{2}{3}$ cup of strawberries. Do you have enough? If not, how many more cups of strawberries do you need?

424

© Big Ideas Learning, LLC

Name _____

Learning Target: Multiply whole numbers and fractions.

Example Find $2 \times \frac{5}{8}$.

One Way: Multiply the numerator by the whole number.

$$2 \times \frac{5}{8} = \frac{\boxed{2} \times \boxed{5}}{8}$$

$$= \frac{\boxed{10}}{\boxed{8}}$$

Another Way: Rewrite the expression as a multiple of a unit fraction.

$$2 \times \frac{5}{8} = 2 \times \left(\underline{\quad 5 \quad} \times \frac{1}{8} \right)$$

$$= (2 \times \underline{\quad 5 \quad}) \times \frac{1}{8} \qquad \text{Associative Property of Multiplication}$$

$$= \underline{\quad 10 \quad} \times \frac{1}{8}$$

$$= \frac{\boxed{10}}{\boxed{8}}$$

So, $2 \times \frac{5}{8} = \underline{\quad \frac{10}{8} \quad}$.

Multiply.

1. $2 \times \frac{1}{4} =$ _____

2. $3 \times \frac{3}{5} =$ _____

3. $1 \times \frac{6}{8} =$ _____

4. $4 \times \frac{10}{12} =$ _____

5. $7 \times \frac{6}{10} =$ _____

6. $\frac{4}{6} \times 5 =$ _____

7. $8 \times \frac{5}{2} =$ _____

8. $\frac{70}{100} \times 6 =$ _____

9. $10 \times \frac{9}{3} =$ _____

Compare.

10. $2 \times \dfrac{4}{2} \bigcirc 8 \times \dfrac{1}{2}$

11. $9 \times \dfrac{1}{5} \bigcirc 9 \times \dfrac{1}{12}$

12. $\dfrac{6}{10} \times 4 \bigcirc 9 \times \dfrac{3}{10}$

13. Writing Explain one way to multiply a whole number by a fraction.

14. 🔵 **Number Sense** Between which two whole numbers does the product of 10 and $\dfrac{5}{6}$ lie?

15. Modeling Real Life A seamstress makes fabric dog collars. An extra small dog collar is $\dfrac{1}{3}$ yard long. A large dog collar is 2 times as long as the extra small dog collar. How long is the large dog collar?

16. **DIG DEEPER!** Newton has 16 baseball cards. Descartes has $\dfrac{1}{4}$ as many cards as Newton, and your friend has $\dfrac{1}{2}$ as many cards as Descartes. How many baseball cards do Newton, Descartes, and your friend have in all?

Review & Refresh

Divide.

17. $4\overline{)76}$

18. $7\overline{)571}$

19. $5\overline{)923}$

Learning Target: Multiply whole numbers and mixed numbers.

Success Criteria:
- I can write a mixed number as a fraction to multiply.
- I can use the Distributive Property to multiply.
- I can find the product of a whole number and a mixed number.

 Explore and Grow

Use models to help you complete the table.

Expression	Product
$2 \times 1\frac{3}{8}$	☐ ☐/☐
$2 \times 2\frac{1}{3}$	☐ ☐/☐
$3 \times 2\frac{1}{4}$	☐ ☐/☐
$3 \times 1\frac{3}{10}$	☐ ☐/☐

 Structure How does the Distributive Property relate to your models? Explain.

Think and Grow: Multiply Whole Numbers and Mixed Numbers

You can find the product of a whole number and a mixed number by writing the mixed number as a fraction or by using the Distributive Property.

Example   Find $3 \times 1\frac{1}{2}$.

One Way: Write the mixed number as a fraction, then multiply.

$$3 \times 1\frac{1}{2} = 3 \times \frac{3}{2}$$

$$= \frac{\square \times \square}{2}$$

$$= \frac{\square}{2}$$

$$= \square\frac{\square}{\square}$$

Another Way: Use the Distributive Property.

$$3 \times 1\frac{1}{2} = 3 \times \left(1 + \frac{1}{2}\right)$$

$$= (3 \times 1) + \left(3 \times \frac{1}{2}\right) \quad \text{Distributive Property}$$

$$= 3 + \frac{3 \times \square}{2}$$

$$= 3 + \frac{\square}{2}$$

$$= 3 + \square\frac{\square}{2}$$

$$= \square\frac{\square}{\square}$$

So, $3 \times 1\frac{1}{2} =$ _____.

1
1
1

3×1

$\frac{1}{2}$	$\frac{1}{2}$
$\frac{1}{2}$	$\frac{1}{2}$
$\frac{1}{2}$	$\frac{1}{2}$

$3 \times \frac{1}{2}$

$\Big\}\, 3 \times 1\frac{1}{2}$

Show and Grow   I can do it!

Multiply.

1. $3 \times 2\frac{1}{4} =$ _____

2. $2 \times 1\frac{7}{12} =$ _____

3. $4 \times 3\frac{5}{8} =$ _____

Name _____

Multiply.

4. $10 \times 1\frac{2}{3} =$ _____

5. $5 \times 2\frac{1}{2} =$ _____

6. $7\frac{4}{6} \times 4 =$ _____

7. $9 \times 5\frac{2}{5} =$ _____

8. $3\frac{9}{10} \times 8 =$ _____

9. $6 \times 9\frac{11}{100} =$ _____

10. **Reasoning** How can you check whether your answer in Exercise 9 is reasonable?

11. **YOU BE THE TEACHER** Your friend finds the product of 9 and $6\frac{1}{3}$. Is your friend correct? Explain.

$$9 \times 6\frac{1}{3} = 9 \times \frac{19}{3}$$

$$= \frac{171}{3}$$

$$= 57$$

12. **DIG DEEPER!** Without multiplying, can you tell which expression is greater, $5 \times 6\frac{1}{4}$ or $6 \times 5\frac{1}{4}$? Explain.

Think and Grow: Modeling Real Life

Example An elephant sleeps $2\frac{1}{2}$ hours in 1 day. A koala sleeps 6 times as long as the elephant in the same day. How many hours does the koala sleep that day?

Multiply the number of hours the elephant sleeps by 6.

$$6 \times 2\frac{1}{2} = 6 \times \frac{5}{2}$$

$$= \frac{\square \times \square}{2}$$

$$= \frac{\square}{2}$$

$$= \underline{\hspace{1cm}}$$ So, the koala sleeps _____ hours that day.

Show and Grow   *I can think deeper!*

13. A small bag of popcorn has $1\frac{7}{8}$ cups of popcorn. A large bag has 7 times as many cups of popcorn as the small bag. How many cups of popcorn are in the large bag?

14. **DIG DEEPER!** A deli worker prepares 4 packages of meat. Each package contains $3\frac{1}{3}$ pounds of meat. Your friend says the deli worker uses between 12 and 13 pounds of meat. Is your friend correct? Explain.

15. **DIG DEEPER!** An athlete's goal is to run at least 80 miles in 1 week. He runs $5\frac{3}{4}$ miles 2 times each day for 1 week. Does the athlete meet his goal? Explain.

Name _____

Learning Target: Multiply whole numbers and mixed numbers.

Example Find $2 \times 1\frac{3}{4}$.

One Way: Write the mixed number as a fraction, then multiply.

$$2 \times 1\frac{3}{4} = 2 \times \frac{7}{4}$$

$$= \frac{\boxed{2} \times \boxed{7}}{4}$$

$$= \frac{14}{4}$$

$$= \boxed{3}\frac{\boxed{2}}{\boxed{4}}$$

Another Way: Use the Distributive Property.

$$2 \times 1\frac{3}{4} = 2 \times \left(1 + \frac{3}{4}\right)$$

$$= (2 \times 1) + \left(2 \times \frac{3}{4}\right) \quad \text{Distributive Property}$$

$$= 2 + \frac{2 \times \boxed{3}}{4}$$

$$= 2 + \frac{\boxed{6}}{4}$$

$$= 2 + \boxed{1}\frac{\boxed{2}}{4}$$

$$= \boxed{3}\frac{\boxed{2}}{\boxed{4}}$$

So, $2 \times 1\frac{3}{4} = \underline{3\frac{2}{4}}$.

Multiply.

1. $2 \times 1\frac{1}{12} = $ _____

2. $2 \times 3\frac{5}{6} = $ _____

3. $4 \times 3\frac{6}{10} = $ _____

4. $2\frac{3}{8} \times 5 = $ _____

5. $4 \times 6\frac{4}{5} = $ _____

6. $8\frac{20}{100} \times 10 = $ _____

7. (MP) **Reasoning** Without calculating, is the product of 7 and $5\frac{3}{4}$ greater than or less than 35? Explain.

---

8. **YOU BE THE TEACHER** Your friend finds the product of 4 and $2\frac{8}{10}$. Is your friend correct? Explain.

$$4 \times 2\frac{8}{10} = (4 \times 3) - \left(4 \times \frac{2}{10}\right)$$
$$= 12 - \frac{8}{10}$$
$$= \frac{112}{10}$$
$$= 11\frac{2}{10}$$

9. **Number Sense** Between which two whole numbers does the product of 9 and $7\frac{1}{8}$ lie?

---

10. **Modeling Real Life** Athlete A holds a $2\frac{1}{2}$-kilogram plate while doing squats. Athlete B holds a plate that is 4 times heavier than Athlete A's. How many kilograms is the plate held by Athlete B?

11. **DIG DEEPER!** A zoo nutritionist orders $5\frac{1}{4}$ tons of apples and $7\frac{2}{4}$ tons of bananas each year to feed the animals. She orders 6 times as many tons of herbivore pellets than tons of fruit. How many tons of herbivore pellets does the nutritionist order?

Review & Refresh

Subtract.

12. $9\frac{1}{4} - 6\frac{1}{4} = $ _____

13. $6\frac{1}{3} - 2\frac{2}{3} = $ _____

14. $8\frac{4}{12} - 1\frac{10}{12} = $ _____

Learning Target: Solve multi-step word problems involving fractions and mixed numbers.

Success Criteria:
• I can understand a problem.
• I can make a plan to solve.
• I can solve a problem using an equation.

 **Explore and Grow**

You want to make 3 batches of the recipe. Explain how to find how much of each ingredient you need.

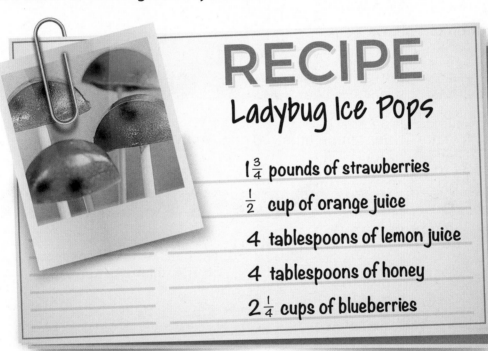

RECIPE
Ladybug Ice Pops

$1\frac{3}{4}$ pounds of strawberries

$\frac{1}{2}$ cup of orange juice

4 tablespoons of lemon juice

4 tablespoons of honey

$2\frac{1}{4}$ cups of blueberries

 Reasoning Explain how you can tell whether you need more than or less than 6 cups of blueberries without calculating.

Think and Grow: Problem Solving: Fraction Operations

Example To convert a temperature from degrees Celsius to degrees Fahrenheit, multiply the Celsius temperature by $\frac{9}{5}$, then add 32. What is the temperature shown by the thermometer in degrees Fahrenheit?

Understand the Problem

What do you know?

- To convert a temperature from degrees Celsius to degrees Fahrenheit, multiply the Celsius temperature by $\frac{9}{5}$, then add 32.
- The thermometer shows 10 degrees Celsius.

What do you need to find?

- You need to find the temperature shown by the thermometer in degrees Fahrenheit.

Make a Plan

How will you solve?

- First, multiply the Celsius temperature, 10 degrees, by $\frac{9}{5}$.
- Then add 32 to the product.

Solve

Step 1: $10 \times \dfrac{9}{5} = p$

p is the unknown product.

$$10 \times \frac{9}{5} = \frac{\square \times \square}{5} = \frac{\square}{\square}$$

$$= \underline{\quad}$$

$$p = \underline{\quad}$$

Step 2: $p + 32 = f$

f is the unknown sum.

$$\underline{\quad} + 32 = \underline{\quad}$$

$$f = \underline{\quad}$$

So, the temperature shown by the thermometer is _____ degrees Fahrenheit.

Show and Grow   I can do it!

1. Show how to solve the example above using one equation.

Name _____

Apply and Grow: Practice

Understand the problem. What do you know? What do you need to find? Explain.

2. You make a friendship bracelet with 3 pink strings and 2 blue strings. Each string is $3\frac{3}{4}$ feet long. How many feet of string do you use?

3. A smoothie store worker makes 4 peanut butter banana smoothies and 2 fruit smoothies. The worker uses $\frac{2}{3}$ cup of bananas in each smoothie. How many cups of bananas does the worker need?

Understand the problem. Then make a plan. How will you solve? Explain.

4. Your friend walks her dog for $\frac{1}{4}$ mile each day. She then runs $2\frac{3}{4}$ miles each day. How many total miles does she walk her dog and run in 1 week?

5. Hair donations must be 12 inches long or longer. Your friend's hair is 7 inches long. Her hair grows about $\frac{1}{2}$ inch each month. Can she donate her hair in 8 months?

6. Today you walk $\frac{6}{10}$ mile from the Martin Luther King Jr. Memorial to the Washington Monument. Tomorrow you will walk about 4 times as far from the Washington Monument to the White House. About how much farther will you walk tomorrow?

© Big Ideas Learning, LLC

Chapter 9 | Lesson 5

435

Think and Grow: Modeling Real Life

Recommended Daily Feeding Chart

10 pounds		$1\frac{1}{4}$ cups
20 pounds		$1\frac{1}{2}$ cups
40 pounds		$2\frac{1}{4}$ cups
60 pounds		3 cups
80 pounds		$3\frac{1}{2}$ cups
100 pounds		$4\frac{1}{4}$ cups

Example A 20-pound dog and a 60-pound dog eat the recommended amounts of dog food each day. How much more food does the 60-pound dog eat in 1 week than the 20-pound dog?

Think: What do you know? What do you need to find? How will you solve?

Step 1: Find how much food the 20-pound dog eats in 1 week.

$$7 \times 1\frac{1}{2} = b$$

b is the unknown product.

$$7 \times 1\frac{1}{2} = 7 \times \frac{3}{2}$$

$$= \frac{\square \times \square}{2}$$

$$= \frac{\square}{2} \qquad b = \underline{\qquad}$$

Step 2: Find how much food the 60-pound dog eats in 1 week.

$$7 \times 3 = c$$

c is the unknown product.

$$7 \times 3 = \underline{\qquad} \qquad c = \underline{\qquad}$$

Step 3: Subtract b from c to find how much more food the 60-pound dog eats in 1 week.

$$c - b = 21 - \frac{21}{2}$$

Write 21 as a fraction with a denominator of 2.

$$21 = \frac{21}{1} = \frac{21 \times 2}{1 \times 2} = \frac{\square}{\square}$$

$$21 - \frac{21}{2} = \frac{\square}{2} - \frac{21}{2}$$

$$= \frac{\square}{2}$$

$$= \frac{\square}{2} + \frac{\square}{2}$$

$$= \square\frac{\square}{\square}$$

So, the 60-pound dog eats _____ more cups of food than the 20-pound dog in 1 week.

Show and Grow   I can think deeper!

7. Use the table above. A 40-pound dog and a 100-pound dog eat the recommended amounts of dog food each day. How much food is needed to feed both dogs for 1 week?

Name _____

Learning Target: Solve multi-step word problems involving fractions and mixed numbers.

Example A farmer has 45 acres of land. He uses $\frac{3}{5}$ of the acres to grow grapes and the rest of the acres to grow apples. How many acres of land does he use for growing apples?

Think: What do you know? What do you need to find? How will you solve?

Step 1: Find how many acres of land the farmer uses for growing grapes.

$$45 \times \frac{3}{5} = g$$

$$45 \times \frac{3}{5} = \frac{\boxed{45} \times \boxed{3}}{5}$$

$$= \frac{\boxed{135}}{\boxed{5}}$$

$$= \underline{\ 27\ }$$

$$g = \underline{\ 27\ }$$

Step 2: Subtract the acres of land the farmer uses for growing grapes from the total acres of land.

$$45 - g = a$$

$$45 - \underline{\ 27\ } = \underline{\ 18\ }$$

$$a = \underline{\ 18\ }$$

The farmer uses __18__ acres of land for growing apples.

Understand the problem. Then make a plan. How will you solve? Explain.

1. Your friend makes strawberry jam and raspberry jam. He makes enough strawberry jam to fill $\frac{1}{2}$ of a jar. He makes 5 times as much raspberry jam as strawberry jam. How many full jars of raspberry jam does he make?

2. You buy a pair of jeans that originally cost $22. The pair of jeans is $\frac{1}{2}$ off the original price. You pay with a $20 bill. How much change do you receive?

3. The observation deck of the Space Needle in Seattle is 520 feet above ground. The tip of the Space Needle is 85 feet above the observation deck. An artist makes a replica that is $\frac{1}{100}$ the height of the entire Space Needle. How tall is the replica?

Space Needle
Seattle, Washington

4. Modeling Real Life How many sheets of orange and black paper does a teacher need so that 30 students can each complete the art project?

Paper Needed for Art Project
$\frac{1}{8}$ sheet of yellow
$\frac{3}{8}$ sheet of orange
$\frac{5}{8}$ sheet of black
$\frac{7}{8}$ sheet of purple

5. Writing Write and solve a two-step word problem with mixed numbers that can be solved using multiplication.

6. Modeling Real Life In science class, you test how many grams different-sized bundles of spaghetti can hold. You predict that a bundle of 5 spaghetti noodles can hold 10 quarters before breaking. You predict that a bundle of 10 spaghetti noodles can hold 20 quarters before breaking. Each quarter weighs $5\frac{67}{100}$ grams. According to your predictions, how many more grams can the bundle of 10 noodles hold than the bundle of 5 noodles?

Review & Refresh

Compare.

7. $\frac{9}{10}$ ◯ $\frac{4}{5}$

8. $\frac{3}{8}$ ◯ $\frac{5}{6}$

9. $\frac{1}{3}$ ◯ $\frac{4}{12}$

Performance Task 9

1. You use identical glass jars, colored water, and a spoon to learn about sounds. When you tap a spoon on a jar, the vibrations make a sound. The jar that has the least amount of water makes the lowest sound.

Color	Number of $\frac{3}{4}$-cups	Total Water (cups)
Green	1	
Blue	2	
Orange	3	
Red	4	
Purple	5	

a. You fill each glass using a $\frac{3}{4}$-cup measuring cup. Complete the table to find the total amount of water in each jar.

b. How much more water is in the purple jar than the green jar?

c. How many cups of water are used in all?

d. Each jar can hold 4 cups of water. Is it possible to add another $\frac{3}{4}$ cup of water to the purple jar? Explain.

e. Which jars are more than half full?

f. You add another $\frac{3}{4}$ cup of water to the green jar. How does that affect the sound?

Three In a Row: Fraction Multiplication

Directions:

1. Players take turns.
2. On your turn, spin both spinners.
3. Multiply the whole number and the fraction or mixed number. Cover the product.
4. If the product is already covered, you lose your turn.
5. The first player to get three in a row wins!

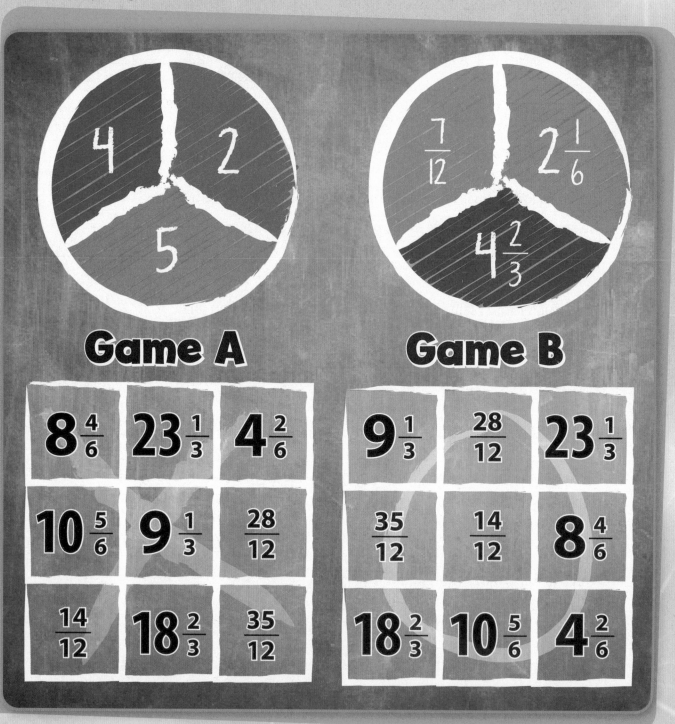

9.1 Understand Multiples of Unit Fractions

Write the fraction as a multiple of a unit fraction.

1. $\dfrac{3}{10} = \dfrac{\square}{\square} + \dfrac{\square}{\square} + \dfrac{\square}{\square}$

$= \underline{\quad} \times \dfrac{1}{10}$

2. $\dfrac{4}{8} = \dfrac{\square}{\square} + \dfrac{\square}{\square} + \dfrac{\square}{\square} + \dfrac{\square}{\square}$

$= \underline{\quad} \times \dfrac{1}{8}$

3. $\dfrac{7}{2}$

4. $\dfrac{56}{100}$

5. **MP Logic** What is Newton's fraction? Write the fraction as a multiple of a unit fraction.

My fraction can be written as a sum of 5 unit fractions. Each unit fraction is one sixth of a whole.

9.2 Understand Multiples of Fractions

Write the product as a multiple of a unit fraction. Then find the product.

6. $2 \times \dfrac{2}{4}$

7. $3 \times \dfrac{9}{12}$

8. $\dfrac{3}{5} \times 4$

9. $\dfrac{8}{10} \times 7$

10. $8 \times \dfrac{6}{3}$

11. $10 \times \dfrac{30}{8}$

© Big Ideas Learning, LLC

9.3 **Multiply Whole Numbers and Fractions**

Multiply.

12. $2 \times \dfrac{1}{2} =$ _____

13. $4 \times \dfrac{5}{8} =$ _____

14. $3 \times \dfrac{9}{6} =$ _____

15. $5 \times \dfrac{7}{12} =$ _____

16. $7 \times \dfrac{30}{100} =$ _____

17. $\dfrac{8}{4} \times 9 =$ _____

 9.4 **Multiply Whole Numbers and Mixed Numbers**

Multiply.

18. $2 \times 1\dfrac{1}{4} =$ _____

19. $3 \times 3\dfrac{10}{12} =$ _____

20. $4 \times 2\dfrac{5}{8} =$ _____

21. $5 \times 2\dfrac{4}{6} =$ _____

22. $6\dfrac{2}{3} \times 7 =$ _____

23. $10 \times 9\dfrac{2}{5} =$ _____

 9.5 **Problem Solving: Fraction Operations**

24. **Modeling Real Life** Your friend rides her bike $\dfrac{2}{6}$ mile to your house and $\dfrac{2}{6}$ mile back home 4 times in 1 week. How far does she bike in all?

10 Relate Fractions and Decimals

Chapter Learning Target:
Understand fractions and decimals.

Chapter Success Criteria:
- I can identify fractions involving tenths as decimals.
- I can write fractions involving hundredths as decimals.
- I can compare two decimals.
- I can justify the operation I used to solve a problem.

- Muffins can be flavored with fresh fruits and vegetables. What is a muffin flavor you would try?

- Each muffin cup holds about 4 ounces of batter. How can you use fractions to decide how much of a cup of batter to pour into each muffin cup?

10 Vocabulary

Organize It

Use the review words to complete the graphic organizer.

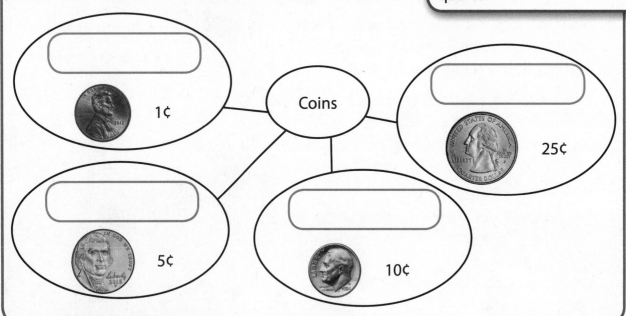

Define It

Use your vocabulary cards to identify the word. Find the word in the word search.

1. 1 of 10 equal parts of a whole

2. 1 of 100 equal parts of a whole

3. A number with one or more digits to the right of the decimal point

```
N  I  H  T  E  S  B  E  F  A
T  E  P  A  M  L  R  C  N  K
H  U  N  D  R  E  D  T  H  Z
K  D  I  O  E  W  N  S  U  B
A  G  T  Q  U  C  Y  L  T  N
S  R  E  M  L  N  I  D  E  M
U  C  N  O  J  A  R  M  O  D
N  X  T  D  E  H  B  U  A  I
H  L  H  I  L  T  C  N  E  L
O  G  Q  V  N  P  Z  S  R  E
```

Chapter 10 Vocabulary Cards

decimal

decimal fraction

decimal point

equivalent decimals

hundredth

hundredths place

tenth

tenths place

A fraction with a denominator of 10 or 100

$$\frac{26}{100}$$

$$\frac{9}{10}$$

$$\frac{60}{100}$$

A number with one or more digits to the right of the decimal point

0.3

0.04

0.59

Two or more decimals that have the same value

$0.40 = 0.4$

A symbol used to separate the ones place and the tenths place in numbers, and to separate the whole dollars and the cents in money

0.1 $5.06

decimal point

The second place to the right of the decimal point

0.01
↑
hundredths
place

1 of 100 equal parts of a whole

one hundredth →

The first place to the right of the decimal point

0.1
↑
tenths
place

1 of 10 equal parts of a whole

one tenth

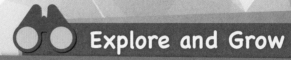

Learning Target: Write a fraction or mixed number involving tenths as a decimal.

Success Criteria:
- I can extend a place value chart to include tenths.
- I can write fractions involving tenths as decimals.
- I can write mixed numbers involving tenths as decimals.

 **Explore and Grow**

How many dimes have a total value of one dollar? Draw a model.

One dime is what fraction of one dollar? Write your answer in words and as a fraction.

MP **Structure** How is one whole related to one tenth? How do you think you can write $\frac{1}{10}$ in a place value chart?

Think and Grow: Understand Tenths

A **decimal** is a number with one or more digits to the right of the **decimal point**. The first place to the right of the decimal point is the **tenths place**.

You can write **tenths** as fractions or decimals.

Example Write $\frac{3}{10}$ as a decimal.

Shade the model. Use a place value chart.

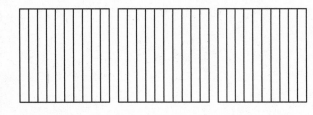

Each part of the model represents one tenth.

Tens	Ones	.	Tenths
	0	.	_____

$\frac{3}{10}$ is 3 tenths.

So, $\frac{3}{10} =$ _____.

The decimal point separates the ones place and the tenths place.

Tens	Ones	.	Tenths
	0	.	1

one tenth, $\frac{1}{10}$, 0.1

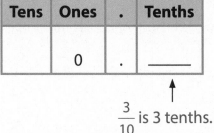

$\frac{3}{10}$ and 0.3 are both read as "three tenths."

Example Write $2\frac{8}{10}$ as a decimal.

Shade the model. Use a place value chart.

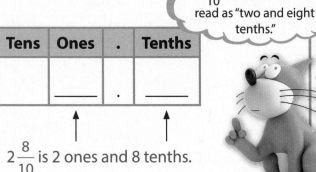

Tens	Ones	.	Tenths
	_____	.	_____

$2\frac{8}{10}$ is 2 ones and 8 tenths.

$2\frac{8}{10}$ and 2.8 are both read as "two and eight tenths."

So, $2\frac{8}{10} =$ _____.

Show and Grow   I can do it!

Write the fraction or mixed number as a decimal.

1. $\frac{5}{10}$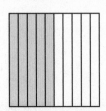

2. $1\frac{7}{10}$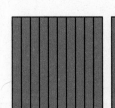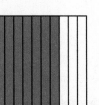

446

Apply and Grow: Practice

Shade the model to represent the fraction or mixed number. Then write the fraction or mixed number as a decimal.

3. $\frac{2}{10}$

4. $1\frac{9}{10}$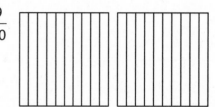

Write the fraction or mixed number as a decimal.

5. $\frac{7}{10}$

6. $\frac{4}{10}$

7. $5\frac{1}{10}$

8. $24\frac{3}{10}$

Write the number as a fraction or mixed number and as a decimal.

9. six tenths

10. eleven and five tenths

11. Newton passes 8 out of 10 obedience classes. What portion of the classes does Newton pass? Write your answer as a decimal.

12. You move a game piece around a game board $3\frac{2}{10}$ times before you lose a turn. Write this number as a decimal.

13. **Writing** Do 0.5 and 5.0 have the same value? Explain.

Think and Grow: Modeling Real Life

Example You have a collection of dinosaur figurines. What portion of the dinosaurs in your collection are carnivores? Write your answer as a decimal.

Draw a model to represent the collection. Shade the same number of parts as there are carnivore dinosaurs in the collection.

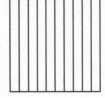

Write the decimal shown by the model.

_____ of the dinosaurs in the collection are carnivores.

Dinosaur Figurine Collection

Name	Type
Triceratops	Herbivore
Ankylosaurus	Herbivore
Stegosaurus	Herbivore
Brachiosaurus	Herbivore
Diplodocus	Herbivore
Velociraptor	Carnivore
Dilophosaurus	Carnivore
Tyrannosaurus Rex	Carnivore
Oviraptor	Omnivore
Ornithomimus	Omnivore

Show and Grow I can think deeper!

14. Use the table above. What portion of the dinosaurs in your collection are herbivores? Write your answer as a decimal.

15. **DIG DEEPER!** You have 10 apps on your tablet. Six of the apps are games. What portion of the apps on your tablet are *not* games? Write your answer as a decimal.

16. **DIG DEEPER!** You make 3 pans of lasagna for a party. You cut each pan of lasagna into 10 equal pieces. The guests eat 22 pieces. Write the fraction and decimal that represent how many pans of lasagna the guests eat.

448

© Big Ideas Learning, LLC

Name _____

Learning Target: Write a fraction or mixed number involving tenths as a decimal.

Example Write $\frac{9}{10}$ as a decimal.

Tens	Ones	.	Tenths
	0	.	9

So, $\frac{9}{10} = \underline{0.9}$.

---

1. Write $\frac{6}{10}$ as a decimal.

2. Shade the model to represent $1\frac{8}{10}$. Then write the mixed number as a decimal.

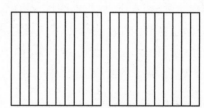

Write the fraction or mixed number as a decimal.

3. $\frac{1}{10}$

4. $\frac{5}{10}$

5. $\frac{2}{10}$

6. $\frac{8}{10}$

7. $4\frac{3}{10}$

8. $1\frac{4}{10}$

9. $31\frac{7}{10}$

10. $40\frac{6}{10}$

Write the number as a fraction or mixed number and as a decimal.

11. three tenths

12. fourteen and nine tenths

13. You knock down 5 out of 10 bowling pins. What portion of the bowling pins do you knock down? Write your answer as a decimal.

14. You drive a go-kart around a track $8\frac{7}{10}$ times before you spin out. Write this number as a decimal.

15. **DIG DEEPER!** Which number cards are represented by the model?

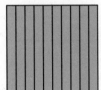 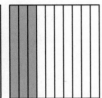

| $1\frac{3}{10}$ | | 13 | | 0.13 | | 1.3 |

Use the table.

16. **Modeling Real Life** A photographer frames her photographs from a safari trip. What portion of the framed photographs are of mammals? Write your answer as a decimal.

17. **DIG DEEPER!** What portion of the framed photographs are *not* of mammals? Write your answer as a decimal.

Framed Safari Photographs

Animal	Type
Lizard	Reptile
Snake	Reptile
Crocodile	Reptile
Ostrich	Bird
Baboon	Mammal
Lion	Mammal
Zebra	Mammal
Giraffe	Mammal
Elephant	Mammal
Cheetah	Mammal

Review & Refresh

Find the product.

18.
   47
× 6

19.
   961
× 3

20.
  2,405
× 8

450

Understand Hundredths  **10.2**

Learning Target: Write a fraction or mixed number involving hundredths as a decimal.

Success Criteria:
- I can extend a place value chart to include hundredths.
- I can write fractions involving hundredths as decimals.
- I can write mixed numbers involving hundredths as decimals.

 Explore and Grow

How many pennies have a total value of one dollar? Draw a model.

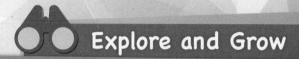

One penny is what fraction of one dollar? Write your answer in words and as a fraction.

MP Structure How is one tenth related to one hundredth? How do you think you can write $\frac{1}{100}$ in a place value chart?

© Big Ideas Learning, LLC

Think and Grow: Understand Hundredths

In a decimal, the second place to the right of the decimal point is the **hundredths place**. You can write **hundredths** as fractions or decimals.

A fraction with a denominator of 10 or 100 is called a **decimal fraction**.

Hundreds	Tens	Ones	.	Ten*ths*	Hundred*ths*
		0	.	0	1

one hundredth, $\frac{1}{100}$, 0.01

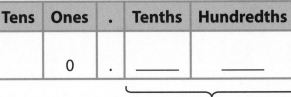

$\frac{75}{100}$ and 0.75 are both read as "seventy-five hundredths."

Example Write $\frac{75}{100}$ as a decimal.

Shade the model. Use a place value chart.

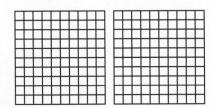

Each part of the model represents one hundredth.

Tens	Ones	.	Tenths	Hundredths
	0	.	_____	_____

So, $\frac{75}{100}$ = _____ .

$\frac{75}{100}$ is 75 hundredths.

$1\frac{25}{100}$ and 1.25 are both read as "one and twenty-five hundredths."

Example Write $1\frac{25}{100}$ as a decimal.

Shade the model. Use a place value chart.

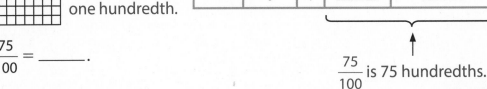

Tens	Ones	.	Tenths	Hundredths
	_____	.	_____	_____

So, $1\frac{25}{100}$ = _____ .

$1\frac{25}{100}$ is 1 one and 25 hundredths.

Show and Grow I can do it!

Write the fraction or mixed number as a decimal.

1. $\frac{45}{100}$

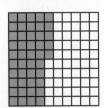

2. $1\frac{90}{100}$

1.9

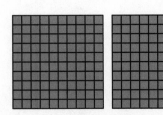

452

Name _____

Apply and Grow: Practice

Shade the model to represent the fraction or mixed number. Then write the fraction or mixed number as a decimal.

3. $\frac{98}{100}$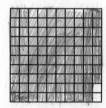

4. $1\frac{34}{100}$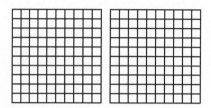

Write the fraction or mixed number as a decimal.

5. $\frac{42}{100}$

hundredth.

6. $\frac{7}{100}$

hundredths.

7. $4\frac{56}{100}$

hundredth

8. $23\frac{9}{100}$

hundredth

Write the number as a fraction or mixed number and as a decimal.

9. sixty-one hundredths $\frac{61}{100}$

10. twelve and eighty-three hundredths

11. A shelter finds homes for 100 dogs. Five of the dogs are Doberman pinschers. What portion of the dogs are Doberman pinschers? Write your answer as a decimal. dogs 100

Dobermans

.05

12. An athlete runs $3\frac{50}{100}$ lengths of a football field. Write this number as a decimal.

$3\frac{50}{100}$

3.50

3.50

13. **MP** **Number Sense** Which number cards show three hundredths?

$\frac{3}{100}$ $\frac{3}{10}$ 300

0.3   0.03

Think and Grow: Modeling Real Life

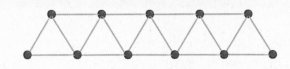

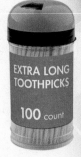

EXTRA LONG
TOOTHPICKS

100 count

Example   You use 51 toothpicks to make a bridge. What portion of the container of toothpicks do you use to make the bridge? Write your answer as a decimal.

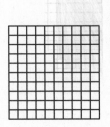

Draw a model to represent the container of toothpicks. Shade the same number of parts as the number of toothpicks you use to make the bridge.

Write the decimal shown by the model.

You use _____ of the container of toothpicks to make the bridge.

Show and Grow   I can think deeper!

14. A book fair has 100 books. 60 of the books are chapter books. What portion of the books in the book fair are chapter books? Write your answer as a decimal.

15. The model represents the members of a marching band. What portion of the marching band plays a brass instrument? woodwind instrument? percussion instrument? Write your answers as decimals.

☐ brass instrument
☐ woodwind instrument
☐ percussion instrument

16. **DIG DEEPER!** What portion of Earth's surface is *not* covered by water? Write your answer as a decimal.

About $\frac{71}{100}$ of Earth's surface is covered by water.

Learning Target: Write tenths and hundredths as equivalent fractions and decimals.

Success Criteria:
- I can write tenths as hundredths in both fraction form and decimal form.
- I can write hundredths as tenths in both fraction form and decimal form.
- I can explain what equivalent decimals are.

 Explore and Grow

Plot each fraction or decimal on a number line.

$\dfrac{3}{10}$

$\dfrac{0}{10}$ $\dfrac{10}{10}$

$\dfrac{30}{100}$

$\dfrac{0}{100}$ $\dfrac{100}{100}$

0.3

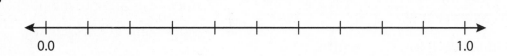

0.0   1.0

0.30

0.00   1.00

MP **Reasoning** What do you notice about the locations of the points? What can you conclude about the numbers?

Think and Grow: Fractions and Decimals

Example   Write $\frac{6}{10}$ as hundredths in fraction form and decimal form.

Fraction form: Shade the model to help write $\frac{6}{10}$ as an equivalent fraction with a denominator of 100.

 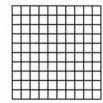

$$\frac{6}{10} = \frac{6 \times \boxed{}}{10 \times \boxed{}} = \frac{\boxed{}}{100}$$

So, $\frac{6}{10}$ = _____.

Decimal form: Use a place value chart.

Tens	Ones	.	Tenths	Hundredths
	0	.	_____	_____

So, $\frac{6}{10}$ = _____.

> Think: Six tenths is the same as 6 tenths 0 hundredths.

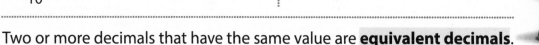

Two or more decimals that have the same value are **equivalent decimals**.

Example   Write 0.40 as tenths in decimal form and fraction form.

Decimal form: Use a place value chart.

Tens	Ones	.	Tenths	Hundredths
	0	.	_____	_____

0.40 is equivalent to _____ tenths.

So, 0.40 = _____.

Fraction form: 0.40 is 40 hundredths, or $\frac{\boxed{}}{\boxed{}}$.

Write $\frac{40}{100}$ as an equivalent fraction with a denominator of 10.

$$\frac{40}{100} = \frac{40 \div \boxed{}}{100 \div \boxed{}} = \frac{\boxed{}}{10}$$

So, 0.40 = _____.

> Think: A common factor of 40 and 100 is 10.

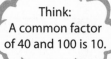

Show and Grow   I can do it!

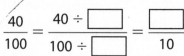

1. Write $\frac{9}{10}$ as hundredths in fraction form and decimal form.

2. Write 0.20 as tenths in decimal form and fraction form.

458

© Big Ideas Learning, LLC

Name _____

Write the number as tenths in fraction form and decimal form.

3. $\dfrac{80}{100}$

4. $\dfrac{50}{100}$

5. 0.30

Write the number as hundredths in fraction form and decimal form.

6. $\dfrac{2}{10}$

7. 0.7

8. $2\dfrac{1}{10}$

Write the number represented by the point as hundredths in fraction form and decimal form.

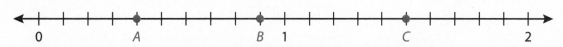

9. *A*

10. *B*

11. *C*

12. **DIG DEEPER!** Complete the table. Think: Can all of the numbers in the table be written as hundredths?

Wow! Fractions and decimals can be written in expanded form, just like 156 can be written as 100 + 50 + 6!

Mixed Number	Decimal	Expanded Form	
		Fraction Notation	**Decimal Notation**
		$20 + 3 + \dfrac{7}{10}$	
			$10 + 8 + 0.2$
$4\dfrac{5}{10}$			
	10.4		

© Big Ideas Learning, LLC

Think and Grow: Modeling Real Life

Example You use 100 tiles to make a mosaic. 80 of them are square tiles. Your friend uses 10 tiles to make a mosaic. Six of them are square tiles. Do the mosaics have the same fraction of square tiles?

Find the fraction of square tiles you use.

☐ ←— number of square tiles

☐ ←— total number of tiles

Find the fraction of square tiles your friend uses.

☐ ←— number of square tiles

☐ ←— total number of tiles

Determine whether the fractions are equivalent.

Write your friend's fraction as hundredths in fraction form. Then compare.

$$\frac{\boxed{}}{\boxed{}} = \frac{\boxed{} \times 10}{\boxed{} \times 10} = \frac{\boxed{}}{100}$$

$$\frac{\boxed{}}{\boxed{}} \overset{?}{=} \frac{\boxed{}}{\boxed{}}$$

The mosaics _____ have the same fraction of square tiles.

Show and Grow   I can think deeper!

13. You use 10 beads to make a bracelet. Seven of them are purple. Your friend uses 100 beads to make a bracelet. 70 of them are purple. Do the bracelets have the same fraction of purple beads?

14. **DIG DEEPER!** The model represents the types of trees on a tree farm. What portion of the tree farm is blue spruce? Fraser fir? white pine? Write your answers as decimals in tenths.

■ blue spruce
☐ Fraser fir
■ white pine

Name _____

Learning Target: Write tenths and hundredths as equivalent fractions and decimals.

Example Write $\dfrac{10}{100}$ as tenths in fraction form.

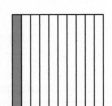

$$\dfrac{10}{100} = \dfrac{10 \div \boxed{10}}{100 \div \boxed{10}} = \dfrac{\boxed{1}}{10}$$

So, $\dfrac{10}{100} = \dfrac{\underline{1}}{\underline{10}}$.

....

Example Write 0.9 as hundredths in decimal form.

Tens	Ones	.	Tenths	Hundredths
	0	.	9	0

0.9 is equivalent to __90__ hundredths.

So, 0.9 = _0.90_ .

Write the number as tenths in fraction form and decimal form.

1. $\dfrac{40}{100}$

2. $\dfrac{70}{100}$

3. 0.20

Write the number as hundredths in fraction form and decimal form.

4. $\dfrac{8}{10}$

5. 0.5

6. $9\dfrac{6}{10}$

Write the number represented by the point as hundredths in fraction form and decimal form.

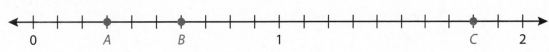

7. *A*

8. *B*

9. *C*

10. **Precision** Which of the following show forty-one and nine tenths?

| 41.9 | 41.09 |

$$40 + 1 + \frac{9}{10}$$ $$40 + 1 + 9$$

$$41\frac{90}{10}$$ $$40 + 1 + 0.9$$

11. **Which One Doesn't Belong?** Which one does *not* belong with the other three?

0.70 $\frac{7}{10}$

0.07 $\frac{70}{100}$

12. **YOU BE THE TEACHER** Is Newton correct? Explain.

0.80 is greater than 0.8 because 80 is greater than 8.

13. **Number Sense** Write two equivalent fractions and two equivalent decimals represented by the model.

14. **Modeling Real Life** Does each player get a base hit on the same fraction of pitches? Explain.

Major League Player: gets a base hit on 30 out of 100 pitches

Youth League Player: gets a base hit on 3 out of 10 pitches

Review & Refresh

Find the equivalent fraction.

15. $\frac{4}{6} = \frac{\square}{3}$

16. $\frac{25}{100} = \frac{5}{\square}$

17. $\frac{14}{8} = \frac{\square}{4}$

Name _____

Compare Decimals 10.4

Learning Target: Compare decimals to the hundredths place.

Success Criteria:
- I can choose a strategy to compare two decimals.
- I can use the symbols <, >, and = to compare two decimals to the hundredths place.

Explore and Grow

Use models to compare the decimals.

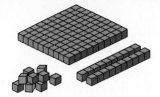

0.38 ◯ 0.4   0.12 ◯ 0.09

2.3 ◯ 2.03

 Reasoning How did you use your models to determine which decimal is greater?

© Big Ideas Learning, LLC

© Big Ideas Learning, LLC

Chapter 10 | Lesson 4

463

Think and Grow: Compare Decimals

Example Compare 0.7 and 0.07.

Use a place value chart. Start at the left. Compare the digits in each place until the digits differ.

Tens	Ones	.	Tenths	Hundredths
	0	.	7	
	0	.	0	7

The digits in the ones place are the same. Compare the tenths.

7 tenths ◯ 0 tenths

So, 0.7 ◯ 0.07.

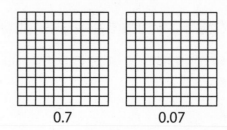

0.7   0.07

....

Example Compare 0.25 and 0.3.

Use a number line. 0.25 is 25 hundredths. 0.3 and 0.30 are equivalent decimals. So, 0.3 is equivalent to 30 hundredths.

> Remember on a number line, numbers to the left are less than numbers to the right.

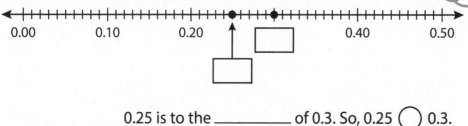

0.25 is to the _____ of 0.3. So, 0.25 ◯ 0.3.

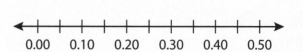

Show and Grow   *I can do it!*

Compare.

1. 0.46 ◯ 0.44

Tens	Ones	.	Tenths	Hundredths
		.		
		.		

2. 0.05 ◯ 0.2

0.00   0.10   0.20   0.30   0.40   0.50

Name _____

Apply and Grow: Practice

Use the number line to compare.

```
←|||||||||||||||||||||||||||||||||||||||||||||||||||||||||||||||||||||→
   0.00   0.10   0.20   0.30   0.40   0.50   0.60   0.70   0.80   0.90   1.00
```

3. 0.85 ◯ 0.96

4. 0.25 ◯ 0.52

5. 0.11 ◯ 0.09

6. 0.72 ◯ 0.59

7. 0.04 ◯ 0.40

8. 0.90 ◯ 0.9

Compare.

9. 0.3 ◯ 0.03

10. 5.29 ◯ 5.24

11. 25.94 ◯ 25.9

Open-Ended Complete the statement to make it true.

12. 0.☐1 > 0.☐1

13. 12.10 = 12.☐

14. 9.43 < _____

15. **MP Precision** Write the number that is halfway between 3.6 and 3.7. Explain how you found your answer.

DIG DEEPER! Write whether the statement is *true* or *false*. If false, explain why.

16. $\dfrac{1}{10} \overset{?}{>} 0.07$ _____

17. $0.6 \overset{?}{<} \dfrac{36}{100}$ _____

© Big Ideas Learning, LLC

Think and Grow: Modeling Real Life

Example   Newton and Descartes make paper airplanes. Newton's paper airplane flies 3.01 meters. Descartes's paper airplane flies 3.10 meters. Whose paper airplane flies farther?

Use a place value chart. Compare the digits in each place until the digits differ.

Tens	Ones	.	Tenths	Hundredths
Newton:	_____	.	_____	_____
Descartes:	_____	.	_____	_____

Compare Newton's distance to Descartes's distance.

_____ paper airplane flies farther.

Show and Grow   I can think deeper!

18. Compare the thickness of a nickel and a quarter. Which coin is thinner?

Coin	Thickness
Penny	1.52 mm
Nickel	1.95 mm
Dime	1.35 mm
Quarter	1.75 mm

19. You, your cousin, and your friend run a 100-meter race. Who finishes first? second? third?

Friend   You   Cousin

20. **DIG DEEPER!**   Your water bottle is 0.25 full. Your friend's water bottle is 0.5 full. You have more water than your friend. Explain how this is possible.

Name _____

Learning Target: Compare decimals to the hundredths place.

Example Compare 1.43 and 1.49.

Use a place value chart. Start at the left. Compare the digits in each place until the digits differ.

Tens	Ones	.	Tenths	Hundredths
	1	.	4	3
	1	.	4	9

The digits in the ones place and the digits in the tenths place are the same. Compare the hundredths.

3 hundredths $<$ 9 hundredths

You can also use a model or a number line to compare decimals.

So, 1.43 $<$ 1.49.

Compare.

1. 0.58 ◯ 0.52

Tens	Ones	.	Tenths	Hundredths
		.		
		.		

2. 0.25 ◯ 0.05

```
0.00   0.10   0.20   0.30   0.40   0.50
```

Use the number line to compare.

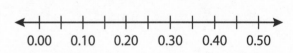

```
0.00  0.10  0.20  0.30  0.40  0.50  0.60  0.70  0.80  0.90  1.00
```

3. 0.76 ◯ 0.59

4. 0.21 ◯ 0.23

5. 0.7 ◯ 0.07

6. 0.05 ◯ 0.08

7. 0.10 ◯ 0.1

8. 0.05 ◯ 0.50

Compare.

9. 0.13 ◯ 0.19

10. 2.2 ◯ 2.02

11. 4.70 ◯ 4.7

12. 8.35 ◯ 8.53

13. 35.01 ◯ 32.98

14. 14.9 ◯ 14.92

15. **MP Precision** Explain how to compare 0.46 and 0.48.

16. **Open-Ended** What might Descartes's number be?

My number is greater than 0.6 and less than 0.7. The greatest digit in the number is in the tenths place.

17. **Modeling Real Life** A traffic light is red for 23.4 seconds and green for 23.6 seconds. Does the traffic light stay red or green longer?

18. **Modeling Real Life** Order the caterpillars from longest to shortest.

Caterpillar	Length (centimeters)
Caterpillar A	3.5
Caterpillar B	3.65
Caterpillar C	3.45

Review & Refresh

Round the number to the nearest hundred thousand.

19. 695,023

20. 246,947

Name _____

Add Decimal Fractions and Decimals

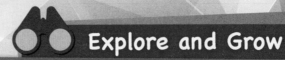

10.5

Learning Target: Use equivalent fractions to add decimal fractions and decimals.

Success Criteria:
- I can use equivalent fractions to add decimal fractions.
- I can use equivalent fractions to add decimals.

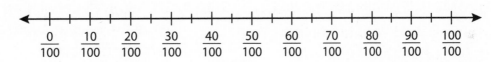

Explore and Grow

How can you use a number line to find the sum?

$$\frac{7}{10} + \frac{25}{100}$$

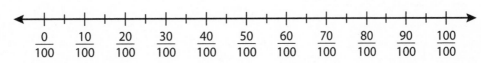

$\frac{0}{100}$ $\frac{10}{100}$ $\frac{20}{100}$ $\frac{30}{100}$ $\frac{40}{100}$ $\frac{50}{100}$ $\frac{60}{100}$ $\frac{70}{100}$ $\frac{80}{100}$ $\frac{90}{100}$ $\frac{100}{100}$

$$0.25 + 0.7$$

$\frac{0}{100}$ $\frac{10}{100}$ $\frac{20}{100}$ $\frac{30}{100}$ $\frac{40}{100}$ $\frac{50}{100}$ $\frac{60}{100}$ $\frac{70}{100}$ $\frac{80}{100}$ $\frac{90}{100}$ $\frac{100}{100}$

How can you use models to check your answers?

 Reasoning How can you add two decimal fractions with a denominator of 10? How can you add two decimal fractions with denominators of 10 and 100?

© Big Ideas Learning, LLC

Chapter 10 | Lesson 5

Think and Grow: Add Decimal Fractions and Decimals

You have learned how to add fractions with the same denominator. You can use equivalent fractions to add fractions that do not have the same denominator.

Example Find $\dfrac{3}{10} + \dfrac{47}{100}$.

Step 1: Use equivalent fractions to write the fractions with the same denominator.

Think: Rewrite $\dfrac{3}{10}$ with a denominator of 100.

$$\dfrac{3}{10} = \dfrac{3 \times \boxed{}}{10 \times \boxed{}} = \dfrac{\boxed{}}{100}$$

Step 2: Add the numerators.

$$\dfrac{\boxed{}}{100} + \dfrac{47}{100} = \dfrac{\boxed{}}{100}$$

So, $\dfrac{3}{10} + \dfrac{47}{100} = $ _____ .

Example Find $0.75 + 0.2$.

Step 1: Write 0.75 and 0.2 as fractions.

Think: 0.75 is 75 hundredths. 0.2 is 2 tenths.

$$0.75 = \dfrac{\boxed{}}{\boxed{}} \qquad 0.2 = \dfrac{\boxed{}}{\boxed{}}$$

Step 2: Use equivalent fractions to write the fractions with the same denominator.

$$\dfrac{2}{10} = \dfrac{2 \times \boxed{}}{10 \times \boxed{}} = \dfrac{\boxed{}}{100}$$

Step 3: Add the numerators.

$$\dfrac{75}{100} + \dfrac{\boxed{}}{100} = \dfrac{\boxed{}}{100}$$

Step 4: Write the sum as a decimal.

$$\dfrac{\boxed{}}{100} = \text{_____}$$

So, $0.75 + 0.2 = $ _____ .

Show and Grow   I can do it!

Find the sum.

1. $\dfrac{1}{10} + \dfrac{36}{100} = \dfrac{\boxed{}}{100} + \dfrac{\boxed{}}{100} = $ _____

2. $0.5 + 0.25 = $ _____

Name _____

✓ Apply and Grow: Practice

Find the sum.

3. $\dfrac{37}{100} + \dfrac{4}{10} =$ _____

4. $\dfrac{2}{10} + \dfrac{23}{100} =$ _____

5. $\dfrac{19}{100} + \dfrac{7}{10} =$ _____

6. $0.35 + 0.1 =$ _____

7. $0.8 + 0.15 =$ _____

8. $0.50 + 0.4 =$ _____

9. $\dfrac{48}{100} + \dfrac{16}{100} + \dfrac{2}{10} =$ _____

10. $0.3 + 0.25 + 0.1 =$ _____

MP Number Sense Find the sum.

11. $0.5 + \dfrac{29}{100} =$ _____

12. $\dfrac{8}{10} + 0.75 =$ _____

13. **YOU BE THE TEACHER** Your friend says Newton and Descartes are both correct. Is your friend correct? Explain.

$0.5 + 0.55 + 0.05 = 1.10$

$0.5 + 0.55 + 0.05 = 1.1$

14. **DIG DEEPER!** Write and solve a decimal addition problem represented by the model. Write your answer as a decimal and as a mixed number.

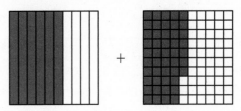

© Big Ideas Learning, LLC

Example You use $\frac{8}{10}$ pound of clay to make a cup. You make

a handle for the cup with $\frac{15}{100}$ pound of clay and attach the handle

to the cup. What fraction of a pound does your cup weigh in all?

Add the fractions.

$$\frac{\boxed{}}{\boxed{}} + \frac{\boxed{}}{\boxed{}}$$

Use equivalent fractions to write the fractions with the same denominator.

Rewrite $\frac{8}{10}$ with a denominator of 100.

$$\frac{8}{10} = \frac{8 \times \boxed{}}{10 \times \boxed{}} = \frac{\boxed{}}{100}$$

Add the numerators.

$$\frac{\boxed{}}{100} + \frac{15}{100} = \frac{\boxed{}}{100}$$

Your cup weighs _____ pound.

Show and Grow   *I can think deeper!*

15. Each morning, you walk $\frac{25}{100}$ mile to your friend's house and then $\frac{5}{10}$ mile to school. What fraction of a mile do you walk each morning?

16. You ride a zip line that is $\frac{15}{100}$ mile long. You ride another zip line that is $\frac{3}{10}$ mile long. Your friend rides a total of $\frac{40}{100}$ mile on zip lines. Who rides farther on zip lines?

17. **DIG DEEPER!** You ship a package that weighs 0.8 pound. Your package is 0.75 pound lighter than your friend's package. How much does your friend's package weigh? Write your answer in decimal form.

Name _____

Learning Target: Use equivalent fractions to add decimal fractions and decimals.

Example Find $\dfrac{2}{10} + \dfrac{58}{100}$.

Step 1: Use equivalent fractions to write the fractions with the same denominator.

$$\dfrac{2}{10} = \dfrac{2 \times \boxed{10}}{10 \times \boxed{10}} = \dfrac{\boxed{20}}{100}$$

Step 2: Add the numerators.

$$\dfrac{\boxed{20}}{100} + \dfrac{58}{100} = \dfrac{\boxed{78}}{100}$$

So, $\dfrac{2}{10} + \dfrac{58}{100} = \dfrac{\underline{78}}{\underline{100}}$.

Find the sum.

1. $\dfrac{4}{10} + \dfrac{32}{100} =$ _____

2. $\dfrac{3}{100} + \dfrac{8}{10} =$ _____

3. $\dfrac{2}{10} + \dfrac{15}{100} =$ _____

4. $\dfrac{45}{100} + \dfrac{1}{10} =$ _____

5. $\dfrac{7}{10} + \dfrac{22}{100} =$ _____

6. $\dfrac{17}{100} + \dfrac{5}{10} =$ _____

7. $0.6 + 0.25 =$ _____

8. $0.3 + 0.40 =$ _____

9. $0.05 + 0.9 =$ _____

Find the sum.

10. $\frac{3}{10} + \frac{41}{100} + \frac{22}{100} =$ _____

11. $0.8 + 0.25 + 0.75 =$ _____

12.  **Patterns** Describe and complete the pattern.

$$\frac{9}{100} + \frac{\Box}{10} = \frac{19}{100}$$

$$\frac{18}{100} + \frac{\Box}{10} = \frac{38}{100}$$

$$\frac{27}{100} + \frac{\Box}{10} = \frac{57}{100}$$

_____ + _____ = _____

_____ + _____ = _____

13. Which One Doesn't Belong? Which expression does *not* belong with the other three?

$$\frac{4}{10} + \frac{4}{100}$$

$$0.4 + 0.40$$

$$0.04 + 0.4$$

$$\frac{4}{100} + \frac{40}{100}$$

15. **DIG DEEPER!** Which gecko is longer? Explain.

Leopard Gecko

├── 0.05 m ──┼──── 0.06 m ────┤

Adult Electric Blue Gecko

├──────── $\frac{7}{100}$ m ────────┤

14. Modeling Real Life In an aquarium, $\frac{5}{10}$ of the fish are red and $\frac{3}{100}$ of the fish are yellow. What fraction of the fish are red or yellow?

Estimate the quotient.

16. $38 \div 4$

17. $641 \div 9$

18. $52 \div 7$

Name _____

Learning Target: Write amounts of money in different ways.

Success Criteria:
- I can write money amounts using a dollar sign and a decimal point.
- I can write money amounts as fractions or mixed numbers.
- I can write money amounts as decimals.

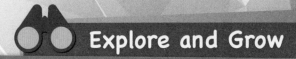

Explore and Grow

Shade the model to show each money amount.

1 dollar

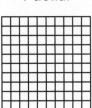

1 quarter

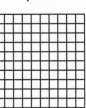

1 dime

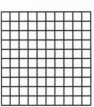

1 nickel

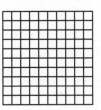

1 penny

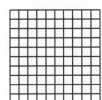

 Reasoning How can you write each money amount as a fraction and a decimal in terms of dollars?

Think and Grow: Fractions, Decimals, and Money

You can use a dollar sign and a decimal point to write a money amount. Just as a decimal point separates ones from tenths and hundredths, it also separates whole dollars from cents.

Think of whole dollars as ones, dimes as tenths, and pennies as hundredths.

Ones	.	Tenths	Hundredths
1	.	2	4

$1 \frac{24}{100}$ dollars, 1.24 dollars, $1.24

$1.24 is read as "1 dollar and 24 cents."

Use the total money amount to complete the table.

Example

Coins	Fraction	Decimal	Money Amount
1 quarter, 2 dimes, 2 pennies	$\frac{47}{100}$ dollar	_____ dollar	_____

Example

Coins	Mixed Number	Decimal	Money Amount
one $1 bill, 2 quarters, 1 nickel, 3 pennies	_____ dollar	1.58 dollar	_____

Show and Grow   I can do it!

Find the total money amount. Then write the amount as a fraction or mixed number and as a decimal.

1.

2.

Name _____

Apply and Grow: Practice

Find the total money amount. Then write the amount as a fraction or mixed number and as a decimal.

3.

4.

Write the fraction or mixed number as a money amount and as a decimal.

5. $\frac{53}{100}$

6. $\frac{4}{100}$

7. $\frac{100}{100}$

8. $1\frac{22}{100}$

9. $1\frac{18}{100}$

10. $1\frac{70}{100}$

---

11. You find 1 dime, 3 nickels, and 2 pennies on the ground. How much money do you find? Write your answer three different ways.

---

12. **YOU BE THE TEACHER** Your friend has three $1 bills and 2 pennies. Your friend writes, "I have $3.2." Is your friend correct? Explain.

13. **DIG DEEPER!** You have $\frac{1}{4}$ dollar in coins. Draw two possible groups of coins that you could have.

© Big Ideas Learning, LLC

Chapter 10 | Lesson 6

477

Think and Grow: Modeling Real Life

$0.99

Example Newton has $\frac{85}{100}$ dollar. Can he buy the spinning toy? Explain.

Write the fraction as a money amount.

$\frac{85}{100}$ as a money amount is _____.

Compare the amount of money Newton has to the price of the toy.

Newton _____ buy the spinning toy.

Explain:

Show and Grow   I can think deeper!

14. Descartes has $\frac{76}{100}$ dollar. Can he buy the bouncy ball? Explain.

$0.50

15. You throw 3 dimes, 3 nickels, and 8 pennies into a fountain. Your friend throws 1 quarter, 4 nickels, and 5 pennies. Who throws a greater amount of money into the fountain?

16. **DIG DEEPER!** Complete the table. Which piggy bank has the greatest amount of money? the least amount of money?

Piggy Bank	Quarters	Dimes	Nickels	Pennies	Total
A	3	1	4	2	
B	1	7	3	0	
C	2	0	8	11	

Name _____

Homework & Practice **10.6**

Learning Target: Write amounts of money in different ways.

Example   Use the total money amount to complete the table.

Coins	Fraction	Decimal	Money Amount
5 dimes, 3 nickels, 4 pennies	$\frac{69}{100}$ dollar	0.69 dollar	$0.69

Write the money amount as a fraction or mixed number and as a decimal.

1. $0.53

2. $0.40

3. $1.01

Find the total money amount. Then write the amount as a fraction or mixed number and as a decimal.

4.

5.

6.

7.

Write the fraction or mixed number as a money amount and as a decimal.

8. $\dfrac{87}{100}$

9. $\dfrac{12}{100}$

10. $1\dfrac{9}{100}$

11. You find 3 quarters, 2 nickels, and 1 penny in your backpack. How much money do you find? Write your answer three different ways.

12. **Which One Doesn't Belong?** Which one does *not* belong with the other three?

| 3 pennies | $\dfrac{3}{10}$ dollar | $0.30 | $\dfrac{30}{100}$ dollar |

13.  **Reasoning** Would you rather have $\dfrac{2}{10}$ of a dollar or 6 nickels? Explain.

14. **Modeling Real Life** Newton has $\dfrac{46}{100}$ dollar. Can he buy the key chain? Explain.

$0.49

15. **DIG DEEPER!** Descartes has $1. Can he buy 2 key chains? Explain how you know without calculating.

~~~~~~~~~~~~~~~~~~
Review & Refresh

Add.

16. $\dfrac{24}{100} + \dfrac{35}{100} =$ _____

17. $\dfrac{10}{8} + \dfrac{3}{8} =$ _____

18. $\dfrac{1}{10} + \dfrac{3}{10} + \dfrac{6}{10} =$ _____

Operations with Money **10.7**

Learning Target: Add, subtract, multiply, and divide amounts of money.

Success Criteria:
• I can use the four operations to solve money problems.
• I can explain why I used the operation I did to solve.

Explore and Grow

Draw bills and coins to solve each problem.

How much do all of the toys cost?

Toy	Cost
Action figure	$5.50
Whistle	$1.25
Board game	$3.75

You pay for one of the toys with a $10 bill.
What is your change?

You buy three of the same toy. How much do the toys cost in all?

You and your friend put your money together to buy some of the toys.
The cashier gives you $4.50 change. You want to share the change equally.
How much money do each of you get?

 Precision Compare your work to your partner's.

Think and Grow: Operations with Money

Example Newton has $1.35. Descartes has $1.25. How much money do they have altogether?

Newton

Descartes

They have _____ altogether.

Example Newton has $2.45. He spends $1.10. How much money does he have left?

You only need to model $2.45. Use Xs to take away the amount spent.

He has _____ left.

Example Three friends each have $0.60. How much money do they have in all?

They have _____ in all.

Example You and a friend have a total of $1.48. You want to share the money equally. How much money should each of you get?

You each should get _____ .

Show and Grow   I can do it!

1. You pay a total of $2.25 for 3 granola bars. How much money does each bar cost? Draw bills and coins to solve.

482

Name _____

Apply and Grow: Practice

Draw bills and coins to solve.

2. You buy 2 stamps. Each stamp costs $0.49. How much money do you spend in all?

3. Newton has $2.50. He spends $1.07 on a flying disk. How much money does Newton have left?

4. A tube of toothpaste costs $2.71 and a toothbrush costs $1.62. How much more money does the toothpaste cost than the toothbrush?

5. Two fingerboards cost a total of $7.20. Each fingerboard costs the same amount. How much does each fingerboard cost?

6. In Exercise 2, you pay for the stamps using a $1 bill. What is your change?

7. You have four $1 bills and 3 dimes. Do you have enough money to buy the tube of toothpaste and the toothbrush in Exercise 4? Explain.

8. **DIG DEEPER!** You have $1.10 less than Descartes. How much money do you, Newton, and Descartes have altogether?

I have $1.50.

Newton

I have $1.25 more than Newton.

Descartes

Think and Grow: Modeling Real Life

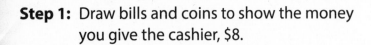
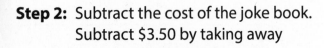

Example You buy a joke book that costs $3.50 and a book about science experiments that costs $4.25. You give the cashier $8. What is your change?

Think: What do you know? What do you need to find? How will you solve?

Step 1: Draw bills and coins to show the money you give the cashier, $8.

Step 2: Subtract the cost of the joke book. Subtract $3.50 by taking away

_____ $1 bills and _____ quarters.

Step 3: Subtract the cost of the science experiment book.

Subtract $4.25 by taking away

_____ $1 bills and _____ quarter.

Step 4: The remaining coin represents your change.

$1	$1
$1	$1
$1	$1

$1

(25¢) (25¢)
(25¢) (25¢)

Your change is _____ .

Show and Grow   I can think deeper!

9. You buy a gel pen that costs $1.10 and a school shirt that costs $5.85. You give the cashier $7. What is your change?

10. You have $2.50. Your friend has 2 times as much money as you. How much money do you and your friend have altogether?

11. **DIG DEEPER!** You have $8.38. Your friend has $3.16. How much money can you give to your friend so that you each have the same amount?

484

Name _____

Learning Target: Add, subtract, multiply, and divide amounts of money.

Example   Newton and Descartes have a total of $3.02. They want to share the money equally. How much money will each of them get?

Regroup 1 dollar as 4 quarters so it can be shared equally.

Newton and Descartes each get ___$1.51___.

Draw bills and coins to solve.

1. A sketch pad is $2.85 and a sketching pencil is $1.25. How much more money is the sketch pad than the sketching pencil?

2. Descartes buys two toys for a total of $2.54. Each toy costs the same amount. How much does each toy cost?

3. You buy 4 bags of the water balloons shown. How much money do you spend in all?

4. You have four $1 bills and 2 nickels. Do you have enough money to buy the sketch pad and the sketching pencil in Exercise 1? Explain.

5. **(MP) Reasoning** You have 3 jars, with $2.32 in each jar. Do you have enough money to buy the model car? If not, how much more money do you need?

$7.49

6. **DIG DEEPER!** Descartes has 3 quarters, 1 dime, and 3 nickels. He wants to put the same amount of money into each of two piggy banks. How can he do this with these coins?

7. **Modeling Real Life** You buy the key chains shown. You pay with a $5 bill. What is your change?

$2.37

$2.53

8. **DIG DEEPER!** Your class collects pennies and nickels in separate jars. Your class collects $5.87 in pennies and $2.65 in nickels. You divide the total amount of money collected between two charities. How many pennies do you put in the nickel jar so that both jars have the same amount of money?

Review & Refresh

Write the product as a multiple of a unit fraction. Then find the product.

9. $6 \times \dfrac{7}{12}$

10. $2 \times \dfrac{5}{6}$

11. $10 \times \dfrac{3}{8}$

Name _____

You have a recipe to make one loaf of homemade whole wheat bread. You want to make 8 loaves of bread.

1. You need between 6.5 cups and 7 cups of whole wheat flour for one loaf of bread.

   a. So far, you measure $3\frac{1}{4}$ cups of flour for one loaf. What is the least amount of cups you need to add?

   b. There are about 4 cups of flour in 1 pound. How many 5-pound bags of whole wheat flour should you buy to make all of the bread?

   c. You use a $10 bill to buy enough bags of whole wheat flour for 8 loaves. What is your change?

2. You need to add $2\frac{1}{4}$ cups of warm water for one loaf of bread. The temperature of the water should be about 110°F.

   a. How many cups of water do you need for all of the bread?

   b. You find the temperatures of 3 different samples of water. Which sample of water should you use? Explain.

Water Sample	Temperature (°F)
A	105.5
B	$100 + 10 + 4 + \frac{4}{10}$
C	$109\frac{6}{10}$

Decimal Boss

Directions:

1. Divide the Decimal Boss Cards equally between both players.
2. Each player flips a Decimal Boss Card.
3. Players compare their numbers. The player with the greater number takes both cards.
4. The player with the most cards at the end of the round wins!

Player A

Player B

Chapter Practice 10

10.1 Understand Tenths

Write the fraction or mixed number as a decimal.

1. $\frac{8}{10}$

2. $\frac{3}{10}$

3. $6\frac{7}{10}$

4. $15\frac{4}{10}$

Write the number as a fraction or mixed number and as a decimal.

5. two tenths

6. thirteen and six tenths

7. **Modeling Real Life** You bake 2 loaves of banana bread for a party. You cut each loaf into 10 equal pieces. The guests eat 18 pieces. Write the fraction and decimal that represent how many loaves the guests eat in all.

10.2 Understand Hundredths

Write the fraction or mixed number as a decimal.

8. $\frac{10}{100}$

9. $\frac{6}{100}$

10. $8\frac{75}{100}$

11. $34\frac{2}{100}$

Write the number as a fraction or mixed number and as a decimal.

12. thirty-seven hundredths

13. nineteen and forty-one hundredths

10.3 **Fractions and Decimals**

Write the number as tenths in fraction form and decimal form.

14. $\dfrac{30}{100}$

15. $\dfrac{90}{100}$

16. 0.50

Write the number as hundredths in fraction form and decimal form.

17. $\dfrac{7}{10}$

18. $\dfrac{4}{10}$

19. 0.6

10.4 **Compare Decimals**

Compare.

20. 0.79 ◯ 0.72

21. 9.16 ◯ 9.56

22. 11.40 ◯ 11.4

Open-Ended Complete the statement to make it true.

23. 0.☐9 < 0.☐5

24. 6.3☐ = 6.3

25. _____ > 40.48

26. Open-Ended What might Newton's number be?

My number is greater than 0.2 and less than 0.3. The greatest digit in the number is in the hundredths place.

10.5 Add Decimal Fractions and Decimals

Find the sum.

27. $\dfrac{6}{10} + \dfrac{14}{100} =$ _____

28. $\dfrac{52}{100} + \dfrac{3}{10} =$ _____

29. $0.12 + 0.6 =$ _____

30. $0.4 + 0.72 =$ _____

31. $\dfrac{23}{100} + \dfrac{36}{100} + \dfrac{2}{10} =$ _____

32. $0.18 + 0.2 + 0.07 =$ _____

MP Number Sense Find the sum.

33. $0.5 + \dfrac{48}{100} =$ _____

34. $\dfrac{9}{10} + 0.25 =$ _____

10.6 Fractions, Decimals, and Money

Find the total money amount. Then write the amount as a fraction or mixed number and as a decimal.

35.

36.

37. Write $\dfrac{18}{100}$ as a money amount and as a decimal.

38. Write $0.94 as a fraction and as a decimal.

10.7 Operations with Money

Draw bills and coins to solve.

39. Bananas cost $0.29 per pound. You buy 3 pounds of bananas. How much money do you spend in all?

40. Descartes has $3.50. He spends $1.75 on a journal. How much money does Descartes have left?

41. You buy the items shown at a book fair. How much money do you spend in all?

11 Understand Measurement Equivalence

- Have you ever driven a go-kart?

- A go-kart fuel tank can hold $2\frac{1}{2}$ quarts of gasoline. Why is it important to know how many quarts are in a gallon when filling the fuel tank of a go-kart?

11 Vocabulary

Name _____

Review Words

kilogram
liter
mass
milliliter

Organize It

Use the review words to complete the graphic organizer.

	Liquid Volume
 gram	

Define It

Use your vocabulary cards to complete the puzzle.

Across
1. A unit of time (sec)
2. A customary unit used to measure capacity (c)

Down
3. A customary unit used to measure length (mi)
4. A customary unit used to measure weight (oz)

Chapter 11 Vocabulary Cards

cup (c)

gallon (gal)

kilometer (km)

mile (mi)

millimeter (mm)

ounce (oz)

pint (pt)

pound (lb)

A customary unit used to
measure capacity
There are 4 quarts in 1 gallon.

The capacity of the jug is 1 gallon.

A customary unit used to
measure capacity

The capacity of the measuring
cup is 1 cup.

A customary unit used to measure length
There are 1,760 yards in 1 mile.

When walking briskly, you can walk
1 mile in about 20 minutes.

A metric unit used to measure length
There are 1,000 meters in 1 kilometer.

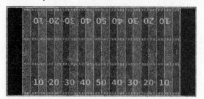

1 kilometer is about the length of
10 football fields including the end zones.

A customary unit used to measure weight

A slice of bread weighs about 1 ounce.

A metric unit used to measure length
1 millimeter

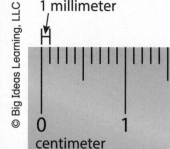

There are
10 millimeters in
1 centimeter.

A customary unit used to measure weight
There are 16 ounces in 1 pound.

A loaf of bread weighs about 1 pound.

A customary unit used to measure capacity
There are 2 cups in 1 pint.

The capacity of the carton is 1 pint.

Chapter 11 Vocabulary Cards

quart (qt)

second (sec)

ton (T)

A unit of time

1 second

11 12 1
10   2
9   3
8   4
7   6   5

There are
60 seconds in
1 minute.

A customary unit used to
measure capacity
There are 2 pints in 1 quart.

MILK

The capacity of the carton is 1 quart.

A customary unit used to measure weight
There are 2,000 pounds in 1 ton.

A small compact car weighs about 1 ton.

Learning Target: Write lengths using equivalent metric measures.

Success Criteria:
• I can compare sizes of metric units of length.
• I can write metric lengths using smaller metric units.
• I can make tables of equivalent metric lengths.

Explore and Grow

Work with a partner. Find 3 objects in your classroom, and use a meter stick to measure them. One of you measure in centimeters, and the other measure in millimeters. Think: What do you notice about the pairs of measurements? How does each measurement compare to 1 meter?

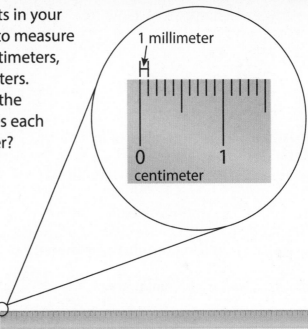

Meter Stick

1 centimeter is _____ times as long as 1 millimeter.

1 meter is _____ times as long as 1 centimeter.

1 meter is _____ times as long as 1 millimeter.

MP **Structure** You know the length of an object in centimeters. Without measuring, how can you find its length in millimeters?

Think and Grow: Find Equivalent Metric Lengths

Metric units of length include **millimeters**, centimeters, meters, and **kilometers**.

Metric Units of Length
1 centimeter (cm) = 10 millimeters (mm)
1 meter (m) = 100 centimeters (cm)
1 kilometer (km) = 1,000 meters (m)

Example   Find the number of meters in 3 kilometers.

There are _____ meters in 1 kilometer.

3 × _____ = _____

So, there are _____ meters in 3 kilometers.

Example   Find the number of millimeters in 9 meters.

There are _____ centimeters in 1 meter.

9 × _____ = _____ centimeters

There are _____ millimeters in 1 centimeter.

900 × _____ = _____ millimeters

So, there are _____ millimeters in 9 meters.

First, find the number of centimeters. Then find the number of millimeters.

Show and Grow   I can do it!

Find the equivalent length.

1. 8 km = _____ m

2. 7 m = _____ cm

3. 5 cm = _____ mm

4. 6 km = _____ cm

 duplicate none

496

© Big Ideas Learning, LLC

Name _____

 Apply and Grow: Practice

Find the equivalent length.

5. 3 cm = _____ mm

6. 8 m = _____ cm

7. 9 cm = _____ mm

8. 4 m = _____ cm

9. 11 km = _____ m

10. 2 km = _____ cm

11. 3 m = _____ mm

12. 5 km = _____ m

13. A pencil is 19 centimeters long. How many millimeters long is the pencil?

14. **MP** **Number Sense** How does the meaning of each prefix relate to the metric units of length in this lesson?

Prefix	Definition
kilo-	one thousand
centi-	one hundredth
milli-	one thousandth

DIG DEEPER! Compare.

15. 4 m ◯ 400 cm

16. 5,000 mm ◯ 50 m

Think and Grow: Modeling Real Life

Example During 1 day of swim practice, your friend swam 2,600 meters. Your friend's goal was to swim $2\frac{1}{2}$ kilometers. Did he reach his goal?

Make a table that shows the relationship between kilometers and meters.

Compare 2,600 meters to $2\frac{1}{2}$ kilometers.

Kilometers	Meters
1	
$1\frac{1}{2}$	
2	
$2\frac{1}{2}$	
3	

1 kilometer = _____ meters

$1\frac{1}{2} \times$ _____ = _____

Your friend _____ reach his goal.

Show and Grow   I can think deeper!

17. You have 42 millimeters of wire. You need $4\frac{1}{2}$ centimeters of wire to make an earring. Do you have enough wire to make the earring?

18. Which insect's wingspan is longer? How much longer is it?

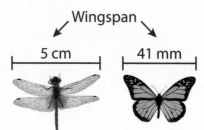

Wingspan

5 cm   41 mm

19. **DIG DEEPER!** There are signs posted every 500 meters along a 5-kilometer race. How many signs are posted?

Name _____

Learning Target: Write lengths using equivalent metric measures.

Example Find the number of centimeters in 2 kilometers.

There are ___1,000___ meters in 1 kilometer.

$2 \times$ ___1,000___ $=$ ___2,000___ meters

There are ___100___ centimeters in 1 meter.

$2,000 \times$ ___100___ $=$ ___200,000___ centimeters

So, there are ___200,000___ centimeters in 2 kilometers.

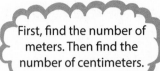

First, find the number of meters. Then find the number of centimeters.

Find the equivalent length.

1. 3 km = _____ m

2. 5 m = _____ mm

3. 12 km = _____ m

4. 8 m = _____ cm

5. 9 km = _____ cm

6. 6 m = _____ mm

7. 7 m = _____ cm

8. 4 m = _____ mm

9. A basketball player is 2 meters tall. How tall is the player in centimeters?

10. **Which One Doesn't Belong?** Which measurement does *not* belong with the other three?

   50 m   500 km   5,000 cm   50,000 mm

---

11.  **Patterns** Describe and complete the pattern.

Meters	Centimeters	Millimeters
4	400	4,000
6	600	6,000
8		
10		
12		

---

12. **Modeling Real Life** A pencil is 190 millimeters long. A pencil box is $20\frac{1}{2}$ centimeters long. Will the pencil fit inside the pencil box?

Centimeters	Millimeters
19	
$19\frac{1}{2}$	
20	
$20\frac{1}{2}$	

---

13. **DIG DEEPER!** An airplane runway is 4 kilometers long. An airplane starts at one end and travels 2,044 meters. How many more meters can the airplane travel before reaching the end of the runway?

Review & Refresh

Find the factor pairs for the number.

14. 11   **15.** 25   **16.** 12

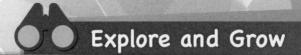
Learning Target: Write masses and capacities using
equivalent metric measures.
Success Criteria:
• I can compare sizes of metric units of mass and capacity.
• I can write metric masses and capacities using smaller
metric units.
• I can make tables of equivalent metric measures.

Explore and Grow

Use a balance and weights to help you complete the statement.

1 kilogram is _____ times as much as 1 gram.

Use a 1-liter beaker to help you complete the statement.

1 liter is _____ times as much as 1 milliliter.

MP **Structure** You know the mass of an object in kilograms.
Without using a scale, how can you find its mass in grams?

Think and Grow: Find Equivalent Metric Measures

Metric units of mass include grams and kilograms.

Metric units of capacity include liters and milliliters.

Metric Units of Mass
1 kilogram (kg) = 1,000 grams (g)

Metric Units of Capacity
1 liter (L) = 1,000 milliliters (mL)

Example Find the number of grams in 3 kilograms.

There are _____ grams in 1 kilogram.

$3 \times$ _____ = _____

So, there are _____ grams in 3 kilograms.

Example The container holds 5 liters of water. How many milliliters of water does the container hold?

There are _____ milliliters in 1 liter.

$5 \times$ _____ = _____

So, the container holds _____ milliliters of water.

Show and Grow   I can do it!

Find the equivalent mass.

1. 6 kg = _____ g

2. 9 kg = _____ g

Find the equivalent capacity.

3. 7 L = _____ mL

4. 10 L = _____ mL

Apply and Grow: Practice

Find the equivalent mass.

5. 8 kg = _____ g

6. 7 kg = _____ g

7. 4 kg = _____ g

8. 67 kg = _____ g

Find the equivalent capacity.

9. 9 L = _____ mL

10. 3 L = _____ mL

11. 23 L = _____ mL

12. 40 L = _____ mL

13. What is the mass of the bag of apples in grams?

2-kg bag

14. **YOU BE THE TEACHER** Your friend says that 4 liters is greater than 4,500 milliliters. Is your friend correct? Explain.

15. **Writing** Compare the relationship between kilograms and grams to the relationship between liters and milliliters.

Example A restaurant chef has $5\frac{3}{4}$ kilograms of rice. A recipe uses 5,875 grams of rice. Does the chef have enough rice to follow the recipe?

Make a table that shows the relationship between kilograms and grams.

Compare $5\frac{3}{4}$ kilograms to 5,875 grams.

Kilograms	Grams
5	
$5\frac{1}{4}$	
$5\frac{2}{4}$	
$5\frac{3}{4}$	
6	

1 kilogram = _____ grams

5 × _____ = _____

$5\frac{1}{4}$ × _____ = _____

The chef _____ have enough rice to follow the recipe.

Show and Grow   I can think deeper!

16. Your goal is to drink 1,500 milliliters of water each day. Yesterday, you drank $2\frac{1}{2}$ liters of water. Did you reach your goal?

17. Which egg has a greater mass? How much greater?

Ostrich: $1\frac{1}{4}$ kg

Chicken: 581 g

18. **DIG DEEPER!** A scientist has 3 liters, 818 milliliters, and 410 milliliters of a solution in each of 3 beakers. The scientist wants to divide the solution equally among 7 beakers. How much of the solution should the scientist put into each beaker?

Name _____

Learning Target: Write masses and capacities using equivalent metric measures.

Example Find the number of grams in 5 kilograms.

There are 1,000 grams in 1 kilogram.

5 × 1,000 = 5,000

So, there are 5,000 grams in 5 kilograms.

Find the equivalent mass.

1. 2 kg = _____ g

2. 10 kg = _____ g

3. 50 kg = _____ g

4. 31 kg = _____ g

Find the equivalent capacity.

5. 7 L = _____ mL

6. 4 L = _____ mL

7. 8 L = _____ mL

8. 11 L = _____ mL

9. A pitcher contains 3 liters of iced tea. How many milliliters of iced tea does the pitcher contain?

10. **MP** **Number Sense** The prefix "kilo-" means one thousand. The prefix "milli-" means one thousandth. How does the meaning of each prefix relate to the metric units of mass and capacity in this lesson?

11. **MP** **Number Sense** When measuring the mass of a chair, how will the size of the unit affect the size of the measurement?

12. **Modeling Real Life** To cook a pound of pasta, you need to boil 4,700 milliliters of water. You fill a pot with $4\frac{1}{4}$ liters of water. Is there enough water in your pot?

Liters	Milliliters
4	
$4\frac{1}{4}$	
$4\frac{2}{4}$	
$4\frac{3}{4}$	
5	

13. **DIG DEEPER!** A 4,500-gram bag of soil costs $3, and an 18-kilogram bag of soil costs $10. Which is the less expensive way to buy 18,000 grams of soil? Explain.

Review & Refresh

Find the difference. Then check your answer.

14.   8,467
     − 6,753

15.   30,052
     − 5,439

16.   85,012
     − 34,769

Learning Target: Write lengths using equivalent customary measures.

Success Criteria:
- I can compare sizes of customary units of length.
- I can write customary lengths using smaller customary units.
- I can make tables of equivalent customary lengths.

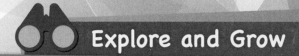
Explore and Grow

Work with a partner. Use a yard stick to draw 3 lines on a whiteboard that are 1 yard, 2 yards, and 3 yards in length. Then measure the lengths of the lines in feet and in inches. Think: How do the lengths, in inches, compare to the lengths in feet? How does each length compare to 1 yard?

1 foot is _____ times as long as 1 inch.

1 yard is _____ times as long as 1 foot.

1 yard is _____ times as long as 1 inch.

Structure You know the length of an object in feet. Without measuring, how can you find its length in inches?

Think and Grow: Find Equivalent Customary Lengths

Customary units of length include inches, feet, yards, and **miles**.

Customary Units of Length
1 foot (ft) = 12 inches (in.)
1 yard (yd) = 3 feet (ft)
1 mile (mi) = 1,760 yards (yd)

Example   Find the number of yards in 2 miles.

There are _____ yards in 1 mile.

2 × _____ = _____

   So, there are _____ yards in 2 miles.

Example   Find the number of inches in 7 yards.

There are _____ feet in 1 yard.

7 × _____ = _____ feet

There are _____ inches in 1 foot.

21 × _____ = _____ inches

   So, there are _____ inches in 7 yards.

First, find the number of feet. Then find the number of inches.

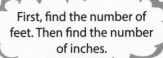

Find the equivalent length.

1. 6 mi = _____ yd

2. 4 ft = _____ in.

3. 11 yd = _____ ft

4. 3 mi = _____ ft

508

© Big Ideas Learning, LLC

Name _____

 Apply and Grow: Practice

Find the equivalent length.

5. 10 ft = _____ in.

6. 8 yd = _____ in.

7. 2 mi = _____ ft

8. 9 mi = _____ yd

9. 4 yd = _____ in.

10. 20 ft = _____ in.

11. 7 mi = _____ yd

12. 5 mi = _____ ft

13. You ran 54 yards. How many feet did you run?

14. (MP) **Precision** Three students measure the height of a bookshelf. Student A measures 72 units, Student B measures 2 units, and Student C measures 6 units. The teacher says all three students are correct. What units did each student use?

15. (MP) **Reasoning** What is one way you can check whether an answer is reasonable when converting from larger units to smaller units?

Think and Grow: Modeling Real Life

Example A football player needs to run $6\frac{1}{3}$ yards to score.

The player runs 17 feet. Does the player score?

Make a table that shows the relationship between yards and feet.

Compare $6\frac{1}{3}$ yards to 17 feet.

Yards	Feet
5	
$5\frac{1}{3}$	
$5\frac{2}{3}$	
6	
$6\frac{1}{3}$	

1 yard = _____ feet

$5 \times$ _____ = _____

$5\frac{1}{3} \times$ _____ = _____

The player _____ score.

Show and Grow   I can think deeper!

16. You have $3\frac{1}{4}$ feet of string. You need 36 inches of string to make a necklace. Do you have enough string to make the necklace?

17. Which snake is longer? How much longer?

Boa Constrictor: 13 feet

Green Anaconda: $9\frac{1}{3}$ yards

18. **DIG DEEPER!** You have 6 yards of ribbon. You wrap 3 feet of ribbon around a present. You wrap 16 inches of ribbon around another present. How many inches of ribbon do you have left?

Name _____

Learning Target: Write lengths using equivalent customary measures.

Example   Find the number of feet in 4 miles.

There are __1,760__ yards in 1 mile.

4 × __1,760__ = __7,040__ yards

There are ___3___ feet in 1 yard.

7,040 × ___3___ = __21,120__ feet

So, there are __21,120__ feet in 4 miles.

First, find the number of yards. Then find the number of feet.

Find the equivalent length.

1. 25 ft = _____ in.

2. 3 mi = _____ yd

3. 7 yd = _____ ft

4. 9 yd = _____ in.

5. 5 mi = _____ yd

6. 6 mi = _____ ft

7. $\frac{1}{4}$ mi = _____ yd

8. $\frac{1}{3}$ yd = _____ ft

9. A street is 2 miles long. How long is the street in yards?

© Big Ideas Learning, LLC

10.  **Number Sense** Does it take more miles or more yards to equal a given length? Explain.

11. **YOU BE THE TEACHER** Your friend says 1 inch is $\frac{1}{12}$ of a foot. Is your friend correct? Explain.

---

12. **Number Sense** Which lengths are equivalent?

15 yards	540 inches	135 feet
180 inches	45 feet	10 yards

---

13. **Modeling Real Life** A plumber has $6\frac{1}{3}$ feet of piping. She needs 75 inches of piping. Does she have enough piping?

Feet	Inches
6	
$6\frac{1}{3}$	
$6\frac{2}{3}$	
7	

---

14. **Modeling Real Life** A teacher has 12 yards of string for her class to make balloon zip lines. Each zip line needs 8 feet of string. How many zip lines can the class make?

© Big Ideas Learning, LLC

Name _____

Weight in Customary Units **11.4**

Learning Target: Write weights using equivalent customary measures.

Success Criteria:
- I can compare sizes of customary units of weight.
- I can write customary weights using smaller customary units.
- I can make tables of equivalent customary weights.

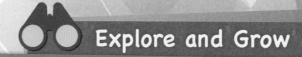

Explore and Grow

Use a platform scale to help you complete the statement.

1 pound is _____ times as heavy as 1 ounce.

How can you use the number line to complete the statement?

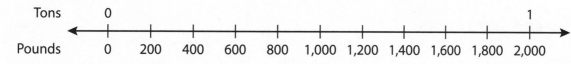

Tons	0										1
Pounds	0	200	400	600	800	1,000	1,200	1,400	1,600	1,800	2,000

1 ton is _____ times as heavy as 1 pound.

MP **Structure** You know the weight of an object in pounds. Without measuring, how can you find its weight in ounces?

© Big Ideas Learning, LLC

Chapter 11 | Lesson 4

513

Customary units of weight include **ounces**, **pounds**, and **tons**.

Customary Units of Weight
1 pound (lb) = 16 ounces (oz)
1 ton (T) = 2,000 pounds (lb)

Example   Find the number of ounces in 6 pounds.

There are _____ ounces in 1 pound.

$6 \times$ _____ = _____

So, there are _____ ounces in 6 pounds.

Example   The vehicle shown weighs 8 tons. What is the weight in pounds?

There are _____ pounds in 1 ton.

$8 \times$ _____ = _____

So, the vehicle weighs _____ pounds.

Show and Grow   I can do it!

Find the equivalent weight.

1. 5 T = _____ lb

2. 9 lb = _____ oz

3. 15 lb = _____ oz

4. 7 T = _____ lb

Name _____

Find the equivalent weight.

5. 6 T = _____ lb

6. 20 lb = _____ oz

7. 12 lb = _____ oz

8. 2 T = _____ lb

9. 4 T = _____ lb

10. 11 lb = _____ oz

11. 15 lb = _____ oz

12. 10 T = _____ lb

13. A bag of flour weighs 5 pounds. What is the weight of the bag of flour in ounces?

Open-Ended Complete the statement.

14. 54 ounces > _____ pounds

15. 5,500 pounds < _____ tons

DIG DEEPER! Compare.

16. 2 lb $\bigcirc$ 25 oz

17. 6,500 lb $\bigcirc$ 7 T

Think and Grow: Modeling Real Life

Example   A river otter eats 64 ounces of food each day. A zookeeper has $3\frac{1}{2}$ pounds of fish to feed the otter. Does the zookeeper have enough food to feed the otter for 1 day?

Make a table that shows the relationship between pounds and ounces.

Compare 64 ounces to $3\frac{1}{2}$ pounds.

Pounds	Ounces
3	
$3\frac{1}{2}$	
4	
$4\frac{1}{2}$	

1 pound = _____ ounces

$3 \times$ _____ = _____

$3\frac{1}{2} \times$ _____ = _____

The zookeeper _____ have enough food to feed the otter for 1 day.

Show and Grow   I can think deeper!

18. The weight limit of a bridge is 10,000 pounds. Can the van cross the bridge?

Weight: $4\frac{1}{4}$ tons

19. Your backpack weighs $3\frac{1}{2}$ pounds. You take a 4-ounce book out of your backpack. How many ounces does your backpack weigh now?

20. **DIG DEEPER!**   A 195-pound man has twenty-five 40-pound packages to deliver. Can he bring all of the packages on the elevator at once? Explain.

THIS ELEVATOR MAXIMUM CAPACITY **2 TONS**

Name _____

Learning Target: Write weights using equivalent customary measures.

Example Find the number of ounces in 10 pounds.

There are ___16___ ounces in 1 pound.

$10 \times$ ___16___ $=$ ___160___

So, there are ___160___ ounces in 10 pounds.

Find the equivalent weight.

1. $3\,T =$ _____ lb

2. $13\,lb =$ _____ oz

3. $22\,lb =$ _____ oz

4. $8\,T =$ _____ lb

5. $2\,T =$ _____ lb

6. $20\,lb =$ _____ oz

7. $5\frac{3}{4}\,lb =$ _____ oz

8. $6\frac{1}{4}\,T =$ _____ lb

© Big Ideas Learning, LLC

9. A hippopotamus weighs 4 tons. What is the weight of the hippopotamus in pounds?

10. **Writing** Explain how to compare tons to ounces.

11. **Modeling Real Life** Workers need 20,000 pounds of concrete to create a driveway. The boss orders $10\frac{3}{4}$ tons of concrete. Does he order enough?

Tons	Pounds
10	
$10\frac{1}{4}$	
$10\frac{2}{4}$	
$10\frac{3}{4}$	
11	

12. **Modeling Real Life** You buy crushed tomatoes in 6-ounce cans. You want to make a recipe that calls for $1\frac{1}{2}$ pounds of crushed tomatoes. How many cans do you need to make the recipe?

13. **DIG DEEPER!** How many more ounces does the heaviest puppy weigh than the lightest puppy?

Weights of Puppies

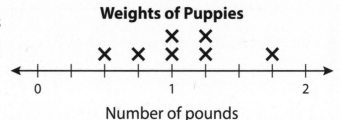

Number of pounds

Review & Refresh

Find the sum.

14. $\frac{2}{8} + \frac{4}{8} =$ _____

15. $\frac{1}{2} + \frac{4}{2} =$ _____

16. $\frac{5}{12} + \frac{3}{12} + \frac{1}{12} =$ _____

Capacity in Customary Units 11.5

Learning Target: Write capacities using equivalent customary measures.

Success Criteria:
• I can compare sizes of customary units of capacity.
• I can write customary capacities using smaller customary units.
• I can make tables of equivalent customary capacities.

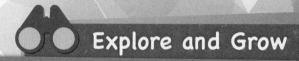 Explore and Grow

Use the diagram to complete each statement. Then check your answers using a gallon measurement set.

1 gallon							
1 quart		1 quart		1 quart		1 quart	
1 pint	1 pint	1 pint	1 pint	1 pint	1 pint	1 pint	1 pint
1 cup / 1 cup	1 cup / 1 cup	1 cup / 1 cup	1 cup / 1 cup	1 cup / 1 cup	1 cup / 1 cup	1 cup / 1 cup	1 cup / 1 cup

1 gallon is _____ times as much as 1 quart.

1 quart is _____ times as much as 1 pint.

1 pint is _____ times as much as 1 cup.

1 gallon is _____ times as much as 1 cup.

 Structure You know the capacity of a container in pints. Without measuring, how can you find its capacity in cups?

Think and Grow: Find Equivalent Customary Capacities

Customary units of capacity include **cups**, **pints**, **quarts**, and **gallons**.

Customary Units of Capacity
1 pint (pt) = 2 cups (c)
1 quart (qt) = 2 pints (pt)
1 gallon (gal) = 4 quarts (qt)

Example   Find the number of quarts in 15 gallons.

There are _____ quarts in 1 gallon.

$15 \times$ _____ = _____

So, there are _____ quarts in 15 gallons.

Example   Find the number of cups in 7 quarts.

There are _____ pints in 1 quart.

$7 \times$ _____ = _____ pints

There are _____ cups in 1 pint.

$14 \times$ _____ = _____ cups

So, there are _____ cups in 7 quarts.

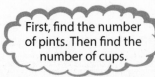
First, find the number of pints. Then find the number of cups.

Show and Grow   I can do it!

Find the equivalent capacity.

1.   4 pt = _____ c

2.   6 qt = _____ pt

3.   9 gal = _____ qt

4.   12 gal = _____ pt

Name _____

 Apply and Grow: Practice

Find the equivalent capacity.

5. 30 qt = _____ pt

6. 5 gal = _____ pt

7. 9 qt = _____ c

8. 8 gal = _____ qt

9. 25 pt = _____ c

10. 11 gal = _____ pt

11. 18 gal = _____ qt

12. 16 qt = _____ c

13. You have a 10-gallon fish tank. How many quarts of water does it take to fill your fish tank?

14. **DIG DEEPER!** Which measurements are greater than 5 gallons?

92 cups   36 pints   15 quarts

10 gallons   80 cups   41 pints

Think and Grow: Modeling Real Life

Example A berry salad uses 6 pints of blackberries, 2 quarts of strawberries, and 7 cups of blueberries. Which fruit do you use the greatest amount of?

Make a table that shows the relationship between quarts, pints, and cups.

Quarts	Pints	Cups
1		
2		
3		

1 quart = _____ pints and 1 pint = _____ cups

Compare 6 pints, 2 quarts, and 7 cups.

You use the greatest amount of _____.

Show and Grow   I can think deeper!

15. A caterer buys 2 gallons of milk, 12 quarts of lemonade, and 32 pints of apple juice. Which drink does the caterer buy the least amount of?

16. You make 4 quarts of soup. You and your friend each eat 1 pint of soup. Will the leftover soup fit into a 10-cup container? Explain.

17. **DIG DEEPER!** You use 16 gallons of water while taking a shower. Your friend uses 288 cups. Who uses less water? How much less?

Name _____

Learning Target: Write capacities using equivalent customary measures.

Example Find the number of pints in 5 gallons.

There are ___4___ quarts in 1 gallon.

$5 \times$ ___4___ $=$ ___20___ quarts

There are ___2___ pints in 1 quart.

$20 \times$ ___2___ $=$ ___40___ pints

So, there are ___40___ pints in 5 gallons.

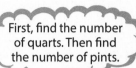

First, find the number of quarts. Then find the number of pints.

Find the equivalent capacity.

1. 7 pt = _____ c

2. 10 qt = _____ pt

3. 8 gal = _____ qt

4. 4 gal = _____ pt

5. 12 qt = _____ c

6. 6 gal = _____ qt

7. $3\frac{1}{4}$ gal = _____ pt

8. $4\frac{1}{2}$ pt = _____ c

9. A bottle holds $\frac{1}{2}$ quart of liquid. How many cups of water does the bottle hold?

10. Writing Compare the relationship between pints and cups to the relationship between quarts and pints.

11. (MP) **Logic** Your friend makes a table of equivalent capacities. What are the labels for the columns?

_____	_____
1	8
2	16
3	24
4	32
5	40

12. Modeling Real Life Turning off the faucet while brushing your teeth can conserve 32 quarts of water. Using a low-flow shower head can conserve 15 gallons of water. Using a dishwasher can conserve 112 pints of water. Which activity conserves the greatest amount of water?

Gallons	Quarts	Pints
13		
14		
15		

13. Modeling Real Life Some pitcher plants are large enough to hold 2 gallons of water. A household pitcher holds 16 cups of water. How much more water can a pitcher plant hold than the household pitcher?

Pitcher Plant

14. A car dealership owner needs to transport 150 cars and 95 trucks to an island. A ferry can hold 8 vehicles. How many trips with vehicles will the ferry need to make?

Name _____

Learning Target: Make line plots and use them to solve problems.

Success Criteria:
• I can make a line plot.
• I can interpret a line plot.
• I can use a line plot to solve a real-life problem.

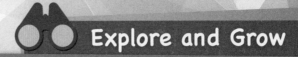
Explore and Grow

Measure your hand length with a ruler. Record the length to the nearest half inch. Collect the hand lengths of all the students in your class, including yourself. Create a line plot of the results.

Think: How will you label the scale? What title will you give your line plot?

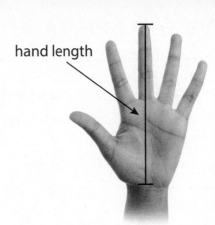
hand length

MP **Construct Arguments** What conclusions can you make from the line plot?

Think and Grow: Make Line Plots

Plant Height (inch)				
$\frac{1}{8}$	$\frac{3}{8}$	$\frac{3}{8}$	$\frac{1}{2}$	$\frac{3}{8}$
$\frac{1}{2}$	$\frac{3}{8}$	$\frac{1}{2}$	$\frac{5}{8}$	$\frac{3}{4}$

Example   You plant 10 seeds. After 6 days, you measure the height of each plant. Make a line plot to display the data.

Step 1: Write the data values as fractions with the same denominator.

The denominators of the data values are 2, 4, and 8. Because 2 and 4 are factors of 8, use a denominator of 8.

$$\frac{1}{2} = \frac{1 \times 4}{2 \times 4} = \frac{\boxed{}}{\boxed{}} \qquad \frac{3}{4} = \frac{3 \times 2}{4 \times 2} = \frac{\boxed{}}{\boxed{}}$$

Step 2: Use a scale on a number line that shows all of the data values.

Step 3: Mark an X for each data value.

Plant Height

Remember: When making a line plot, write a title and label the scale.

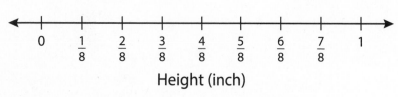

Height (inch)

Which plant height is the most common?

Show and Grow   I can do it!

1. You survey 10 people about the amount of water each person drinks in 1 day. Make a line plot to display the data.

Water Consumption

Amount of Water (gallon)				
$\frac{1}{4}$	$\frac{3}{8}$	$\frac{1}{8}$	$\frac{1}{4}$	$\frac{1}{8}$
$\frac{5}{8}$	$\frac{1}{4}$	$\frac{1}{4}$	$\frac{1}{8}$	$\frac{1}{4}$

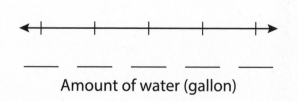

Amount of water (gallon)

Which amount of water consumed is the most common?

526

Name _____

2. The table shows the lengths of 10 chameleons in a pet store. Make a line plot to display the data.

Chameleon Lengths (inch)

$\frac{3}{4}$	$\frac{4}{8}$	$\frac{7}{8}$	$\frac{5}{8}$	$\frac{3}{4}$
$\frac{7}{8}$	$\frac{3}{4}$	$\frac{5}{8}$	$\frac{3}{4}$	$\frac{7}{8}$

Which is most common chameleon length?

Chameleon Lengths

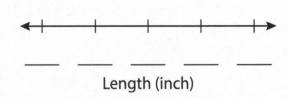

Length (inch)

3. A scientist is studying the weights of 15 sugar gliders. Make a line plot to display the data.

Sugar Glider Weights (pound)

$\frac{1}{8}$	$\frac{1}{4}$	$\frac{3}{8}$	$\frac{1}{4}$	$\frac{1}{4}$
$\frac{1}{4}$	$\frac{3}{8}$	$\frac{1}{4}$	$\frac{3}{8}$	$\frac{1}{4}$
$\frac{1}{8}$	$\frac{1}{4}$	$\frac{1}{8}$	$\frac{1}{4}$	$\frac{3}{8}$

How many sugar gliders weigh more than $\frac{1}{8}$ pound?

Sugar Glider Weights

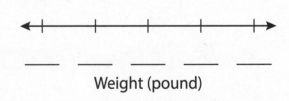

Weight (pound)

4. **DIG DEEPER!** Use your line plot from Exercise 3. How many times as many $\frac{2}{8}$-pound sugar gliders are there as $\frac{3}{8}$-pound sugar gliders? Explain.

Think and Grow: Modeling Real Life

Example   You record the distances you rode your bike for 10 days. What is the difference in the length of your longest ride and the length of your shortest ride?

Make a line plot. Use a scale that shows all of the data values.

Distances Biked (miles)	
$5\frac{1}{2}$	$6\frac{1}{2}$
5	$5\frac{1}{2}$
$6\frac{1}{2}$	$6\frac{1}{2}$
$4\frac{1}{2}$	6
$5\frac{1}{2}$	$6\frac{1}{2}$

$$\longleftarrow \;\;\; | \quad\quad | \quad\quad | \quad\quad | \quad\quad | \;\;\; \longrightarrow$$

_____   _____   _____   _____   _____

_____

Subtract the shortest ride from the longest ride.

_____ − _____ = _____

The difference in the length of your longest ride and

the length of your shortest ride is _____ miles.

Show and Grow   *I can think deeper!*

5. You record the total monthly rainfall for 10 months. What is the difference of the greatest monthly rainfall and the least monthly rainfall?

Monthly Rainfall (inches)	
$1\frac{1}{8}$	$\frac{6}{8}$
$\frac{7}{8}$	$\frac{5}{8}$
$\frac{4}{8}$	1
$\frac{5}{8}$	$\frac{4}{8}$
$1\frac{1}{8}$	$\frac{5}{8}$

_____

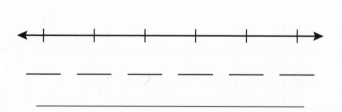

How much did it rain during the 10 months in all?

Learning Target: Make line plots and use them to solve problems.

Example The table shows the amounts of time that 10 basketball players exercise in 1 day. Make a line plot to display the data.

Amount of Time (hour)				
$\frac{3}{4}$	$\frac{1}{2}$	1	$\frac{3}{4}$	$\frac{1}{2}$
$\frac{1}{4}$	$\frac{3}{4}$	$\frac{1}{2}$	$\frac{1}{4}$	$\frac{3}{4}$

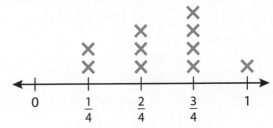

Time Spent Exercising

Amount of time (hour)

Which is the most common amount

of time spent exercising? $\frac{3}{4}$ hour

---

1. The table shows the thicknesses of 10 books in a series. Make a line plot to display the data.

Book Thicknesses (inch)				
$\frac{1}{8}$	$\frac{4}{8}$	$\frac{3}{4}$	$\frac{4}{8}$	$\frac{3}{4}$
$\frac{3}{4}$	$\frac{5}{8}$	$\frac{1}{8}$	$\frac{3}{4}$	$\frac{2}{4}$

Book Thicknesses

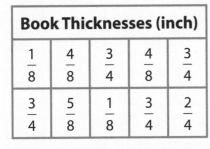

Thickness (inch)

The least common thickness is _____ inch.

There are _____ books that are less than $\frac{5}{8}$ inch thick.

---

2. **DIG DEEPER!** Use your line plot from Exercise 1. How many times as many $\frac{3}{4}$-inch thick books are there as $\frac{1}{8}$-inch thick books?

3. A zoologist is studying the weights of 15 skinks. Make a line plot to display the data.

Skink Weights (pound)

$\frac{3}{4}$	$\frac{4}{8}$	$\frac{3}{4}$	$\frac{5}{8}$	$\frac{3}{4}$
$\frac{5}{8}$	$\frac{3}{4}$	$\frac{5}{8}$	$\frac{3}{4}$	$\frac{2}{4}$
$\frac{3}{4}$	$\frac{3}{4}$	$\frac{3}{4}$	$\frac{4}{8}$	$\frac{3}{4}$

Skink Weights

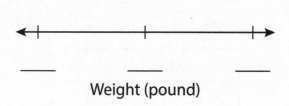

Weight (pound)

4. (MP) **Reasoning** In Exercise 3, do most of the skinks weigh more than $\frac{5}{8}$ pound?

5. **Modeling Real Life** A painter records the amounts of paint he uses in 10 different rooms. What is the difference of the greatest amount of paint used and the least amount of paint used?

_____

Amounts of Paint (gallons)	
2	$3\frac{1}{2}$
3	$2\frac{1}{2}$
$3\frac{1}{2}$	3
2	$2\frac{1}{2}$
$2\frac{1}{2}$	2

How many gallons of paint were used in all 10 rooms combined?

Review & Refresh

Write the fraction as a sum of unit fractions.

6. $\frac{5}{6}$

7. $\frac{8}{3}$

Units of Time **11.7**

Learning Target: Write amounts of time using equivalent measures.

Success Criteria:
• I can compare sizes of units of time.
• I can write amounts of time using smaller units.
• I can make tables of equivalent amounts of time.

 Explore and Grow

Use a clock or a stopwatch to help you complete the statements.

1 minute is _____ times as long as 1 second.

1 hour is _____ times as long as 1 minute.

Structure You know an amount of time in minutes. Without using a clock or a stopwatch, how can you find the amount of time in seconds?

Think and Grow: Find Equivalent Amounts of Time

Units of time include **seconds,** minutes, hours, days, weeks, months, and years.

Units of Time	
1 minute (min) = 60 seconds (sec)	1 week (wk) = 7 days (d)
1 hour (h) = 60 minutes (min)	1 year (yr) = 12 months (mo)
1 day (d) = 24 hours (h)	1 year (yr) = 52 weeks (wk)

Example   Find the number of minutes in 6 hours.

There are _____ minutes in 1 hour.

$6 \times$ _____ = _____

So, there are _____ minutes in 6 hours.

Example   Find the number of hours in 4 weeks.

There are _____ days in 1 week.

$4 \times$ _____ = _____ days

There are _____ hours in 1 day.

$28 \times$ _____ = _____

So, there are _____ hours in 4 weeks.

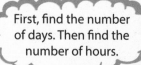
First, find the number of days. Then find the number of hours.

Show and Grow   *I can do it!*

Find the equivalent amount of time.

1. 10 min = _____ sec

2. 5 d = _____ h

3. 8 wk = _____ d

4. 2 d = _____ sec

Name _____

 Apply and Grow: Practice

Find the equivalent amount of time.

5. 7 yr = _____ wk

6. 4 d = _____ min

7. 3 wk = _____ d

8. 6 h = _____ sec

9. 2 yr = _____ mo

10. 1 wk = _____ h

11. 24 h = _____ min

12. 10 yr = _____ d

13. Your friend turns 8 years old today. How many months old is your friend?

14. **Writing** Explain how you can show that 3,000 seconds is less than 1 hour.

15. **MP Structure** The number pairs describe the relationship between which two units of time? Explain.

2 and 104

3 and 156

4 and 208

Think and Grow: Modeling Real Life

Example Your cousin makes a $3\frac{1}{2}$-minute long music video. Your friend makes a 200-second long music video. Who records a longer music video?

Make a table that shows the relationship between minutes and seconds.

Compare $3\frac{1}{2}$ minutes to 200 seconds.

Minutes	Seconds
2	
$2\frac{1}{2}$	
3	
$3\frac{1}{2}$	

1 minute = _____ seconds

$2 \times$ _____ = _____

$2\frac{1}{2} \times$ _____ = _____

Your _____ records a longer music video.

Show and Grow   I can think deeper!

16. You put a puzzle together in 150 minutes. Your friend puts the same puzzle together in $2\frac{1}{4}$ hours. Who put the puzzle together faster?

17. In the wild, a California sea lion can live to be 20 years old. In captivity, it can live to be 360 months old. Does a California sea lion live longer in the wild or in captivity? How much longer?

18. **DIG DEEPER!** Movie A is 98 minutes long. Movie B is $1\frac{1}{2}$ hours long. Movie C is $1\frac{3}{4}$ hours long. Order the movies from longest to shortest.

Learning Target: Write amounts of time using equivalent measures.

Example Find the number of minutes in 3 days.

There are __24__ hours in 1 day.

$3 \times$ __24__ = __72__ hours

There are __60__ minutes in 1 hour.

$72 \times$ __60__ = 4,320 minutes

First, find the number of hours. Then find the number of minutes.

So, there are 4,320 minutes in 3 days.

Find the equivalent amount of time.

1. 9 yr = _____ wk

2. 10 min = _____ sec

3. 1 wk = _____ h

4. 6 yr = _____ mo

5. 3 yr = _____ d

6. 2 d = _____ min

7. $\frac{1}{3}$ d = _____ h

8. $2\frac{3}{4}$ yr = _____ wk

9. How many hours are in 1 week?

10. **YOU BE THE TEACHER** Your friend labels the first column *Weeks* and the second column *Years*. Is your friend correct? Explain.

?	?
1	52
2	104
3	156
4	208
5	260

11. **DIG DEEPER!** How many days is Newton thinking of?

The number of days is greater than 2 weeks, but less than 384 hours.

12. **Modeling Real Life** You have $1\frac{1}{2}$ hours before dinner. You want to watch a movie that is 118 minutes long. Do you have enough time to watch the entire movie?

Hours	Minutes
1	
$1\frac{1}{2}$	
2	
$2\frac{1}{2}$	

13. **DIG DEEPER!** The world record for holding a person vertically overhead with one hand is $1\frac{1}{12}$ minutes. The world record for holding a person horizontally overhead with one hand is 76 seconds. Which world record is longer? How much longer?

Review & Refresh

Find the product. Check whether your answer is reasonable.

14. Estimate: _____

$418 \times 3 =$ _____

15. Estimate: _____

$729 \times 5 =$ _____

16. Estimate: _____

$9 \times 3{,}026 =$ _____

Name _____

Learning Target: Solve multi-step word problems involving elapsed time.
Success Criteria:
• I can understand a problem.
• I can make a plan to solve.
• I can solve a problem.

Explore and Grow

Use a clock to help answer each question.

How much time has passed since you woke up?

How much time has passed since school started?

MP **Construct Arguments** Explain to a partner how you found your answers.

Think and Grow: Problem Solving: Time Intervals

Example A dinosaur museum closes in $1\frac{1}{2}$ hours. Do you have enough time to spend 20 minutes at each of 4 exhibits in the museum?

Understand the Problem

What do you know?
- The museum closes in $1\frac{1}{2}$ hours.
- You want to spend 20 minutes at each of 4 exhibits.

What do you need to find?
- You need to find whether you have enough time to spend 20 minutes at each of 4 exhibits before the museum closes.

Make a Plan

How will you solve?
- Find the number of minutes until the museum closes.
- Find the total number of minutes it takes to visit the exhibits.

Solve

Step 1: Find the number of minutes until the museum closes.

There are _____ minutes in 1 hour.

$1\frac{1}{2} \times$ _____ = _____

There are _____ minutes until the museum closes.

Step 2: Find how many minutes it takes to visit the exhibits.

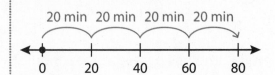

It takes _____ minutes to visit the exhibits, which is _____ than 90 minutes.

You _____ have enough time to visit the exhibits.

Show and Grow   I can do it!

1. You have a total of $9\frac{1}{2}$ minutes to complete 4 tasks in a video game. Do you have enough time to spend 150 seconds on each task?

© Big Ideas Learning, LLC

Name _____

Understand the problem. What do you know? What do you need to find? Explain.

2. You spend $1\frac{1}{4}$ hours exploring the woods. Then you spend 25 minutes sitting at a campfire. How many total minutes do you spend exploring the woods and sitting at the campfire?

3. A bodybuilder spends $2\frac{1}{2}$ hours lifting weights. She spends 20 minutes running. How many more minutes does she spend lifting weights than running?

Understand the problem. Then make a plan. How will you solve? Explain.

4. You visit an animal shelter for $1\frac{3}{4}$ hours. You spend an equal amount of time with each of 7 animals. How many minutes do you spend with each animal?

5. A skate park closes in $3\frac{1}{4}$ hours. Do you have enough time to spend 15 minutes practicing each of 13 different skateboard tricks?

6. A basketball team practices drills for 20 minutes and then scrimmages for 40 minutes. The overall practice time is divided evenly into 3 sessions. How many minutes is each session?

7. A high school music concert is 55 minutes long. The band plays 25 minutes to start the concert. The rest of the concert time is divided equally among the choir, band, orchestra, and jazz ensemble. For how many minutes does the orchestra play?

Think and Grow: Modeling Real Life

Field Day Activities
Bean Bag Toss
Obstacle Course
Paint with Bubbles
Sack Race
Water Balloon Toss

Example   Field day starts at 12:15 P.M. and ends at 3:30 P.M. You spend an equal amount of time at each activity. How much time do you spend at each activity?

Think: What do you know? What do you need to find? How will you solve?

Step 1: How long is field day?

+1 h   +1 h   +1 h   +15 min

12:15 P.M.   1:15 P.M.   2:15 P.M.   3:15 P.M.   3:30 P.M.

Field day is _____ hours

_____ minutes long.

Step 2: How many minutes long is field day?

There are _____ minutes in 1 hour.   _____ × _____ = _____

_____ + 15 = _____   Add 15 minutes.

Field day is _____ minutes long.

Step 3: Divide the total amount of time by the number of field day activities.

5)‾‾

You spend _____ minutes at each activity.

Show and Grow   I can think deeper!

8. You start exercising at 6:30 A.M. and finish at 7:45 A.M. You spend an equal amount of time stretching, walking, and running. How much time do you spend doing each exercise?

540

Name _____

Example   Your school carnival takes place for 15 minutes before it rains. The carnival continues the next day for 120 minutes. You divide your time equally for the 2 days among 9 activities. How many minutes do you spend at each activity?

Think: What do you know? What do you need to find? How will you solve?

Step 1: Find how long the carnival lasts over the 2 days.

$$\underline{\ 15\ } + \underline{\ 120\ } = \underline{\ 135\ }$$

The carnival lasts __135__ minutes.

Step 2: Find how many minutes you spend at each activity.

$$\underline{\ 135\ } \div \underline{\ 9\ } = \underline{\ 15\ }$$

You spend __15__ minutes at each activity.

Understand the problem. Then make a plan. How will you solve? Explain.

1. It takes Descartes $1\frac{1}{4}$ minutes to run 3 laps around his house. Each lap takes him the same amount of time. How many seconds does it take him to run each lap?

2. You watch television for 60 minutes. There are 18 minutes of commercials. The rest of the time is divided evenly between 2 shows. How many minutes long is each show?

3. You spend $5\frac{1}{2}$ hours at the park this week. You spend 210 fewer minutes at the library than you do at the park. How many minutes do you spend at the library?

4. Your class spends $\frac{1}{4}$ hour setting up an experiment. You spend 55 more minutes recording data than you do setting up the experiment. For how many minutes do you record data?

5. You have $7\frac{1}{2}$ minutes left to successfully complete 3 rock climbing walls. It normally takes 155 seconds to climb each wall. Do you have enough time to climb all three walls?

6. **Writing** Write and solve a two-step word problem involving elapsed time.

7. **Modeling Real Life** A family attends a family expo from 1:30 P.M. to 5:15 P.M. They spend an equal amount of time at each activity. How many minutes do they spend at each activity?

Family Expo Activities
- Costumed Characters
- Dog Show
- Foam Pit
- Giant Slide
- Magician

~~~~~~~~~~~~~~~~~~~~~~
Review & Refresh

Find the product.

8. 20×50

9. 38×30

10. 60×82

Learning Target: Add and subtract mixed measures.
Success Criteria:
• I can write measures using smaller units.
• I can use regrouping to rewrite a mixed measure.

 Explore and Grow

Measure your height, the height of a classmate, and the height of your teacher. Write each height in the table.

Heights		
You	_____ ft	_____ in.
Classmate	_____ ft	_____ in.
Teacher	_____ ft	_____ in.

Who is taller, you or your classmate? How much taller?

Who is taller, you or your teacher? How much taller?

 Structure Without measuring, how can you find each height in inches?

Think and Grow: Adding and Subtracting Mixed Measures

Example Add 3 feet 4 inches and 2 feet 5 inches.

Step 1: Add the inches.

3 ft	4 in.
+ 2 ft	5 in.
	_____ in.

You could also write each measurement as an equivalent length in inches, and then find the sum in inches.

Step 2: Add the feet.

3 ft	4 in.
+ 2 ft	5 in.
_____ ft	9 in.

The sum is _____ feet _____ inches.

Example Subtract 4 hours 22 minutes from 7 hours 10 minutes.

Step 1: Subtract the minutes.

6	70
7̶ h	1̶0̶ min
− 4 h	22 min
	_____ min

Think: 22 is greater than 10. So, regroup 1 hour as 60 minutes.

Step 2: Subtract the hours.

6	70
7̶ h	1̶0̶ min
− 4 h	22 min
_____ h	48 min

The difference is _____ hours _____ minutes.

Show and Grow   *I can do it!*

Add or subtract.

1. 2 d 12 h
  + 3 d   9 h

2. 12 T 400 lb
  − 8 T 900 lb

3. 4 gal 5 c
  − 1 gal 7 c

Name _____

Apply and Grow: Practice

Add or subtract.

4. 5 yr   8 mo
   − 2 yr   1 mo
   _____

5. 10 lb   4 oz
   − 1 lb   9 oz
   _____

6. 3 yd   1 ft
   + 6 yd   1 ft
   _____

7. 4 gal   1 qt
   + 8 gal   2 qt
   _____

8. 2 min   55 sec
   − 2 min   12 sec
   _____

9. 7 mi   482 yd
   + 9 mi   109 yd
   _____

10. 4 wk   3 d
    − 2 wk   5 d
   _____

11. 8 pt
    − 5 pt   1 c
   _____

12. 1 yr   22 wk
    + 3 yr   14 wk
   _____

13. 2 qt   1 pt
    + 1 qt
   _____

14. 6 mi   1,875 ft
    − 2 mi   2,304 ft
   _____

15. 9 gal   2 pt
    + 3 gal   7 pt
   _____

16. A truck driver transports new vehicles. The total weight of the cargo is 14 tons 1,544 pounds. The truck driver drops off 1 car that weighs 1 ton 1,693 pounds. What is the weight of the cargo now?

17. **DIG DEEPER!** Find the unknown numbers.

   16 gal   ☐ c
  + ☐ gal   3 c
   _____
   34 gal   9 c

18. **YOU BE THE TEACHER** Newton finds the difference between 5 yards 1 foot and 2 yards 2 feet. Is Newton correct? Explain.

   $\overset{4}{\cancel{5}}$ yd $\overset{11}{\cancel{1}}$ ft
  − 2 yd   2 ft
   _____
   2 yd   9 ft

© Big Ideas Learning, LLC

Think and Grow: Modeling Real Life

Example   A commercial airplane is 121 feet 6 inches shorter than Air Force One. How long is the commercial airplane?

Subtract 121 feet 6 inches from the length of Air Force One.

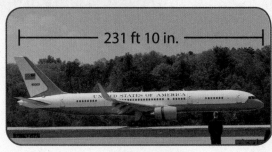

231 ft 10 in.

Air Force One

$$
\begin{array}{r}
231 \text{ ft} \quad\quad 10 \text{ in.} \\
-\quad 121 \text{ ft} \quad\quad\ 6 \text{ in.} \\
\hline
\underline{\quad\quad} \text{ ft} \quad\underline{\quad\quad} \text{ in.}
\end{array}
$$

The commercial airplane is _____ feet _____ inches long.

Show and Grow   I can think deeper!

19. An art teacher has 3 quarts 1 pint of yellow paint. The teacher has 1 quart 2 pints less red paint than yellow paint. How much red paint does the teacher have?

20. A 1-month-old puppy weighs 7 pounds 3 ounces. How much does the puppy weigh after 3 months?

Month	Weight Gain
2nd month	9 lb 6 oz
3rd month	10 lb 2 oz

21. **DIG DEEPER!** How long do you work on your science fair project in all?

Day	Start Time	End Time
1	4:25 P.M.	5:45 P.M.
2	5:30 P.M.	7:50 P.M.

546

Name _____

Learning Target: Add and subtract mixed measures.

Example Add 3 weeks 4 days and 1 week 2 days.

Step 1: Add the days.

$$
\begin{array}{r}
3 \text{ wk} \quad 4 \text{ d} \\
+ \quad 1 \text{ wk} \quad 2 \text{ d} \\
\hline
\underline{6} \text{ d}
\end{array}
$$

Step 2: Add the weeks.

$$
\begin{array}{r}
3 \text{ wk} \quad 4 \text{ d} \\
+ \quad 1 \text{ wk} \quad 2 \text{ d} \\
\hline
\underline{4} \text{ wk} \quad 6 \text{ d}
\end{array}
$$

The sum is ___4___ weeks ___6___ days.

Add or subtract.

1. $\begin{array}{r} 3 \text{ lb} \quad 5 \text{ oz} \\ + 1 \text{ lb} \quad 2 \text{ oz} \\ \hline \end{array}$

2. $\begin{array}{r} 5 \text{ min} \quad 20 \text{ sec} \\ - 3 \text{ min} \quad 15 \text{ sec} \\ \hline \end{array}$

3. $\begin{array}{r} 10 \text{ mi} \quad 1{,}500 \text{ ft} \\ + 7 \text{ mi} \quad 675 \text{ ft} \\ \hline \end{array}$

4. $\begin{array}{r} 2 \text{ T} \quad 300 \text{ lb} \\ - 1 \text{ T} \quad 300 \text{ lb} \\ \hline \end{array}$

5. $\begin{array}{r} 9 \text{ gal} \quad 1 \text{ qt} \\ - 2 \text{ gal} \quad 3 \text{ qt} \\ \hline \end{array}$

6. $\begin{array}{r} 4 \text{ h} \quad 35 \text{ min} \\ + 1 \text{ h} \quad 12 \text{ min} \\ \hline \end{array}$

7. $\begin{array}{r} 3 \text{ yd} \quad 1 \text{ ft} \\ + 6 \text{ yd} \quad 1 \text{ ft} \\ \hline \end{array}$

8. $\begin{array}{r} 8 \text{ gal} \quad 5 \text{ pt} \\ - 7 \text{ gal} \quad 7 \text{ pt} \\ \hline \end{array}$

9. $\begin{array}{r} 6 \text{ ft} \quad 5 \text{ in.} \\ - 3 \text{ ft} \quad 7 \text{ in.} \\ \hline \end{array}$

10. You are making punch. You use 3 quarts 1 pint of pineapple juice and 2 quarts 1 pint of orange juice. How much juice do you use?

11. **Writing** Explain when you need to regroup when subtracting mixed measures.

12. **Modeling Real Life** How much longer did it take one person to cycle the length of South America than a two-person team?

Fastest Time to Cycle the Length of South America	
One person	58 days, 3 hours, 45 minutes
Two-person team	49 days, 23 hours, 43 minutes

13. **DIG DEEPER!** It rains 1 inch each day for 3 days. A meteorologist says that if the rain had been snow, each inch of rain would have been 1 foot 1 inch of snow. What would have been the total snowfall for the 3 days?

Think: Why is there such a big difference between the measurements of rain and snow?

Review & Refresh

Subtract.

14. $\dfrac{5}{10} - \dfrac{1}{10} =$ _____

15. $\dfrac{9}{5} - \dfrac{4}{5} =$ _____

16. $\dfrac{11}{12} - \dfrac{7}{12} =$ _____

Name _____

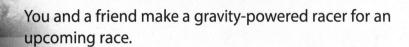

You and a friend make a gravity-powered racer for an upcoming race.

1. The rules state that the racer must be less than 40 inches wide and less than 96 inches long. The weight of the racer must be less than 70 pounds.

   a. Your racer is 2 feet wide and 1 yard long. Does your racer meet the size requirements? Explain.

   b. Your racer weighs 65 pounds without wheels, and each wheel weighs 22 ounces. Is your racer under the weight limit? Explain.

2. You test your racer on a track. The length of the track is $\frac{1}{2}$ mile. What is the length of the track in feet?

3. The table shows the race times for all of the teams.

   a. Make a line plot to display the data.

   b. How many seconds later did the last team finish than the first team?

Race Times (minutes)		
$1\frac{3}{6}$	$1\frac{2}{6}$	1
$1\frac{1}{6}$	$1\frac{1}{2}$	$1\frac{5}{6}$
2	$1\frac{2}{6}$	$1\frac{1}{3}$

4. After the race, you drink 5 cups of water and your friend drinks 3 pints of water. Who drinks more water? How much more?

Conversion Flip and Find

Directions:

1. Choose which conversion cards you will play with.

2. Place the cards face down on the board.

3. Players take turns flipping two cards.

4. If your two cards show equivalent measures, keep the cards.
   If your cards show different measures, flip the cards back over.

5. The player with the most matches wins!

11.1 Length in Metric Units

Find the equivalent length.

1. 7 km = _____ m

2. 9 m = _____ mm

3. 3 cm = _____ mm

4. 5 km = _____ cm

11.2 Mass and Capacity in Metric Units

Find the equivalent mass.

5. 3 kg = _____ g

6. 7 kg = _____ g

7. 8 kg = _____ g

8. 46 kg = _____ g

Find the equivalent capacity.

9. 2 L = _____ mL

10. 10 L = _____ mL

11. 4 L = _____ mL

12. 98 L = _____ mL

13. What is the mass of the potatoes in grams?

5-kg bag

11.3 Length in Customary Units

Find the equivalent length.

14. 8 ft = _____ in.

15. 10 yd = _____ ft

16. 12 yd = _____ in.

17. $\frac{3}{4}$ mi = _____ yd

18. Modeling Real Life You have a 4-foot-long roll of magnetic tape. You use 2 inches for each picture you hang on the refrigerator. How many pictures can you hang?

11.4 Weight in Customary Units

Find the equivalent weight.

19. 4 T = _____ lb

20. 15 lb = _____ oz

21. 12 lb = _____ oz

22. 15 T = _____ lb

23. $2\frac{1}{2}$ lb = _____ oz

24. $\frac{3}{4}$ T = _____ lb

11.5 Capacity in Customary Units

Find the equivalent capacity.

25. 6 pt = _____ c

26. 3 qt = _____ pt

27. 9 gal = _____ qt

28. 2 gal = _____ pt

29. $10\frac{3}{4}$ gal = _____ pt

30. $6\frac{1}{2}$ pt = _____ c

11.6 Make and Interpret Line Plots

31. A scientist is studying the lengths of 15 sea horses. Make a line plot to display the data.

Sea Horse Lengths

Sea Horse Lengths (inch)				
$\frac{1}{4}$	$\frac{3}{8}$	$\frac{1}{2}$	$\frac{3}{8}$	$\frac{1}{2}$
$\frac{3}{8}$	$\frac{1}{2}$	$\frac{3}{8}$	$\frac{1}{2}$	$\frac{3}{8}$
$\frac{1}{2}$	$\frac{3}{8}$	$\frac{1}{4}$	$\frac{3}{8}$	$\frac{3}{8}$

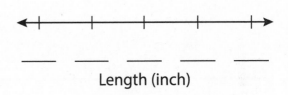

Length (inch)

32. **MP Precision** Use the line plot in Exercise 31. How many times as many $\frac{3}{8}$-inch sea horses are there as $\frac{1}{4}$-inch sea horses? Explain.

Hippocampus
Denise Sea Horse

33. **MP Reasoning** In Exercise 31, are most of the sea horses less than $\frac{5}{8}$ inch long? Explain.

11.7 Units of Time

Find the equivalent amount of time.

34. 5 yr = _____ wk

35. 15 min = _____ sec

36. $\frac{1}{3}$ d = _____ h

37. $1\frac{1}{2}$ yr = _____ wk

11.8 Problem Solving: Elapsed Time

38. A gymnastics competition is $2\frac{3}{4}$ hours long. The competition time is divided equally among 5 age groups. For how many minutes does each age group perform?

11.9 Mixed Measures

Add or subtract.

39.   7 yr   3 mo
    + 4 yr   7 mo

40.   11 gal   2 qt
    − 3 gal   1 qt

41.   5 pt   1 c
    + 6 pt

42.   8 yd   1 ft
    − 1 yd   2 ft

43.   10 d   3 h
    − 5 d   12 h

44.   13 mi   352 yd
    − 4 mi   461 yd

1. Four laps around a track is equal to 1 mile. You run 3 laps around the track. Which number line shows how many miles you run?

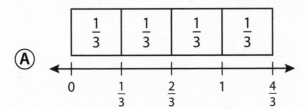

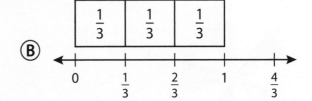

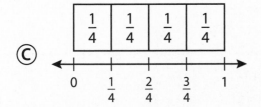

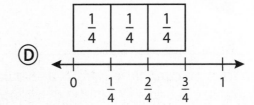

2. When estimating to find the product of 25 and 32, which expressions will give an estimate that is greater than the product of 25 and 32?

⬜ 30×32

⬜ 25×30

⬜ 25×40

⬜ 20×30

3. A bottle of sand art is $\frac{3}{8}$ full of purple sand and $\frac{3}{8}$ full of blue sand. The rest of the bottle is full of green sand. How much of the bottle is filled with both purple sand and blue sand?

Ⓐ $\frac{6}{16}$

Ⓑ $\frac{2}{8}$

Ⓒ $\frac{6}{8}$

Ⓓ $\frac{5}{8}$

4. Which statements are true?

⬜ 5 minutes $\overset{?}{=}$ 300 seconds

⬜ 8 days $\overset{?}{=}$ 192 hours

⬜ 70 weeks $\overset{?}{=}$ 10 days

⬜ 10 years $\overset{?}{=}$ 5,200 weeks

5. Compare the fractions using benchmarks. Which comparisons are true?

◯ $\frac{3}{4} \overset{?}{<} \frac{2}{8}$

◯ $\frac{10}{12} \overset{?}{>} \frac{3}{1}$

◯ $\frac{4}{8} \overset{?}{=} \frac{2}{4}$

◯ $\frac{1}{6} \overset{?}{<} \frac{4}{2}$

---

6. What number is shown by the model?

(A) 5.10

(B) 0.510

(C) 0.5

(D) 0.05

---

7. Which fraction *cannot* be written as a mixed number?

(A) $\frac{5}{2}$

(B) $\frac{12}{10}$

(C) $\frac{8}{3}$

(D) All of the fractions can be written as mixed numbers.

---

8. What is the missing number in _____ ÷ 2 = 400?

(A) 200

(B) 800

(C) 8,000

(D) 600

---

9. Which statements are true?

◯ 1,000 centimeters $\overset{?}{=}$ 1 meter

◯ 10 millimeters $\overset{?}{=}$ 1 centimeter

◯ 1,000 meters $\overset{?}{=}$ 1 kilometer

◯ 100 millimeters $\overset{?}{=}$ 1 meter

10. Multiply $2 \times 3\frac{5}{6}$.

(A) $6\frac{5}{6}$

(B) $7\frac{4}{6}$

(C) 5

(D) $\frac{5}{36}$

---

11. Which one does *not* belong?

(A) $\frac{3}{10}$

(B) 0.30

(C) 0.03

(D) $\frac{30}{100}$

---

12. Which expression shows $\frac{4}{3}$ as a sum of unit fractions?

(A) $\frac{1}{3} + \frac{1}{3} + \frac{1}{3} + \frac{1}{3} + \frac{1}{3} + \frac{1}{3} + \frac{1}{3} + \frac{1}{3} + \frac{1}{3} + \frac{1}{3} + \frac{1}{3} + \frac{1}{3}$

(B) $\frac{2}{3} + \frac{2}{3}$

(C) $\frac{1}{4} + \frac{1}{4} + \frac{1}{4}$

(D) $\frac{1}{3} + \frac{1}{3} + \frac{1}{3} + \frac{1}{3}$

---

13. Look at the dot pattern below. How many dots are in the 112th figure?

 Figure 1

Figure 2

 Figure 3

---

14. Which show 5 hundredths?

☐ $\frac{5}{100}$

☐ $\frac{5}{10}$

☐ 0.5

☐ 0.05

15. A child ticket costs $12 less than an adult ticket. In 1 day, 25 adult tickets and 34 child tickets are sold.

1 Adult $65

Part A How much money was raised from adult tickets?

Part B How much money was raised from child tickets?

Part C How much more money was raised from child tickets than from adult tickets? Explain.

---

16. Which measures are equivalent to 8 gallons?

◯ 2 quarts ◯ 64 pints

◯ 1 pint ◯ 32 quarts

---

17. You want to find 4×598 using the Distributive Property. You begin solving as shown. What is your next step?

$$4 \times 598 = 4 \times (600 - 2)$$

(A) $4 \times 600 \times 2$ (B) $(4 \times 600) + (4 \times 2)$

(C) $(4 \times 600) - (4 \times 2)$ (D) $(4 \times 600) - 2$

---

18. A recipe calls for $\frac{3}{4}$ cup of peanut butter. You make 3 batches of the recipe. Which expressions show how many cups of peanut butter you use?

◯ $2 + \frac{1}{4}$ ◯ $3 + \frac{3}{4}$

◯ $\frac{3 \times 3}{4}$ ◯ $3 \times \left(3 \times \frac{1}{4}\right)$

STEAM **1-11**
Performance
Task

An electrical circuit is a pathway of wires that electricity can flow through. Many homes have an electrical panel that provides power to electrical circuits. The circuits are connected to electrical outlets throughout the home.

1. *Watts* are the measure of how much power a circuit can provide. Every electrical current has two components: volts and amps.

    $$\text{Watts} = \text{volts} \times \text{amps}$$

    a. For a wire that carries 120 volts and 20 amps, how many watts of power are available?

    ....

    b. For a wire that carries 240 volts and 15 amps, how many watts of power are available?

2. An electrician checks the circuits in your house.

    a. One of the circuits has a maximum capacity of 15 amps. The electrician recommends that you only use $\frac{4}{5}$ of the total amps on the circuit. How many amps should be used?

    ....

    b. The wire from this 15-amp circuit carries 120 volts. How many watts should be used on this circuit?

Appliance	Watts
Refrigerator	750
Blender	500
Toaster	900
Microwave	1,200
Space heater	1,500
Waffle iron	1,000

Remember to check the watts before you plug something in!

c. Your toaster is plugged in to the 15-amp circuit. Use the table to find another appliance that can be used on the same circuit and stay within the recommended amount of amps.

....

d. Can you run the microwave and the refrigerator on the 15-amp circuit? Explain.

© Big Ideas Learning, LLC

3. You are decorating for a party at your house.

  a. There are 15 bulbs on a string of lights. Each bulb uses 12 watts of energy. How many watts of energy does one string of lights use?

  b. You connect 7 strings of lights together. Can the lights be plugged into a 15-amp circuit, or is a 20-amp circuit needed? Explain.

  c. The length of each string is $20\frac{3}{4}$ feet. What is the total length of all 7 strings of lights?

  d. Five of the bulbs burn out. Of the bulbs that are lit, $\frac{3}{10}$ are purple, $\frac{1}{10}$ are blue, $\frac{2}{10}$ are green, and the rest are red. What fraction of the bulbs are red?

  e. How many more bulbs are purple than blue?

  f. The lights are plugged in from 4:35 P.M. until 9:35 P.M. Each hour that the lights are on costs about $0.18 in electricity. What is the total cost to have the lights on for the party?

12

Use Perimeter and Area Formulas

Chapter Learning Target:
Understand perimeter and area formulas.

Chapter Success Criteria:
- I can define perimeter.
- I can find the perimeter of a shape.
- I can compare perimeter and area.
- I can model perimeter and area.

- What is your favorite television show? Is the show filmed on a stage in front of a live studio audience?

- You know the length of one side of a square stage. How can you find the perimeter and the area of the stage?

12 Vocabulary

Review Words

parallelogram
rectangle
right angles

Organize It

Use the review words to complete the graphic organizer.

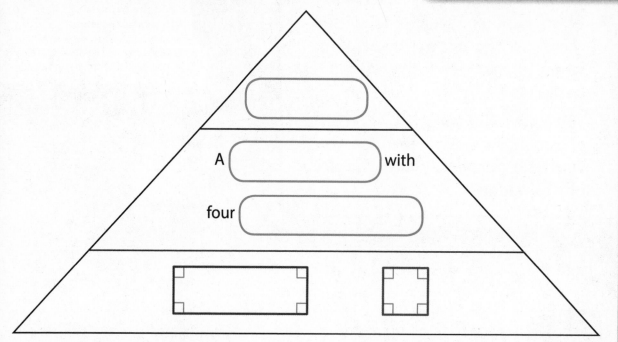

Define It

Use your vocabulary cards to complete the puzzle.

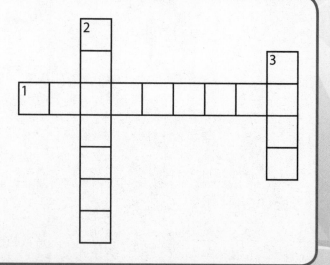

Across

1. The distance around a figure

Down

2. An equation that uses letters and numbers to show how quantities are related

3. The amount of surface a figure covers

Chapter 12 Vocabulary Cards

area

formula

perimeter

An equation that uses letters and numbers to show how quantities are related

$$P = (2 \times \ell) + (2 \times w)$$

$$A = \ell \times w$$

© Big Ideas Learning, LLC

The amount of surface a figure covers

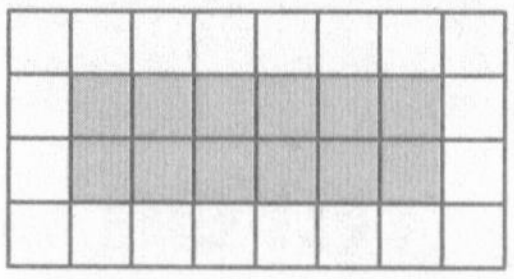

$\square$ = 1 square unit

The area of the rectangle is 12 square units.

© Big Ideas Learning, LLC

© Big Ideas Learning, LLC

The distance around a figure

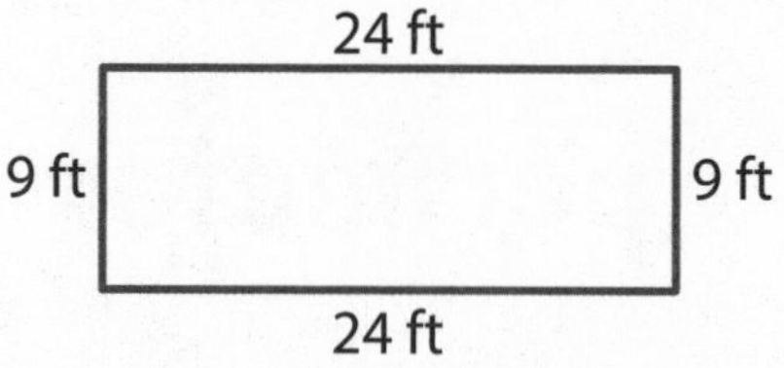

24 ft

9 ft   9 ft

24 ft

The perimeter is 66 feet.

© Big Ideas Learning, LLC

© Big Ideas Learning, LLC

© Big Ideas Learning, LLC

© Big Ideas Learning, LLC

© Big Ideas Learning, LLC

Learning Target: Use a formula to find the perimeter of a rectangle.

Success Criteria:
• I can write a formula for the perimeter of a rectangle.
• I can find the perimeter of a rectangle.

Explore and Grow

Use color tiles to create a rectangle with a perimeter of 12 units. Compare your rectangle to your partner's. How are they the same? How are they different?

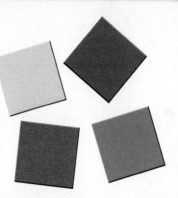

How do you know that the perimeter of your rectangle is 12 units?

MP **Structure** How is the perimeter of a rectangle related to its length and width?

Think and Grow: Use a Formula for Perimeter

Perimeter is the distance around a figure. A **formula** is an equation that uses letters and numbers to show how quantities are related. You can use a formula to show how the length, width, and perimeter of a rectangle are related.

length (ℓ)

width (w)

Perimeter of a Rectangle

$$P = (2 \times \ell) + (2 \times w)$$

↑   ↑   ↑

perimeter   length   width

Example   Find the perimeter of the rectangle.

24 ft

9 ft

The length is _____ feet and the width is _____ feet.

$P = (2 \times \ell) + (2 \times w)$ Formula for perimeter of a rectangle

$= (2 \times \underline{\quad}) + (2 \times \underline{\quad})$

$= \underline{\quad} + \underline{\quad}$

$= \underline{\quad}$ The perimeter is _____ feet.

Show and Grow   I can do it!

Find the perimeter of the rectangle.

1. 16 cm

   13 cm

2.

   $4\frac{1}{2}$ in.

   8 in.

Apply and Grow: Practice

Find the perimeter of the rectangle.

3.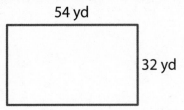
54 yd
32 yd

4.
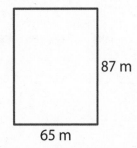
87 m
65 m

5.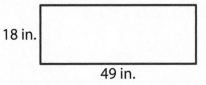
18 in.
49 in.

6.
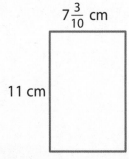
$7\frac{3}{10}$ cm
11 cm

7. You want to string lights around a rectangular room that is 12 feet long and 10 feet wide. How many feet of lights do you need?

8. **YOU BE THE TEACHER** Your friend finds the perimeter of the rectangle. Is your friend correct? Explain.

13 ft
5 ft

$P = (2 \times 13) \times (2 \times 5)$
$\quad = 26 \times 10$
$\quad = 260$ ft

9. **DIG DEEPER!** You can use the formula for the perimeter of a rectangle to find the perimeter of the square. What other formula can you use to find the perimeter of the square?

s

Example In a video game, you make a rectangular castle that is 4 times longer than it is wide. What is the perimeter of the castle?

25 yd

Multiply 4 and the width of the castle to find the length.

$4 \times 25 =$ _____

The length of the castle is _____ yards.

Use a formula to find the perimeter. $P = (2 \times \text{_____}) + (2 \times \text{_____})$

$= \text{_____} + \text{_____}$

$= \text{_____}$

The perimeter of the castle is _____ yards.

Show and Grow *I can think deeper!*

10. A teacher wants to put a border around a rectangular whiteboard. The whiteboard is 2 times longer than it is wide. What is the perimeter of the whiteboard?

1 m

11. You want to put a ribbon border around each rectangular card. Which card requires more ribbon? How much more ribbon?

18 cm

18 cm

14 cm

21 cm

12. **DIG DEEPER!** A rectangular flower bed has a length of 6 feet. The width is 48 inches shorter than the length. What is the perimeter of the flower bed?

Name _____

Learning Target: Use a formula to find the perimeter of a rectangle.

Example Find the perimeter of the rectangle.

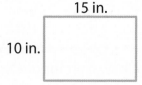

The length is __15__ inches and the width is __10__ inches.

$P = (2 \times \ell) + (2 \times w)$ Formula for perimeter of a rectangle

$= (2 \times \underline{\ 15\ }) + (2 \times \underline{\ 10\ })$

$= \underline{\ 30\ } + \underline{\ 20\ }$

$= \underline{\ 50\ }$

The perimeter is __50__ inches.

Find the perimeter of the rectangle.

1.
22 yd
18 yd

2.
36 mm
25 mm

3.
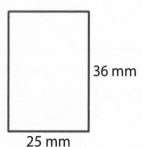
14 cm
30 cm

4.
8 ft
$12\frac{1}{4}$ ft

5. **(MP) Number Sense** What is the perimeter of a square tabletop with side lengths of 48 inches?

6. **(MP) Structure** Use the Distributive Property to write $P = (2 \times \ell) + (2 \times w)$ another way.

7. **Open-Ended** Draw a rectangle that has the same perimeter as the one shown, but different dimensions.

25 m

50 m

8. **Modeling Real Life** A worker places tape around a rectangular shipping label that is 2 times longer than it is wide. How much tape does the worker need?

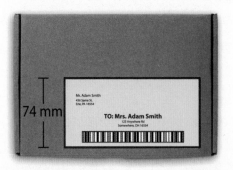

74 mm

9. **Modeling Real Life** A coach is painting lines around the perimeter of two rectangular fields. Which field requires more paint?

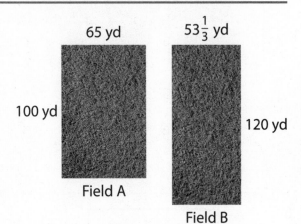

65 yd

$53\frac{1}{3}$ yd

100 yd

120 yd

Field A

Field B

Write the first six numbers in the pattern. Then describe another feature of the pattern.

10. Rule: Subtract 11.
First number: 99

11. Rule: Multiply by 5.
First number: 5

© Big Ideas Learning, LLC

Name _____

Area Formula for a Rectangle 12.2

Learning Target: Use a formula to find the area of a rectangle.

Success Criteria:
- I can write a formula for the area of a rectangle.
- I can find the area of a rectangle.

 Explore and Grow

Use color tiles to create a rectangle with an area of 12 square units. Compare your rectangle to your partner's. How are they the same? How are they different?

How do you know that the area of your rectangle is 12 square units?

MP **Structure** How is the area of a rectangle related to its length and width?

 © Big Ideas Learning, LLC

Think and Grow: Use a Formula for Area

Area is the amount of surface a figure covers. You can use a formula to show how the length, width, and area of a rectangle are related.

Remember, area is measured in square units.

Area of a Rectangle

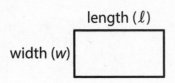

length (ℓ)

width (w)

$$A = \ell \times w$$

area   length   width

Example   Find the area of the rectangle.

The length is _____ inches and the width is _____ inches.

$A = \ell \times w$ Formula for area of a rectangle

$= \underline{\quad} \times \underline{\quad}$

$= \underline{\quad}$

The area is _____ square inches.

14 in.

19 in.

Show and Grow   I can do it!

Find the area of the rectangle.

1.

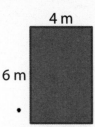

4 m

6 m

2.

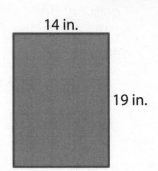

12 yd

20 yd

3.

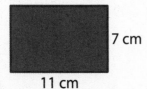

7 cm

11 cm

4.

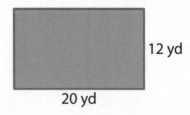

5 ft

$1\frac{1}{2}$ ft

Name _____

Apply and Grow: Practice

Find the area of the rectangle.

5.

35 mm

32 mm

6.
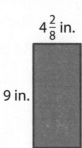
$4\frac{2}{8}$ in.

9 in.

7.
$5\frac{1}{2}$ ft

8 ft

8.
37 cm

79 cm

9. You are installing wall-to-wall carpet in a rectangular bedroom that is 10 feet long and 9 feet wide. How many square feet of carpet do you need?

10. **YOU BE THE TEACHER** Newton says the area of the rectangle is 33 square meters. Descartes says the area is 33 meters. Who is correct? Explain.

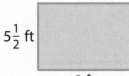
3 m

11 m

11. **DIG DEEPER!** Write a formula for the area of a square that has a side length of *s*. Then use your formula to find the area of the square shown.

12 yd

Think and Grow: Modeling Real Life

Example The length of the rectangular dance floor is 6 feet longer than the width. What is the area of the dance floor?

24 ft

Add 6 feet to the width to find the length.

24 + 6 = _____

The length of the dance floor is _____ feet.

Use a formula to find the area. $A =$ _____ × _____

= _____

The area of the dance floor is _____ square feet.

Show and Grow   *I can think deeper!*

12. A designer creates a rectangular advertisement for a website. The length of the advertisement is $1\frac{1}{2}$ centimeters longer than the width. What is the area of the advertisement?

7 cm

13. You create a mural using 4 rectangular posters that are each $4\frac{1}{4}$ feet long and 2 feet wide. You put the posters next to each other with no gaps or overlaps. What is the area of the mural?

14. **DIG DEEPER!** Two rolls of wrapping paper have the same price. The red roll is 3 feet wide and is 10 yards long when unrolled. The striped roll is $3\frac{1}{2}$ feet wide and 8 yards long when unrolled. Which roll is the better buy? Explain.

Name _____

Learning Target: Use a formula to find the area of a rectangle.

Example Find the area of the rectangle.

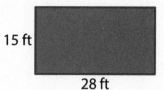

15 ft

28 ft

The length is __28__ feet and the

width is __15__ feet.

$A = \ell \times w$ Formula for area of a rectangle

= __28__ × __15__

= __420__

The area is __420__ square feet.

Find the area of the rectangle.

1.

8 m

7 m

2.

9 cm

21 cm

3.

12 yd

56 yd

4.

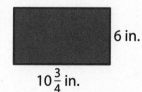

6 in.

$10\frac{3}{4}$ in.

© Big Ideas Learning, LLC

5. What is the area of the window?

48 in.

18 in.

6.  **Structure** A rectangle has an area of 40 square feet. The dimensions are whole numbers. What are all of the possible dimensions of the rectangle?

7. **Open-Ended** Draw a rectangle that has the same area as the one shown, but different dimensions.

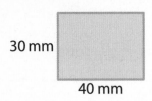

30 mm

40 mm

8. **Modeling Real Life** An interior designer says that a rug under a dining room table should be 4 feet longer and 4 feet wider than the table. What is the area of a rug a customer should buy for under the table?

3 ft

6 ft

9. **DIG DEEPER!** A wolf hunts within a rectangular area that is 10 miles long and 5 miles wide. A cougar hunts within a rectangular area that is 8 miles long and 6 miles wide. Which animal hunts within a greater area? How much more area does the animal hunt in?

Review & Refresh

Find the quotient.

10. $70 \div 7 =$ _____

11. $420 \div 6 =$ _____

12. $2{,}400 \div 8 =$ _____

Name _____

Learning Target: Find unknown measures of rectangles.
Success Criteria:
- I can find an unknown measure of a rectangle given the area.
- I can find an unknown measure of a rectangle given the perimeter.

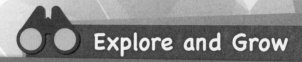 **Explore and Grow**

For each row of the table, use color tiles to create the rectangle described. Then complete the table.

Area or Perimeter	Length	Width
Area = 20 square units	5 units	_____ units
Area = 24 square units	_____ units	4 units
Perimeter = 20 units	_____ units	3 units
Perimeter = 24 units	8 units	_____ units

For each rectangle, how did you determine the missing measure?

 Reasoning Compare your strategy to your partner's. How are they the same or different?

© Big Ideas Learning, LLC

Think and Grow: Find Unknown Measures

Example The area of the rectangle is 36 square feet. Find the length.

l ft

3 ft

$A = l \times w$ Formula for area of a rectangle

_____ $= l \times$ _____   Write an equation.

$36 =$ _____ $\times 3$ What number times 3 equals 36?

The length is _____ feet.

Example The perimeter of the rectangle is 30 centimeters. Find the width.

8 cm

w cm

$P = (2 \times l) + (2 \times w)$ Formula for perimeter of a rectangle

_____ $= (2 \times$ _____ $) + (2 \times w)$ Write an equation.

$30 =$ _____ $+ (2 \times w)$ Multiply 2 times the length.

$30 = 16 +$ _____   16 plus what number equals 30?

So, 2 times the width equals _____ .

$2 \times$ _____ $= 14$ 2 times what number equals 14?

The width is _____ centimeters.

Show and Grow I can do it!

Find the unknown measure of the rectangle.

1. Area = 75 square meters

l m

5 m

2. Perimeter = 42 inches

12 in.

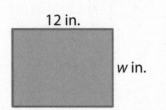

w in.

Apply and Grow: Practice

Find the unknown measure of the rectangle.

3. Area = 50 square millimeters

2 mm [ ]
ℓ mm

4. Perimeter = 30 centimeters

w cm

9 cm

5. Area = 240 square meters

w m [ ]
80 m

6. Perimeter = 86 yards

23 yd

w yd

7. Perimeter = $44\frac{2}{4}$ inches

$8\frac{1}{4}$ in.

ℓ in.

8. Area = 108 square feet

ℓ ft

9 ft

9. **DIG DEEPER!** What are the dimensions of Newton's rectangle?

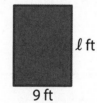

My rectangle has an area of 24 square meters. The length is 2 meters longer than the width.

10. **DIG DEEPER!** The area of a square is 81 square centimeters. What is the perimeter of the square?

Example   The rectangular park has an area of 200 square yards. You kick a soccer ball straight across the width of the park. How far did you kick the soccer ball?

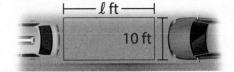

w yd

25 yd

Use a formula to find the width.

$A = \ell \times w$ Formula for area of a rectangle

_____ = _____ × w Write an equation.

$200 = 25 \times$ _____   25 times what number equals 200?

You kick the soccer ball _____ yards.

Show and Grow   *I can think deeper!*

11. The rectangular parking spot has an area of 220 square feet. What is the length of the longest car that can fit in the parking spot?

ℓ ft

10 ft

w in.

14 in.

12. You want to put a frame around the rectangular painting. The painting has a perimeter of 50 inches. How wide should the frame be?

---

13. A rectangular zoo enclosure for a red panda has a perimeter of 116 meters. The length is 50 meters. What is the area of the enclosure?

14. **DIG DEEPER!**   A rectangular patio at a restaurant has an area of 98 square feet. The dimensions of the patio are whole numbers. The length of the patio is 2 times the width. What are the dimensions of the patio?

Learning Target: Find unknown measures of rectangles.

Example The area of the rectangle is 65 square meters.

Find the length.

5 m

$A = \ell \times w$

$\underline{\hspace{0.5cm}65\hspace{0.5cm}} = \ell \times \underline{\hspace{0.5cm}5\hspace{0.5cm}}$

ℓ m

$65 = \underline{\hspace{0.5cm}13\hspace{0.5cm}} \times 5$

The length is __13__ meters.

Example The perimeter of the rectangle is 24 yards.

Find the length.

ℓ yd

4 yd

$P = (2 \times \ell) + (2 \times w)$

$\underline{\hspace{0.5cm}24\hspace{0.5cm}} = (2 \times \ell) + (2 \times \underline{\hspace{0.5cm}4\hspace{0.5cm}})$

$24 = (2 \times \ell) + \underline{\hspace{0.5cm}8\hspace{0.5cm}}$

$24 = \underline{\hspace{0.5cm}16\hspace{0.5cm}} + 8$

So, 2 times the length equals __16__.

$2 \times \underline{\hspace{0.5cm}8\hspace{0.5cm}} = 16$

The length is __8__ yards.

Find the unknown measure of the rectangle.

1. Area = 63 square feet

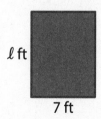

ℓ ft

7 ft

2. Perimeter = 26 yards

1 yd

ℓ yd

Find the unknown measure of the rectangle.

3. Perimeter = 40 centimeters

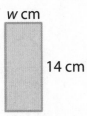

w cm

14 cm

4. Area = 88 square millimeters

8 mm

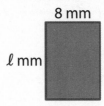

ℓ mm

5. Area = 2,800 square meters

40 m

ℓ m

6. Perimeter = 41 inches

w in.

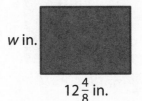

$12\frac{4}{8}$ in.

7. **MP** **Structure** A rectangle has an area of 18 square inches and a perimeter of 18 inches. What are the dimensions of the rectangle?

8. **Modeling Real Life** The rectangular fire pit has a perimeter of 176 inches. What is the width of the fire pit?

|— 50 in. —|

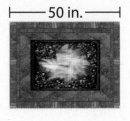

9. **DIG DEEPER!** A painting canvas has an area of 384 square inches. The length and width of the canvas are whole numbers. The length of the canvas is 8 inches greater than the width. What are the dimensions of the canvas?

© Big Ideas Learning, LLC

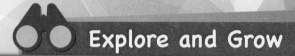

Learning Target: Solve multi-step word problems involving perimeter or area.

Success Criteria:
• I can understand a problem.
• I can make a plan to solve.
• I can solve a problem.

Explore and Grow

An office has a large rectangular window overlooking a city. Describe two methods for finding the area of the rectangular wall around the window.

 Make Sense of Problems Use one of your methods to estimate the area of a wall with a window.

Think and Grow: Problem Solving: Perimeter and Area

Example A rectangular board has an area of 1,700 square inches. You cut out a rectangular piece that is 10 inches long and 9 inches wide to make a carnival prop similar to the one shown. What is the area of the prop?

Understand the Problem

What do you know?

- The original board has an area of 1,700 square inches.
- The piece you cut out is 10 inches long and 9 inches wide.

What do you need to find?

- You need to find the area of the carnival prop.

Make a Plan

How will you solve?

- Find the area of the piece you cut out.
- Subtract the area of the piece you cut out from the original area.

Solve

Step 1: Find the area of the piece you cut out.

$A = \ell \times w$

$= \underline{\hspace{1cm}} \times \underline{\hspace{1cm}}$

$= \underline{\hspace{1cm}}$

Step 2: Subtract the area of the piece you cut out from the original area.

$1,700 - \underline{\hspace{1cm}} = \underline{\hspace{1cm}}$

The area of the prop is _____ square inches.

Show and Grow   I can do it!

1. Explain how you can check whether your answer above is reasonable.

Name _____

Understand the problem. What do you know? What do you need to find? Explain.

2. A construction worker has 40 feet of caution tape. Is this enough tape to surround a rectangular region that is 120 inches long and 90 inches wide?

3. One ton of salt de-ices a rectangular section of a road that is 10,500 meters long and 3 meters wide. How many square meters does 6 tons of salt de-ice?

Understand the problem. Then make a plan. How will you solve? Explain.

4. A worker installs fencing around two rectangular properties. One is 99 feet long and 80 feet wide. The other is 95 feet long and 83 feet wide. Which property requires more fencing? How much more?

5. A roofer covers the rectangular roof with shingles. A chimney occupies a rectangular area that is 4 feet long and 2 feet wide. How many square feet of the roof are with shingles?

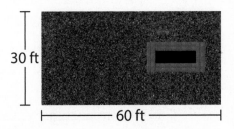

30 ft

60 ft

---

6. You want to buy a cover for the lid of your laptop. Your laptop is $1\frac{1}{3}$ feet long and 1 foot wide. Which cover will fit best on your laptop?

192 square in.
16 in. by 12 in.

$126\frac{3}{4}$ square in.
13 in. by $9\frac{3}{4}$ in.

$159\frac{1}{2}$ square in.
$14\frac{1}{2}$ in. by 11 in.

Think and Grow: Modeling Real Life

Example A worker wants to cover the miniature golf putting surface with artificial turf. The putting surface is in the shape of two rectangles. How much turf does the worker need?

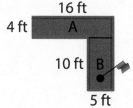

16 ft
4 ft
10 ft
5 ft

Think: What do you know? What do you need to find? How will you solve?

Step 1: Divide the surface into two rectangles. Then find the area of each rectangle.

16 ft
4 ft   A
10 ft B
5 ft

Rectangle A:

$A = \ell \times w$

$= 16 \times 4$

$= \underline{\hphantom{XXX}}$

Rectangle B:

$A = \ell \times w$

$= 10 \times 5$

$= \underline{\hphantom{XXX}}$

Step 2: Add the areas of the rectangles.

$\underline{\hphantom{XXX}} + \underline{\hphantom{XXX}} = \underline{\hphantom{XXX}}$

The worker needs \underline{\hphantom{XXX}} square feet of artificial turf.

Show and Grow   I can think deeper!

7. You want to install new carpet in the rectangular bedroom and the rectangular closet. How much carpet do you need to cover the floor?

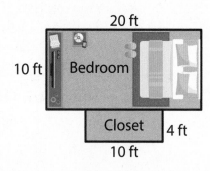

20 ft
10 ft   Bedroom
Closet   4 ft
10 ft

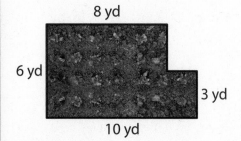

8 yd
6 yd
3 yd
10 yd

8. A gardener wants to enclose the garden with fencing. The garden is in the shape of two rectangles. How much fencing does the gardener need?

Name _____

Homework & Practice 12.4

Learning Target: Solve multi-step word problems involving perimeter or area.

Example A rectangular region of a forest is on fire. The region is 52 miles long and 27 miles wide. To create a fireline, a plane dispersing water flies around the perimeter of the region 4 times. How many miles does the plane fly?

Think: What do you know? What do you need to find? How will you solve?

Step 1: Find the perimeter of the region.

$$P = (2 \times \ell) + (2 \times w)$$

$$= (2 \times \underline{52}) + (2 \times \underline{27})$$

$$= \underline{158}$$

Step 2: Multiply the perimeter by the number of times the plane flies around the region.

$$158 \times \underline{4} = \underline{632}$$

The plane flies __632__ miles.

Understand the problem. Then make a plan. How will you solve? Explain.

1. An indoor dog park has an area of 50,000 square feet. The owner creates a square welcome center inside the park that is 100 feet long. What is the area of the section that dogs can play in?

2. You tile a hallway with square tiles that are 12 inches wide. You completely cover the hallway with 3 rows of 5 tiles. What is the area of the hallway?

Play Section

Welcome Center

© Big Ideas Learning, LLC

Chapter 12 | Lesson 4

585

3. Your friend makes a rectangular poster for a school play. The poster is 4 feet long and 3 feet wide. Ribbon costs $1 per foot. How much does it cost to add a ribbon border to the poster?

4. **Writing** Explain how you know when you need to find the perimeter or the area of a rectangle when solving a word problem.

5. **Modeling Real Life** Your teacher joins two rectangular tables for students to complete a craft. How much newspaper does your teacher need to cover the tops of the tables with no overlap and no paper hanging over the sides?

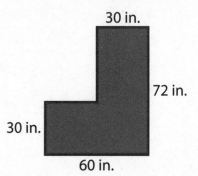

30 in.

72 in.

30 in.

60 in.

6. **Modeling Real Life** A landscaper buys 2 bags of grass seed. Each bag covers 5,000 square feet. A rectangular lawn is 200 feet long and 40 feet wide. Does the landscaper have enough seed to cover the lawn once? twice? Explain.

Review & Refresh

Multiply.

7. $4 \times \dfrac{1}{8}$

8. $3 \times \dfrac{4}{5}$

9. $6 \times \dfrac{10}{8}$

Performance Task 12

Stop-motion animation videos are made by taking multiple photographs of an object. Each photograph shows the object in a slightly different position. When all of the photographs are combined into a video, the object appears to be moving.

1. You decide to make a stop-motion video. You make a background with an area of 12 square feet and a perimeter of 14 feet.

   a. What are the dimensions of your background?

   b. The part of the background in each photograph is 45 inches long and 30 inches wide. What is the perimeter of the background in each photograph?

   c. What is the area of the background that is *not* in each photograph?

2. You take photographs for your video. Your video shows 15 photographs each second. How many photographs are in a 24-second video?

3. You start working on your animation at 3:05 P.M. and finish at 5:20 P.M. You spend equal amounts of time creating your background, taking photographs, and editing your video. How much time do you spend on each activity?

Area Roll and Conquer

Directions:

1. Players take turns rolling two dice.

2. On your turn, create a rectangle with the numbers on the dice as the length and width. Your rectangle cannot cover another rectangle.

3. Shade the rectangle in your color. Record the multiplication equation for the rectangle.

4. If you cannot create a rectangle on the board, then you lose your turn. Play 10 rounds, if possible.

5. The player with the greatest area covered wins!

Example:

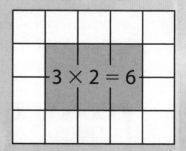

$3 \times 2 = 6$

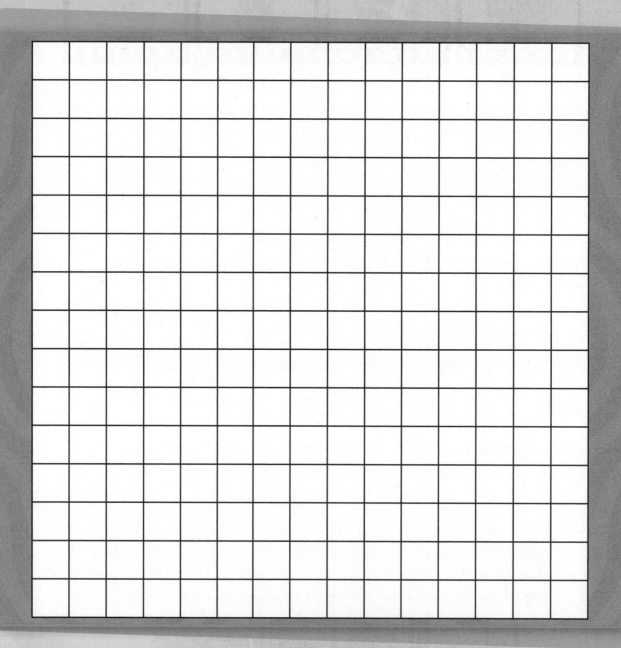

12.1 Perimeter Formula for a Rectangle

Find the perimeter of the rectangle.

1.

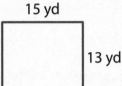

15 yd

13 yd

2.

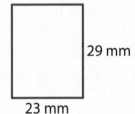

29 mm

23 mm

3.

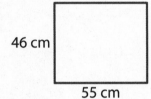

46 cm

55 cm

4.

7 ft

$10\frac{2}{12}$ ft

12.2 Area Formula for a Rectangle

Find the area of the rectangle.

5.

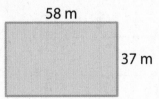

58 m

37 m

6.

7 in.

$13\frac{1}{2}$ in.

7. **MP Structure** A rectangle has an area of 60 square feet. The dimensions are whole numbers. What are all of the possible dimensions of the rectangle?

12.3 Find Unknown Measures

Find the unknown measure of the rectangle.

8. Area = 48 square yards

ℓ yd

3 yd

9. Perimeter = 90 centimeters

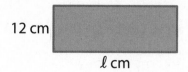

12 cm

ℓ cm

10. **Logic** What are the dimensions of Descartes's rectangle?

My rectangle has a perimeter of 10 meters. The length and width have a product of 6 square meters.

12.4 Problem Solving: Perimeter and Area

11. **Modeling Real Life** You want to paint the wall. What is the area of the wall you will paint?

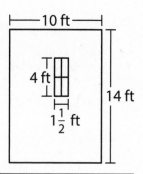

10 ft

4 ft

$1\frac{1}{2}$ ft

14 ft

12. A park director orders 360 feet of fencing. Does he have enough to surround the tennis court?

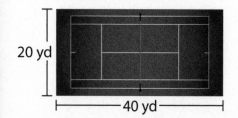

20 yd

40 yd

13 Identify and Draw Lines and Angles

- In a grid plan, city streets intersect to form right angles. Why would this be a useful way to plan a city?

- How do you know whether two roads are parallel?

Chapter Learning Target:
Understand lines and angles.

Chapter Success Criteria:
- ☐ I can name angles.
- ☐ I can measure angles.
- ☐ I can compare sizes of angles to create different patterns.
- ☐ I can measure and draw angles.

591

13 Vocabulary

Organize It

Use the review words to complete the graphic organizer.

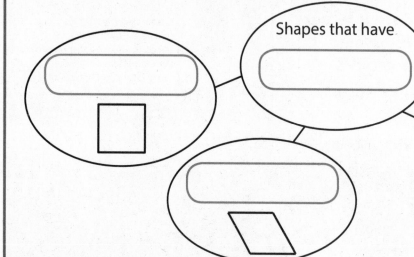

Shapes that have

Define It

Use your vocabulary cards to identify the word. Find the word in the word search.

1. A straight path of points that goes on without end in both directions

2. An exact location in space

3. A part of a line that has one endpoint and goes on without end in one direction

4. Two rays or line segments that have a common endpoint

5. The endpoint at which two rays or line segments of an angle meet

```
P O E I N A R C L G
N R F L M D U O I J
S D A W R L X T N A
A V N Y H A K M E X
E O G B L C P O V C
T N L O I D Z G T I
N X E T H N V U R E
Y P O I N T J Q O B
A D U C G E U N L P
L M R V E R T E X Y
```

Chapter 13 Vocabulary Cards

acute
angle

adjacent
angles

angle

complementary
angles

degree (°)

endpoints

intersecting
lines

line

Two angles that share a common side and a common vertex, but have no other points in common

∠ABD and ∠DBC are adjacent angles.

An angle that is open less than a right angle

Two angles whose measures have a sum of 90°

∠ABD and ∠DBC are complementary angles.

Two rays or line segments that have a common endpoint

Label: ∠ABC, ∠CBA, ∠B

Points that represent the ends of a line segment or ray

endpoints

endpoint

The unit used to measure angles

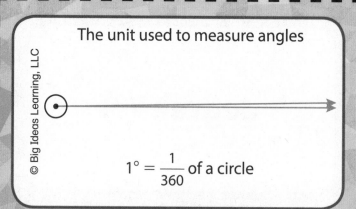

$$1° = \frac{1}{360} \text{ of a circle}$$

A straight path of points that goes on without end in both directions

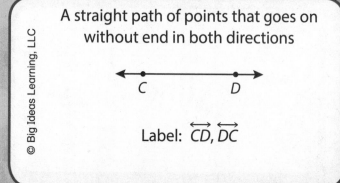

Label: $\overleftrightarrow{CD}, \overleftrightarrow{DC}$

Lines that cross at exactly one point

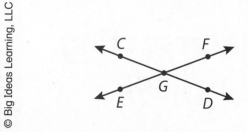

Chapter 13 Vocabulary Cards

line segment

obtuse angle

parallel lines

perpendicular lines

point

protractor

ray

right angle

An angle that is open more than a right angle and less than a straight angle

---

A part of a line that includes two endpoints and all of the points between them

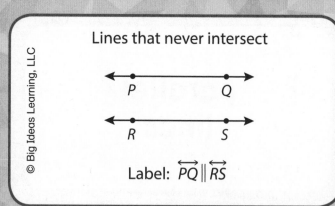

Label: $\overline{FG}, \overline{GF}$

Lines that intersect to form four right angles

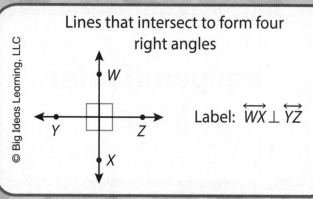

Label: $\overleftrightarrow{WX} \perp \overleftrightarrow{YZ}$

Lines that never intersect

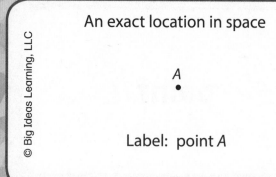

Label: $\overleftrightarrow{PQ} \parallel \overleftrightarrow{RS}$

A tool for measuring and drawing angles

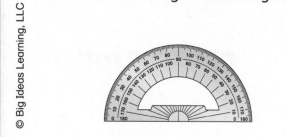

An exact location in space

A
•

Label: point A

An L-shaped angle

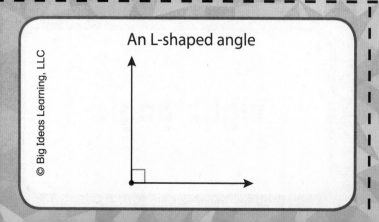

A part of a line that has one endpoint and goes on without end in one direction

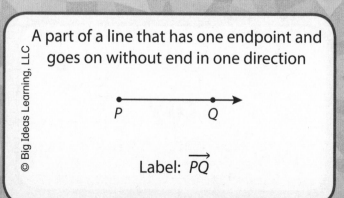

Label: $\overrightarrow{PQ}$

Chapter 13 Vocabulary Cards

straight
angle

supplementary
angles

vertex

Two angles whose measures
have a sum of 180°

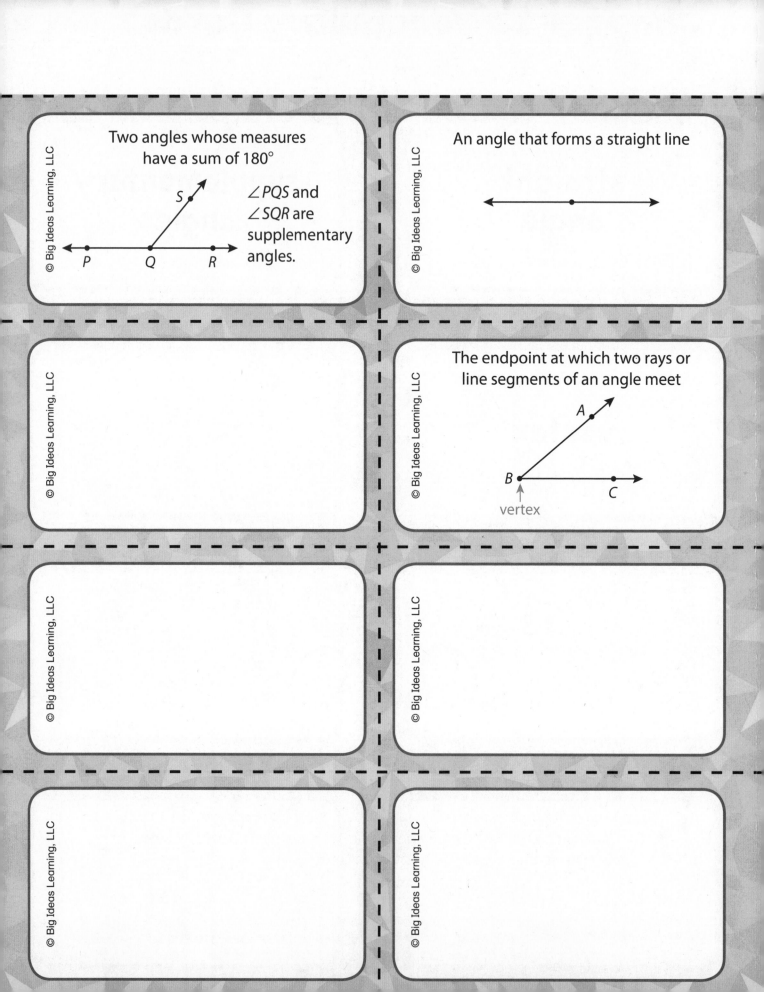

∠*PQS* and
∠*SQR* are
supplementary
angles.

An angle that forms a straight line

The endpoint at which two rays or
line segments of an angle meet

A

B

C

vertex

Learning Target: Identify and draw points, lines, line segments, and rays.

Success Criteria:
- I can identify points, lines, line segments, and rays.
- I can name points, lines, line segments, and rays.
- I can draw points, lines, line segments, and rays.

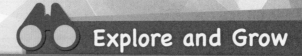

Explore and Grow

Use a straightedge to connect the dots A through Z. Describe the picture you make. How many points do you connect? How many line segments do you make?

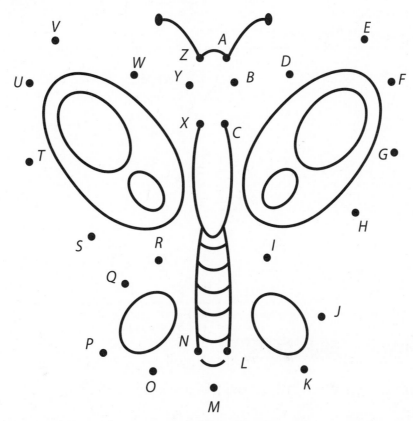

 Structure Draw your own connect-the-dots picture on another sheet of paper. Have your partner use a straightedge to connect the dots to make your picture. How many points did your partner connect? How many line segments did your partner make?

Think and Grow: Points, Lines, Line Segments, and Rays

Definition	Example	Name	Say
A **point** is an exact location in space.	A •		"point A"
A **line** is a straight path of points that goes on without end in both directions.	C D	$\overleftrightarrow{CD}$ $\overleftrightarrow{DC}$	"line CD" "line DC"
A **line segment** is a part of a line that includes two **endpoints** and all of the points between them.	F G	$\overline{FG}$ $\overline{GF}$	"line segment FG" "line segment GF"
A **ray** is a part of a line that has one endpoint and goes on without end in one direction.	P Q	$\overrightarrow{PQ}$	"ray PQ"

Example Draw and label $\overline{LM}$.

$\overline{LM}$ is a _____.

Another name for $\overline{LM}$ is _____.

Example Draw and label $\overrightarrow{ST}$.

$\overrightarrow{ST}$ is a _____.

Why isn't there another name for $\overrightarrow{ST}$?

Show and Grow   I can do it!

1. Name the figure shown. Write how to say the name.

2. Draw and label two points P and Q on the line shown.

3. Draw and label $\overleftrightarrow{XY}$. What is another name for $\overleftrightarrow{XY}$?

Apply and Grow: Practice

Name the figure shown. Write how to say the name.

4.

B
•

5.

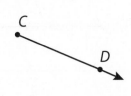

6.

E

F

Draw and label the figure.

7. $\overline{GH}$

8. $\overleftrightarrow{JK}$

9. $\overrightarrow{LM}$

Use the figure.

10. Name a ray.

_____

11. Name a point that lies on two lines.

_____

12. Name two different line segments.

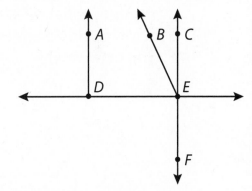

---

13. **MP Logic** Your friend says he can draw two line segments between two points, and maybe even more. His drawing is shown. Explain why this is *not* possible.

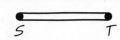

S   T

Think and Grow: Modeling Real Life

Example There are direct ferry routes between each pair of cities on the map. Draw line segments to represent all of the possible ferry routes. How many ferry routes did you draw in all?

Start at Poole. Draw a line segment from Poole to each of the other cities. Repeat this process until a route is shown between each city.

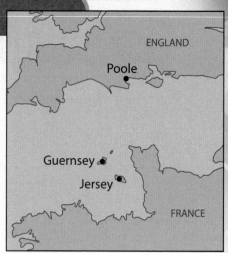

You draw _____ ferry routes in all.

Show and Grow   I can think deeper!

14. There are direct flights between each pair of cities on the map. Draw line segments to represent all of the possible flight routes. How many flights routes did you draw in all?

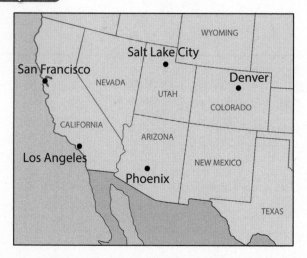

15. Which road signs contain a figure that looks like a ray?

16. Which letters in the banner can be made by drawing line segments? Explain.

596

© Big Ideas Learning, LLC

Name _____

Learning Target: Identify and draw points, lines, line segments, and rays.

Example Draw and label $\overrightarrow{AB}$.

A ———————• B

$\overrightarrow{AB}$ is a __ray__.

Example Draw and label $\overleftrightarrow{CD}$.

$\overleftrightarrow{CD}$ is a __line__.

Another name for $\overleftrightarrow{CD}$ is __$\overleftrightarrow{DC}$__.

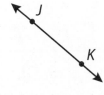

Name the figure shown. Write how to say the name.

1.
    • E

    • F

2. G ———————• H →

3. • J

    K

Draw and label the figure.

4. two points L and M on the line shown

5. $\overrightarrow{NO}$

6. $\overleftrightarrow{PQ}$

Use the figure.

7. Name a line segment.

_____

8. Name two different rays.

_____

9. Name two different lines.

10. Writing Explain the difference between a line and a line segment.

11. 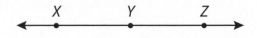 **Structure** Name the figure in as many ways as possible.

X   Y   Z

12. 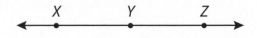 **Structure** Draw and label a figure that has four points, two rays, and one line segment.

DIG DEEPER! Write whether the statement is *true* or *false*. If false, explain.

13. A line segment is part of a line. _____

_____

14. A ray is part of a line segment. _____

_____

15. There are an infinite number of points on a line. _____

16. Modeling Real Life There are direct helicopter flights between each pair of resorts on the map. Draw line segments to represent all of the possible flight routes. How many flight routes did you draw in all?

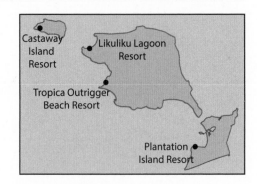

Castaway Island Resort

Likuliku Lagoon Resort

Tropica Outrigger Beach Resort

Plantation Island Resort

17. Modeling Real Life Which road signs contain a figure that looks like it is made of only line segments?

Review & Refresh

Compare.

18. 0.15 ◯ 0.16

19. 2.4 ◯ 2.42

20. 6.90 ◯ 6.9

Learning Target: Identify and draw angles.
Success Criteria:
• I can identify angles as right, straight, acute, or obtuse.
• I can name angles.
• I can draw angles.

 Explore and Grow

Draw the hands of the clock to represent the given time.

For each clock, describe the angle that is formed by the minute hand and the hour hand.

 Reasoning Explain how line segments, rays, and angles can be related.

© Big Ideas Learning, LLC

Think and Grow: Angles

Definition	Example	Name	Say
An **angle** is formed by two rays or line segments that have a common endpoint, called the **vertex**. The rays or line segments are the sides of the angle.	*A* *B* *C*	$\angle ABC$ $\angle CBA$ $\angle B$	"angle *ABC*" "angle *CBA*" "angle *B*"

Angles can be either right, straight, acute, or obtuse.

A **right angle** is an L-shaped angle.	A **straight angle** forms a straight line.	An **acute angle** is open less than a right angle.	An **obtuse angle** is open more than a right angle and less than a straight angle.

Example   Write three names for the angle and classify it.

Three names for the angle are

_____ , _____ , and _____ .

The angle opens _____ a right angle and less than a straight angle.

So, it is an _____ angle.

Show and Grow   I can do it!

Write a name for the angle and classify it.

1.

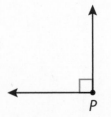

2.

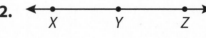

3. $\angle FGH$ is acute. Draw and label the angle.

✓ Apply and Grow: Practice

Write a name for the angle and classify it.

4.
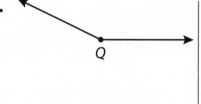
Q

5.
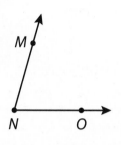
M
N   O

6.
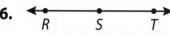
R   S   T

Draw and label the angle.

7. ∠XYZ is right.

8. ∠JKL is straight.

Use the figure. Use three letters to name each angle.

9. Name an acute angle.

_____

10. Name two different obtuse angles.

_____

11. Name two different straight angles.

_____

12. Name three different right angles.

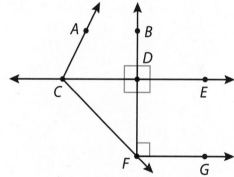

---

13. **Ⓜ️ Structure** Draw to complete each angle.

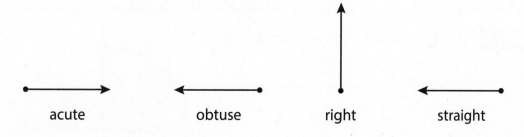

acute   obtuse   right   straight

Example Which angle of the skateboard ramp is acute?

You need to find an angle that is open less than a right angle.

Angle *A* opens _____ a right angle and less than a straight angle.

Angle *B* _____ a right angle.

Angle *C* opens _____ a right angle.

Angle _____ is an acute angle.

Show and Grow   I can think deeper!

14. Use three letters to name an angle of the wind turbine that is obtuse.

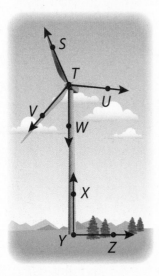

15. Trace and label two right angles, two obtuse angles, and two acute angles in the painting.

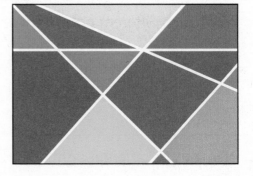

16. **DIG DEEPER!** How many different angles are in the window? Name all of the different angles.

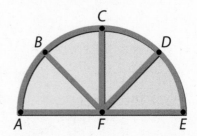

602

Name _____

Learning Target: Identify and draw angles.

Example   Write three names for the angle and classify it.

Three names for the angle are

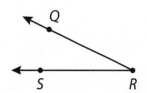

∠QRS , ∠SRQ , and   ∠R   .

The angle opens <u>less than</u> a right angle. So, it is an   <u>acute</u>   angle.

Write a name for the angle and classify it.

1.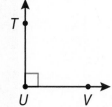
O

2.
T
U   V

3.
Z
X   Y

Draw and label the angle.

4. ∠ABC is obtuse.

5. ∠MNO is acute.

Use the figure. Use three letters to name each angle.

6. Name an acute angle.

_____

7. Name a straight angle.

_____

8. Name two different right angles.

_____

9. Name three different obtuse angles.

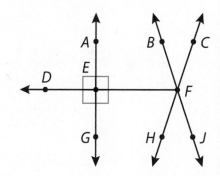

10. **YOU BE THE TEACHER** Is Descartes correct? Explain.

The names for the angle are ∠KJL, ∠LKJ, and ∠K.

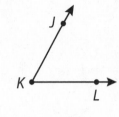

11. **DIG DEEPER!** Can you make a straight angle using an acute angle and an obtuse angle that share a common ray? Draw a picture to support your answer.

12. **MP Structure** Write a capital letter that has more than two right angles.

13. **Modeling Real Life** Use three letters to name the angles of the flag of the Czech Republic that are obtuse.

14. **Modeling Real Life** Horses see an object with both eyes at the same time using *binocular vision*. Classify the angle that describes the horse's binocular vision.

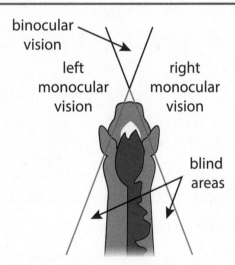

binocular vision

left monocular vision

right monocular vision

blind areas

Review & Refresh

15. Write $1\frac{7}{12}$ as a fraction.

16. Write $\frac{9}{6}$ as a mixed number.

Learning Target: Identify and draw intersecting lines, parallel lines, and perpendicular lines.
Success Criteria:
- I can identify intersecting lines, parallel lines, and perpendicular lines.
- I can draw intersecting lines, parallel lines, and perpendicular lines.

Explore and Grow

Use a straightedge to draw and label a figure for each description. If a figure *cannot* be drawn, explain why.

• two lines $\overleftrightarrow{AB}$ and $\overleftrightarrow{CD}$ that never cross	• two lines $\overleftrightarrow{FG}$ and $\overleftrightarrow{HJ}$ that cross once at point K	• two lines $\overleftrightarrow{PQ}$ and $\overleftrightarrow{RS}$ that cross twice
• two rays $\overrightarrow{TU}$ and $\overrightarrow{VW}$ that never cross	• two rays $\overrightarrow{EF}$ and $\overrightarrow{GH}$ that cross once	• two line segments $\overline{JK}$ and $\overline{LM}$ that never cross

MP **Reasoning** Find the figure that shows two lines that cross once. How many angles are formed by two lines? Name and classify the angles of the figure above.

Think and Grow: Parallel and Perpendicular Lines

You can describe a pair of lines as intersecting, parallel, or perpendicular.

Definition	Example	Name	Say
Intersecting lines cross at exactly one point.	*C* *F* *G* *E* *D*	$\overleftrightarrow{CD}$ and $\overleftrightarrow{EF}$ intersect at point *G*.	"Line *CD* intersects line *EF* at point *G*."
Parallel lines never intersect. The symbol ∥ means "is parallel to."	*P* *Q* *R* *S*	$\overleftrightarrow{PQ} \parallel \overleftrightarrow{RS}$	"Line *PQ* is parallel to line *RS*."
Perpendicular lines intersect to form four right angles. The symbol ⊥ means "is perpendicular to."	*W* *Y* *Z* *X*	$\overleftrightarrow{WX} \perp \overleftrightarrow{YZ}$	"Line *WX* is perpendicular to line *YZ*."

Example Draw and label the lines with the given description.

- $\overleftrightarrow{JK} \perp \overleftrightarrow{LM}$
- $\overleftrightarrow{JK}$ and $\overleftrightarrow{LM}$ intersect at point *P*.

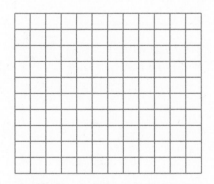

Show and Grow   I can do it!

Draw and label the lines with the given description.

1. $\overleftrightarrow{AB} \parallel \overleftrightarrow{CD}$

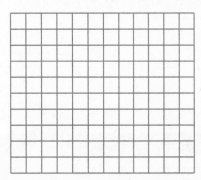

2. $\overleftrightarrow{RS}$ and $\overleftrightarrow{TU}$ intersect at point *V*.

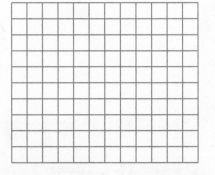

606

Apply and Grow: Practice

Draw and label the lines with the given description.

3. $\overleftrightarrow{MN} \perp \overleftrightarrow{PQ}$
$\overleftrightarrow{MN}$ and $\overleftrightarrow{PQ}$ intersect at point R.

4. $\overleftrightarrow{ST}$ and $\overleftrightarrow{UV}$ intersect at point Z.

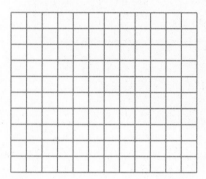

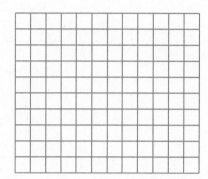

Use the figure.

5. Name a pair of lines that appear to be parallel.

_____

6. Name two lines that are perpendicular.

_____

7. Name two intersecting lines.

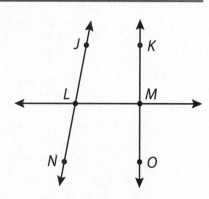

8. **MP Reasoning** All perpendicular lines are also intersecting lines. Are all intersecting lines perpendicular? Explain.

9. **YOU BE THE TEACHER** Your friend says that $\overleftrightarrow{JN}$ and $\overleftrightarrow{KO}$ are parallel because they do *not* cross. Is your friend correct? Explain.

Think and Grow: Modeling Real Life

Example Which street appears to be parallel to 2nd Street?

Look for a street that will *not* intersect with 2nd Street.

_____ Street appears to be parallel to 2nd Street.

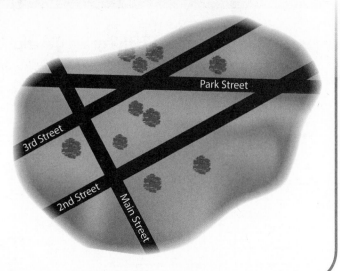

Show and Grow   *I can think deeper!*

10. Which trail appears to be parallel to Fox Trail?

_____

11. Which trail appears to be perpendicular to Fox Trail?

_____

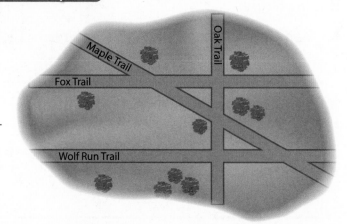

12. Trace and label a pair of line segments that appear to be parallel and a pair of line segments that appear to be perpendicular.

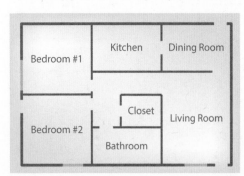

13. **DIG DEEPER!** Design three paths for a park. Two of the paths are perpendicular. Label these paths as Path 1 and Path 2. The third path intersects both perpendicular paths at exactly one point. Label this path as Path 3.

Name _____

Learning Target: Identify and draw intersecting lines, parallel lines, and perpendicular lines.

Example Draw and label $\overleftrightarrow{EF} \parallel \overleftrightarrow{GH}$.

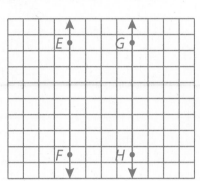

The symbol $\parallel$ means "is parallel to." The symbol $\perp$ means "is perpendicular to."

Draw and label the lines with the given description.

1. $\overleftrightarrow{EF} \perp \overleftrightarrow{GH}$

$\overleftrightarrow{EF}$ and $\overleftrightarrow{GH}$ intersect at point X.

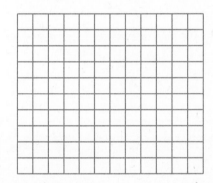

2. $\overleftrightarrow{PQ} \parallel \overleftrightarrow{RS}$

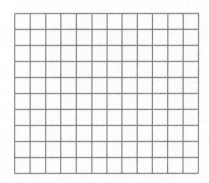

Use the figure.

3. Name a pair of lines that appear to be parallel.

_____

4. Name two lines that are perpendicular.

_____

5. Name two intersecting lines.

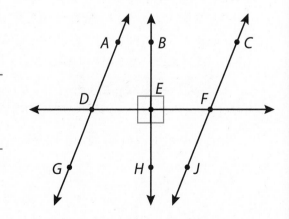

6. (MP) **Structure** Name two line segments that appear to be parallel. Then name two line segments that appear to be perpendicular.

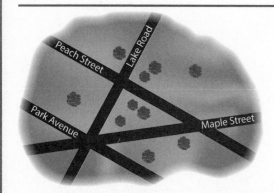

7. (MP) **Reasoning** Can two lines that share a point be parallel? Explain.

8. **DIG DEEPER!** $\overleftrightarrow{SW}$ is parallel to $\overleftrightarrow{TX}$, and $\overleftrightarrow{SW}$ is perpendicular to $\overleftrightarrow{UV}$. Can angle $\angle TVU$ be acute? Explain.

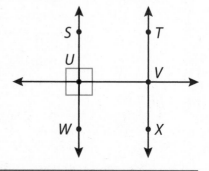

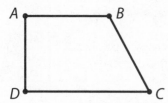

9. **Modeling Real Life** Which street appears to be parallel to Park Avenue?

10. **Modeling Real Life** Which street appears to be perpendicular to Peach Street?

11. **Modeling Real Life** Trace and label a pair of line segments that appear to be parallel and a pair of line segments that appear to be perpendicular.

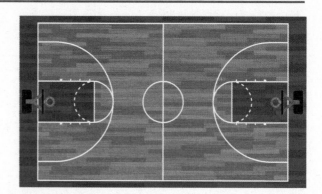

Review & Refresh

Find the equivalent amount of time.

12. 20 min = _____ sec

13. 6 yr = _____ wk

Learning Target: Measure angles using degrees.
Success Criteria:
- I can use fractional parts of a circle to measure angles.
- I can explain how degrees are related to fractional parts of a circle.

 Explore and Grow

Find the elapsed time for each set of clocks. Describe, in your own words, the turn that the minute hand makes.

 Reasoning Explain how elapsed time shown by an analog clock relates to angles formed in a circle.

Think and Grow: Degrees

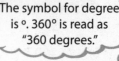
Angles are measured in units called **degrees**. Think of dividing a circle into 360 equal parts. An angle that turns through $\frac{1}{360}$ of a circle measures 1°, and is called a "one-degree angle." A full turn through the entire circle is 360°.

$$1° = \frac{1}{360} \text{ of a circle}$$

Example Find the measure of the angle.

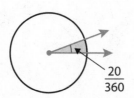

$\frac{20}{360}$

An angle that turns $\frac{1}{360}$ of a circle measures _____ degree.

An angle that turns through $\frac{20}{360}$ of a circle measures _____ degrees.

So, the measure of the angle is _____.

Example Find the measure of a right angle.

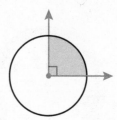

Think: A right angle turns through $\frac{1}{4}$ of a circle.

Step 1: Write $\frac{1}{4}$ as an equivalent fraction with a denominator of 360.

$$\frac{1}{4} = \frac{1 \times \boxed{}}{4 \times \boxed{}} = \frac{\boxed{}}{360}$$

Step 2: Write $\frac{90}{360}$ in degrees. An angle that turns through $\frac{90}{360}$ of a circle measures _____ degrees.

So, a right angle measures _____.

Show and Grow   I can do it!

Find the measure of the angle.

1.
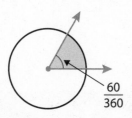

$\frac{60}{360}$

2.
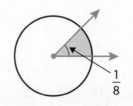

$\frac{1}{8}$

$$\frac{1}{8} = \frac{1 \times \boxed{}}{8 \times \boxed{}} = \frac{\boxed{}}{360}$$

Apply and Grow: Practice

Find the measure of the angle.

3.

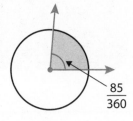

$\dfrac{85}{360}$

4.

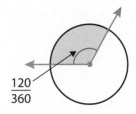

$\dfrac{120}{360}$

5.

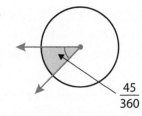

$\dfrac{45}{360}$

6.

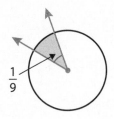

$\dfrac{1}{9}$

7.

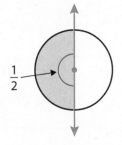

$\dfrac{1}{2}$

8.

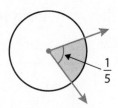

$\dfrac{1}{5}$

9. A circle is divided into 8 equal parts. What is the measure of the angle that turns through 2 parts?

10. A circle is divided into 4 equal parts. What is the measure of the angle that turns through 3 parts?

Classify the angle as *right, straight, acute,* or *obtuse.*

11. 30°

12. 120°

13. 90°

14. 180°

15. **YOU BE THE TEACHER** Both circles are divided into sixths. Your friend says the measure of Angle *D* is greater than the measure of Angle *C*. Is your friend correct? Explain.

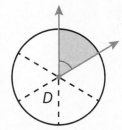

16. **Reasoning** Does each figure show the same angle? If not, which two angles are shown? Explain your reasoning.

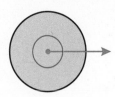
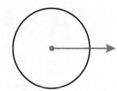

Think and Grow: Modeling Real Life

Example Spokes divide the Ferris wheel into 20 equal parts. What is the angle measure of 1 part?

Write a fraction that represents 1 part.

Because the Ferris wheel has 20 equal parts,

1 part can be represented by the fraction $\dfrac{\square}{\square}$.

Write $\dfrac{1}{20}$ as an equivalent fraction with a denominator of 360.

$$\frac{1}{20} = \frac{1 \times \square}{20 \times \square} = \frac{\square}{360}$$

Write $\dfrac{18}{360}$ in degrees.

An angle that turns through $\dfrac{18}{360}$ of a circle measures _____ degrees.

So, the angle measure of 1 part is _____.

Show and Grow   I can think deeper!

17. The game spinner is divided into 10 equal parts. What is the angle measure of 1 part?

---

18. **DIG DEEPER!** A circular quesadilla is cut into 8 equal pieces. Five pieces are eaten. What is the angle measure formed by the remaining pieces?

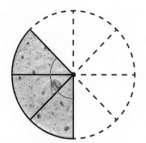

19. **DIG DEEPER!** When a light wave hits an object, the object reflects a colored light at an angle to your eye. The color of the reflected light is the color you see. What fraction of a circle is shown by the angle? Explain.

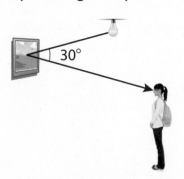

30°

Name _____

Learning Target: Measure angles using degrees.

Example   Find the measure of the angle.

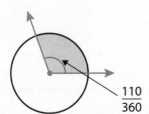

An angle that turns $\frac{1}{360}$ of a circle

measures ___1___ degree.

An angle that turns through $\frac{110}{360}$ of

a circle measures _110_ degrees.

So, the measure of the angle

is _110°_.

Example   Find the measure of a straight angle.

Think: A straight angle turns through $\frac{1}{2}$ of a circle.

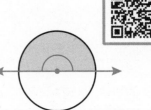

Step 1: Write $\frac{1}{2}$ as an equivalent fraction with a denominator of 360.

$$\frac{1}{2} = \frac{1 \times \boxed{180}}{2 \times \boxed{180}} = \frac{\boxed{180}}{360}$$

Step 2: Write $\frac{180}{360}$ in degrees. An angle that

turns through $\frac{180}{360}$ of a circle

measures _180_ degrees.

So, a straight angle measures _180°_.

Find the measure of each angle.

1.

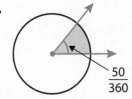

2.

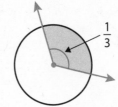

$$\frac{1}{3} = \frac{1 \times \boxed{}}{3 \times \boxed{}} = \frac{\boxed{}}{360}$$

3.

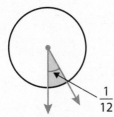

4.

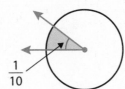

5.

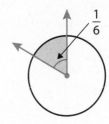

6. A circle is divided into 5 equal parts. What is the measure of the angle that turns through 2 parts?

7. A circle is divided into 10 equal parts. What is the measure of the angle that turns through 3 parts?

Classify the angle as *right*, *straight*, *acute*, or *obtuse*.

8. 90°

9. 45°

10. 160°

11. 60°

---

12. **Which One Doesn't Belong?** Which angle measure does *not* belong with the other three?

$\frac{1}{10}$ of a circle

$\frac{36}{360}$ of a circle

36°

$\frac{1}{8}$ of a circle

13. **DIG DEEPER!** Your friend uses the equation to find an angle measure. Explain what the letters *a* and *b* represent.

$$360° \div a = b$$

---

14. **Modeling Real Life** The steering wheel is divided into 3 equal parts. Find the angle measure of 1 part.

15. **DIG DEEPER!** You and your friend take pie-shaped pieces from a circular quiche. Your friend takes $\frac{2}{8}$ of the quiche. You take a piece with an angle measure of 72°. Who takes a larger piece? Explain.

🌀🌀🌀🌀🌀🌀🌀🌀🌀🌀
Review & Refresh

Multiply.

16. $7 \times 3\frac{1}{2}$

17. $10 \times 8\frac{5}{6}$

18. $4 \times 6\frac{3}{8}$

Name _____

Find Angle Measures **13.5**

Learning Target: Find the measures of angles.
Success Criteria:
• I can find the angle measures of a pattern block.
• I can use a pattern block to find an angle measure.

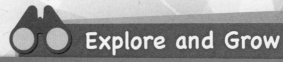

Explore and Grow

How many triangular pattern blocks can you put together around one vertex?

How can you determine the measure of each angle in a triangular pattern block?

 Repeated Reasoning Find all of the angle measures of the other pattern blocks. Organize your results in the table.

Shape	Angle Measure(s)
Square	
Hexagon	
Tan Rhombus	
Trapezoid	
Blue Rhombus	

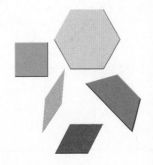

© Big Ideas Learning, LLC

Think and Grow: Find Angle Measures

Example Use the pattern block to find the measure of the angle.

Each angle of the pattern block has a

measure of _____ .

The angle is equal to _____ of the angles of the pattern block.

So, the measure of the angle is _____ .

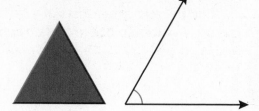

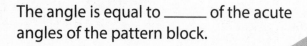

Example Use the pattern block to find the measure of the angle.

Each acute angle of the pattern block has a

measure of _____ .

The angle is equal to _____ of the acute angles of the pattern block.

So, the measure of the angle is _____ .

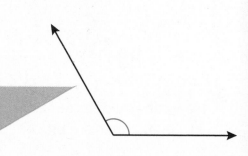

Show and Grow   *I can do it!*

Use pattern blocks to find the measure of the angle.

1.

2.

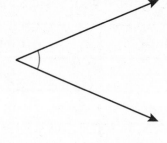

3. Use pattern blocks to find how many 60° angles are in a straight angle.

618

© Big Ideas Learning, LLC

Name _____

Use pattern blocks to find the measure of the angle.

4.

5.

6.

7.

8.

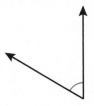

9.

10. How many 90° angles are in a straight angle? Explain.

11. How many 30° angles are in a 150° angle? Explain.

12. **(MP) Structure** Use two different pattern blocks to form an obtuse angle. Find the angle measure. Draw a model to support your answer.

13. **DIG DEEPER!** Find the measure of the smaller angle formed by the clock hands. Then explain how you could find the measure of the larger angle.

Think and Grow: Modeling Real Life

Example   A circular compass is divided into 8 equal sections. What is the measure of each angle formed at the center of the compass?

A full turn through a circle is 360°. So, divide 360° by 8.

$$8\overline{)360}$$

Each angle formed at the center of the compass is _____.

Show and Grow   I can think deeper!

14. You have a circular craft table. You divide the table into 3 equal sections. What is the measure of each angle formed at the center of the table?

15. A chef has a wheel of cheese that is cut into 6 equal pieces. The chef uses 2 pieces. What is the angle measure formed by the missing pieces?

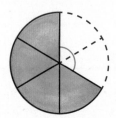

16. You cut a pizza into 5 equal pieces. You and your friend each eat a piece as shown. What is the angle measure formed by the remaining slices?

17. **DIG DEEPER!** You make a tile pattern for a border on a wall. Each tile is the same size and shape as a pattern block. Draw two ways you can arrange 1 triangle tile and 1 hexagon tile to create a straight angle.

Learning Target: Find the measures of angles.

Example Use the pattern block to find the measure of the angle.

Each acute angle of the pattern block has a
measure of __30°__ .

The angle is equal to __5__ of the
acute angles of the pattern block.

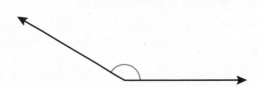

So, the measure of the angle is __150°__ .

Use pattern blocks to find the measure of the angle.

1.

2.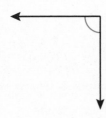

3.

4.

5.

6.

7. How many 30° angles are in a right angle? Explain.

8. **MP Structure** Draw to show how you can use three different pattern blocks to form a straight angle.

9. **YOU BE THE TEACHER** Your friend says the measure of the angle shown is 120°. Is your friend correct? Explain.

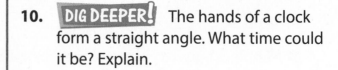

10. **DIG DEEPER!** The hands of a clock form a straight angle. What time could it be? Explain.

11. **Modeling Real Life** The scale is divided into 5 equal sections by each whole kilogram measurement. What is the measure of each angle formed at the center of the scale? What is the mass of the bananas?

12. **DIG DEEPER!** The gasoline tank gauge is divided into 4 equal sections. What are the measures of the angles formed at the starting point of the red arrow?

1/2

E   F

<u>Review & Refresh</u>

Find the area of the rectangle.

13.

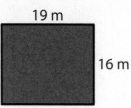

19 m

16 m

14.

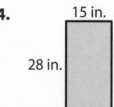

15 in.

28 in.

Learning Target: Measure and draw angles.
Success Criteria:
• I can use a protractor to measure an angle.
• I can use a protractor to draw an angle.

Explore and Grow

Find the measure of each angle. Then classify it.

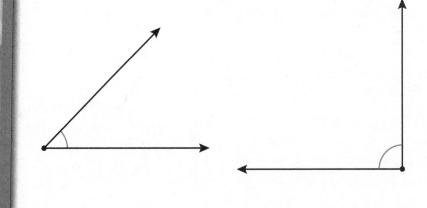

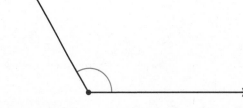
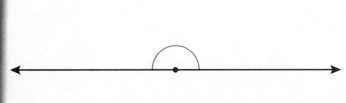
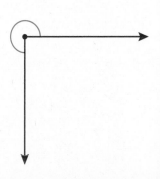

MP Construct Arguments Does the angle shown have a measure of 90°? Explain.

Think and Grow: Measure and Draw Angles

A **protractor** is a tool for measuring and drawing angles.

Example Find the measure of ∠STU. Then classify it.

Step 1: Place the center of the protractor on the vertex of the angle.

Step 2: Align one side of the angle, $\overrightarrow{TU}$, with the 0° mark on the inner scale of the protractor.

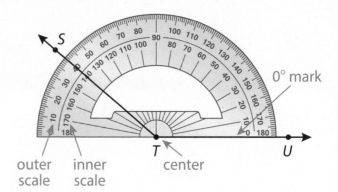

Step 3: Find where the other side of the angle, $\overrightarrow{TS}$, passes through the inner scale.

So, the measure of ∠STU is _____. It is an _____ angle.

Example Draw ∠ABC that measures 65°.

Step 1: Place the center of the protractor on point B. Align $\overrightarrow{BC}$ with the 0° mark on the inner scale of the protractor.

Step 2: Use the same scale to draw a point at 65°. Label the point A.

Step 3: Use the protractor to draw $\overrightarrow{BA}$.

> When measuring and drawing angles, make sure you are using the correct scale.

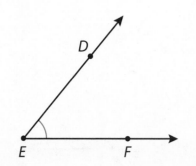

Show and Grow   *I can do it!*

1. Find the measure of ∠DEF. Then classify it.

2. Use a protractor to draw ∠XYZ that measures 110°.

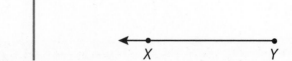

624

© Big Ideas Learning, LLC

Name _____

Find the measure of the angle. Then classify it.

3.
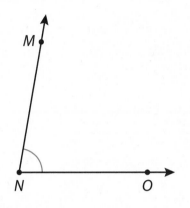

4.
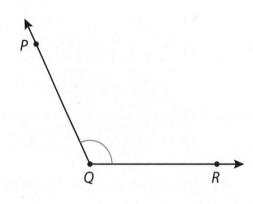

Use a protractor to draw the angle.

5. 25°

6. 160°

---

7. 180°

8. 48°

---

9. **Writing** Why does one side of the angle you are measuring have to be lined up with the straight side of the protractor?

10. **MP Precision** Newton says the measure of $\angle ABC$ is 130°. Explain what he did wrong.

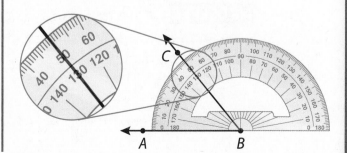

Think and Grow: Modeling Real Life

Example   A contractor builds two roofs. How much greater is the angle measure of Roof A than the angle measure of Roof B?

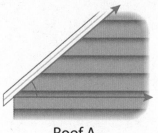

Roof A

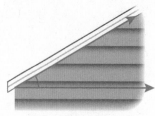

Roof B

Use a protractor to measure the angle of each roof.

The angle measure of Roof A is _____ and the angle measure of Roof B is _____.

Subtract the angle measure of Roof B from the angle measure of Roof A.

_____ − _____ = _____

The angle measure of Roof A is _____ greater than the angle measure of Roof B.

Show and Grow   *I can think deeper!*

11. An inspector compares two ramps. How much greater is the angle measure of Ramp B than the angle measure of Ramp A?

Ramp A

Ramp B

12. **DIG DEEPER!**   On a trail map, two straight trails intersect. One of the angles formed by the intersection is 70°. What are the other three angle measures?

Name _____

Learning Target: Measure and draw angles.

Homework & Practice 13.6

Example Find the measure of ∠ABC.
Then classify it.

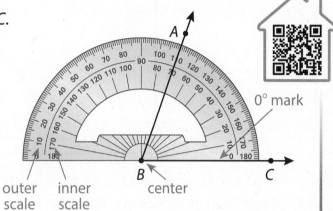

Step 1: Place the center of the
protractor on the vertex
of the angle.

Step 2: Align one side of the angle,
$\overrightarrow{BC}$, with the 0° mark on the
inner scale of the protractor.

Step 3: Find where the other side
of the angle, $\overrightarrow{BA}$, passes through
the inner scale.

So, the measure of ∠ABC is __70°__. It is an __acute__ angle.

Find the measure of the angle. Then classify it.

1.

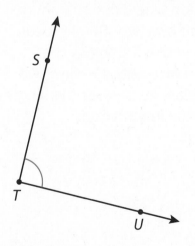

2.

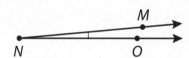

Use a protractor to draw the angle.

3. 40°

4. 125°

© Big Ideas Learning, LLC

Chapter 13 | Lesson 6

5. **MP** **Reasoning** Measure the angles of each quadrilateral. What do you notice about the sum of the angle measures of each quadrilateral?

 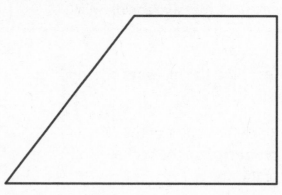

---

6. **MP** **Precision** Use a protractor to draw an angle with a measure of 0°. Describe your drawing.

7. **DIG DEEPER!** Use a protractor to draw a triangle with the angle measures of 90°, 35°, and 55°.

---

8. **Modeling Real Life** A snowboarder compares 2 mountain trails. How much greater is the angle measure of Trail B than the angle measure of Trail A?

Trail A   Trail B

9. **DIG DEEPER!** On a map, there is a Y-intersection where one straight road branches off into two straight roads. One of the angles formed by the intersection measures 45°. Give two possible measures for the other angles formed by the intersection.

Review & Refresh

Find the equivalent length.

10. 5 km = _____ m

11. 7 m = _____ mm

Name _____

Add Angle Measures 13.7

Learning Target: Find the measure of an angle using its parts.

Success Criteria:
- I can identify the parts of an angle.
- I can find the measure of an angle by adding its parts.
- I can write an equation to find an angle measure.

Explore and Grow

Use a protractor to draw ∠*PQR* that measures 70°.

Draw another angle that measures 30° and shares side $\overrightarrow{QR}$. Label your angle. How many angles are in your figure? What do you notice about their measures?

Make a copy of ∠*PQR*. Draw and label a different angle that measures 30° and shares side $\overrightarrow{QR}$. How many angles are in your figure? What do you notice about their measures?

Construct Arguments What conclusions can you make from your figures above?

© Big Ideas Learning, LLC

Think and Grow: Add Angle Measures

When an angle is decomposed into parts that do not overlap, the angle measure of the whole equals the sum of the angle measures of the parts.

Two angles are **adjacent** when they share a common side and a common vertex, but no other points in common. When two or more adjacent angles form a larger angle, the sum of the measures of the smaller angles is equal to the measure of the larger angle.

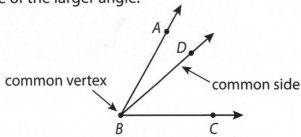

common vertex

common side

> Think: ∠ABC is the whole. ∠ABD and ∠DBC are the parts.

∠ABD and ∠DBC are adjacent angles.

measure of ∠ABD + measure of ∠DBC = measure of ∠ABC

Example Find the measure of ∠WXY.

∠WXZ and ∠ZXY are adjacent. The measure of ∠WXY is equal to the sum of the measures of ∠WXZ and ∠ZXY. Complete the equation.

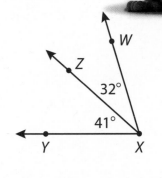

_____ + _____ = _____

So, the measure of ∠WXY is _____.

Show and Grow   I can do it!

1. Complete the equation to find the measure of ∠PQR.

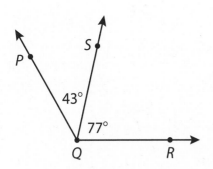

_____ + _____ = _____

2. Use a protractor to find the measure of each angle in the circle. Use the angle measures to complete the equation.

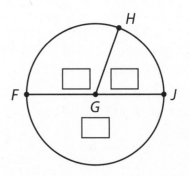

_____ + _____ + _____ = _____

✓ Apply and Grow: Practice

Write an equation to find the measure of the angle.

3. ∠QRS

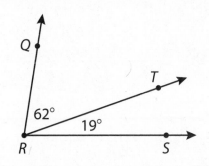

4. ∠ABC

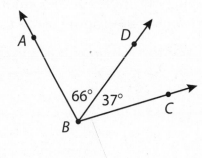

5. ∠MNO

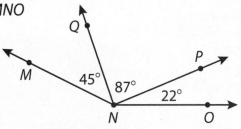

6. ∠VWX

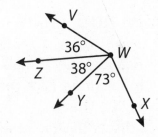

Use a protractor to find the measure of each angle in the circle. Use the angle measures to write an equation.

7.

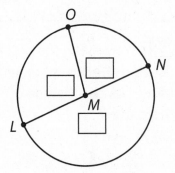

8.

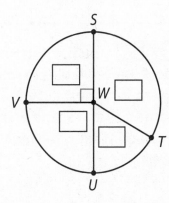

9. **MP Number Sense** The sum of seven adjacent angle measures that share a vertex is 154°. Each angle has the same measure. What is the measure of each angle?

10. **DIG DEEPER!** ∠PRS is adjacent to ∠QRS in Exercise 3. The measure of ∠PRS is 9°. Find the measure of ∠QRP. Classify angle ∠QRP.

Think and Grow: Modeling Real Life

Example A store installs 3 security cameras on the same light post. Each camera has a viewing angle of 28°. The viewing angles of the cameras are adjacent. What is the total viewing angle of the cameras?

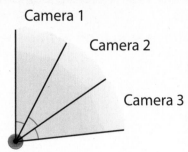

Camera 1
Camera 2
Camera 3

Add the viewing angle measures of the cameras.

28° + 28° + 28° = _____

The total viewing angle of the cameras is _____.

Show and Grow   *I can think deeper!*

11. A landscaper installs 3 sprinklers in 1 location in the grass. Each sprinkler has a spraying angle of 90°. The spraying angles of the sprinklers are adjacent. What is the total spraying angle of the sprinklers?

Sprinkler 1   Sprinkler 2

Sprinkler 3

12. **DIG DEEPER!** You use 4 rhombus tiles and 4 trapezoid tiles to make the pattern for a mosaic. Each tile is the same size and shape as a pattern block. What is the measure of ∠NUQ?

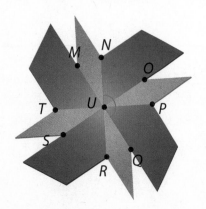

13. **DIG DEEPER!** You make the pattern for a quilt. Each rhombus is the same size and shape. Name all of the 60° angles in the pattern.

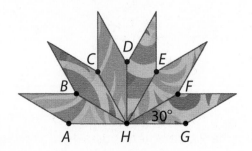

Name _____

Learning Target: Find the measure of an angle using its parts.

Example Find the measure of ∠ABC.

∠ABD and ∠DBC are adjacent. The measure of ∠ABC is equal to the sum of the measures of ∠ABD and ∠DBC. Complete the equation.

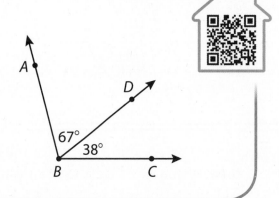

$$\underline{67°} + \underline{38°} = \underline{105°}$$

So, the measure of ∠ABC is $\underline{105°}$.

Write an equation to find the measure of the angle.

1. ∠EFG

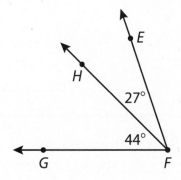

2. ∠JKL

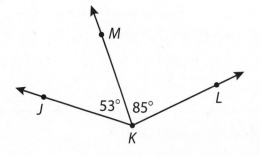

---

3. ∠PQR

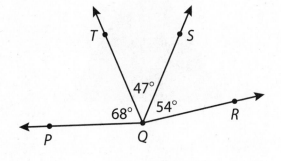

4. ∠VWX

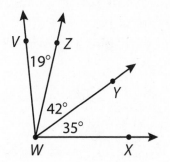

Use a protractor to find the measure of each angle in the circle. Use the angle measures to write an equation.

5.

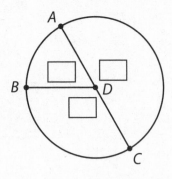

6.

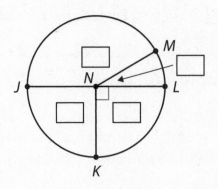

7. **Open-Ended** Is it possible for the sum of two acute adjacent angle measures to be greater than the measure of a right angle? If so, draw a sketch to support your answer.

8. **DIG DEEPER!** Use a protractor to measure the angle. Then decompose the angle into 2 parts so that one part is 25° greater than the other. What is the measure of each part?

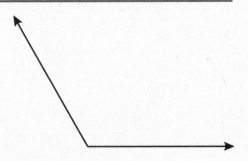

9. **Modeling Real Life** A carpenter glues 3 identical pieces of wood next to each other to make the table shown. The 30° angles of the pieces of wood are adjacent. What is the total angle of the table formed by the pieces of wood?

30°

10. **DIG DEEPER!** You use 3 triangle pattern blocks and 3 rhombus pattern blocks to make the pattern for an art project. What is the measure of ∠ADE?

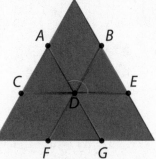

Review & Refresh

Compare.

11. $\frac{4}{10}$ ◯ $\frac{2}{5}$

12. $\frac{8}{12}$ ◯ $\frac{2}{3}$

13. $\frac{3}{4}$ ◯ $\frac{5}{6}$

Learning Target: Find the measures of unknown angles.

Success Criteria:
• I can describe how a pair of angles are related.
• I can write an equation to find an unknown angle measure.
• I can solve an equation to find an unknown angle measure.

Explore and Grow

Draw and label ∠EDF where point F is between the rays of ∠CDE. Explain how you can find the measure of ∠CDF.

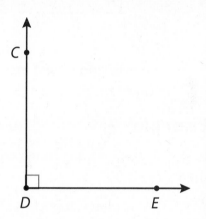

Draw and label ∠LMP. Explain how you can find the measure of ∠NMP.

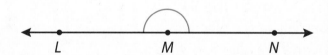

MP **Reasoning** Draw $\overleftrightarrow{MP}$ in your figure above. Explain how you can find all of the angle measures in your figure. What do you notice?

When a right angle is decomposed into two adjacent angles, the sum of their measures is 90°. These angles are **complementary**.

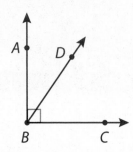

∠ABD and ∠DBC are complementary angles.

When a straight angle is decomposed into two adjacent angles, the sum of their measures is 180°. These angles are **supplementary**.

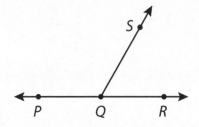

∠PQS and ∠SQR are supplementary angles.

Example   Find the measure of ∠DEG.

∠DEG and ∠GEF are complementary. The sum of their measures is 90°.

Step 1: Write an equation to find the measure of ∠DEG.

$$x + \underline{\hspace{1cm}} = \underline{\hspace{1cm}}$$

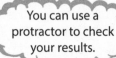

You can use a protractor to check your results.

Step 2: Use subtraction to solve.

$$x = \underline{\hspace{1cm}} - \underline{\hspace{1cm}}$$

$$x = \underline{\hspace{1cm}}$$

So, the measure of ∠DEG is _____.

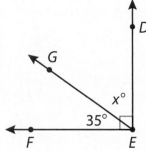

Show and Grow   I can do it!

1. Write and solve an equation to find the measure of ∠NLM.

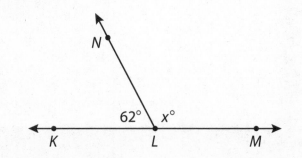

Name _____

Apply and Grow: Practice

Write and solve an equation to find the measure of the angle.

2. ∠MKL

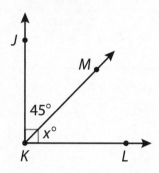

3. ∠MNP

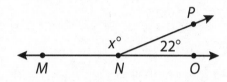

4. ∠TRU

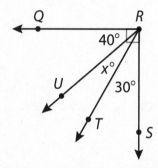

5. ∠YWZ

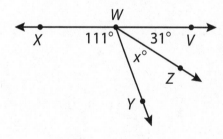

6. Find the measures of ∠AEB, ∠AED, and ∠DEC.

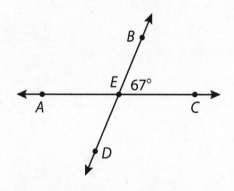

7. **DIG DEEPER!** Write and solve equations to find the measure of ∠KMJ.

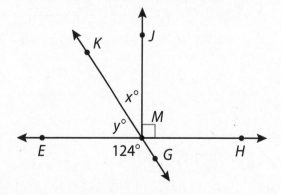

8. **Writing** Define complementary angles and supplementary angles in your own words.

Think and Grow: Modeling Real Life

path of baseball

3rd base foul line

26° $t°$

1st base foul line

Example The foul lines on a baseball field are perpendicular. A baseball player hits a ball as shown. What is the measure of the angle between the path of the ball and the 1st base foul line?

Think: What do you know? What do you need to find? How will you solve?

The 3rd base foul line and 1st base foul line are perpendicular.

So, the measure of the angle between the foul lines is _____.

Write an equation to find the measure of the angle between the path of the ball and the 1st base foul line.

$$\underline{\qquad} + x = \underline{\qquad}$$

Use subtraction to solve.

$$x = \underline{\qquad} - \underline{\qquad}$$

$$x = \underline{\qquad}$$

The measure of the angle between the path of the ball and the

1st base foul line is _____.

Show and Grow   I can think deeper!

9. Runway 1 and Runway 2 are perpendicular. What is the measure of the missing angle between Runway 1 and Runway 3?

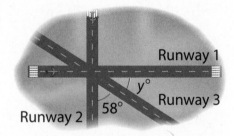

Runway 1

$y°$

Runway 3

58°

Runway 2

10. **DIG DEEPER!** What is the measure of the missing angle between View Street and Elm Street?

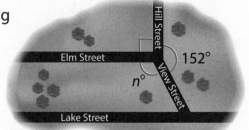

Hill Street

Elm Street

152°

$n°$

View Street

Lake Street

638

© Big Ideas Learning, LLC

Learning Target: Find the measures of unknown angles.

Example Find the measure of ∠ABD.

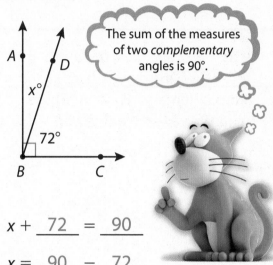

The sum of the measures of two *complementary* angles is 90°.

$x +$ ___72___ $=$ ___90___

$x =$ ___90___ $-$ ___72___

$x =$ ___18___

So, the measure of ∠ABD is ___18°___ .

Example Find the measure of ∠HFE.

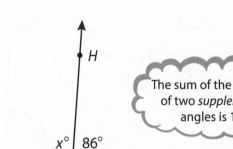

The sum of the measures of two *supplementary* angles is 180°.

$x +$ ___86___ $=$ ___180___

$x =$ ___180___ $-$ ___86___

$x =$ ___94___

So, the measure of ∠HFE is ___94°___ .

Write and solve an equation to find the measure of the angle.

1. ∠JKM

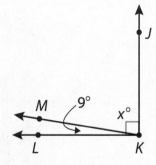

2. ∠PNM

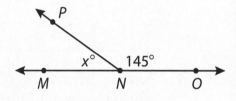

3. ∠QRU

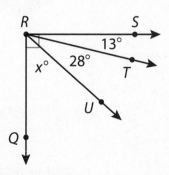

4. ∠ZWV

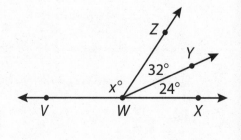

5. **MP Reasoning** ∠ABC and ∠CBD are adjacent. ∠ABC is a right angle. ∠CBD is acute.

Draw and label ∠ABC and ∠CBD.	Classify ∠ABD.	Write an equation to show one possible sum of the measures of ∠ABC and ∠CBD.

---

6. **MP Structure** Which equations can you use to find the measure of angle ∠MKJ?

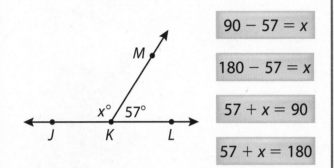

$$90 - 57 = x$$

$$180 - 57 = x$$

$$57 + x = 90$$

$$57 + x = 180$$

7. **Open-Ended** An acute angle and an obtuse angle are adjacent and supplementary. What might the measures of each angle be?

---

8. **Modeling Real Life** Newton bounces a ball off of a wall to Descartes. $\overline{AD} \perp \overline{DB}$. The measures of ∠ADC and ∠BDE are equivalent. Find the measures of ∠ADC and ∠BDE.

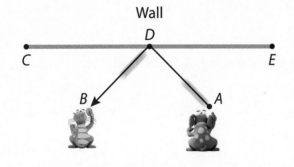

Wall

9. **Modeling Real Life** Owls see an object with both eyes at the same time using *binocular vision*. What angle measure describes the owl's binocular vision? Explain.

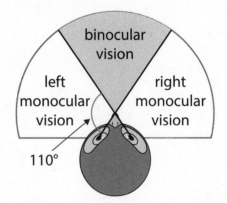

binocular vision

left monocular vision

right monocular vision

110°

Review & Refresh

Write the fraction as a money amount and as a decimal.

10. $\frac{49}{100}$

11. $\frac{25}{100}$

12. $\frac{7}{100}$

Performance Task 13

A rural town is expanding and needs to plan the construction of new roads.

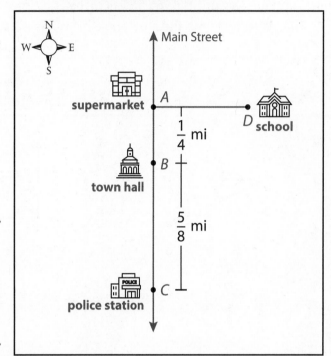

1. What is another name for Main Street?

_____

2. Use the directions to complete the map.
 a. Draw $\overleftrightarrow{BD}$ and label it with a street name of your choice.

....

 b. The library will be at point E on $\overleftrightarrow{BD}$ and on the other side of Main Street as the school. Plot and label the library at point E.

....

 c. Draw a new road through point E that is perpendicular to Main Street. Label it with a street name of your choice.

_____

3. City planners want to construct a new residential neighborhood southeast of the town hall.

 a. The measure of $\angle ABD$ is $\frac{1}{6}$ of 360°. What is the measure of the angle?

....

 b. Classify $\angle DBC$. What is its measure?

....

 c. Draw a road from point B to the new neighborhood. The road divides $\angle DBC$ exactly in half.

_____

4. Is the distance between the supermarket and the police station more than or less than a mile? Explain.

Geometry Dots

Directions:

1. Players take turns connecting two dots, each using a different color.

2. On your turn, connect two dots, vertically or horizontally. If you close a square around an angle, find the measure of the angle inside the square. If you do not close a square, your turn is over.

3. Continue playing until you find all of the angle measures.

4. The player that finds the most angle measures wins!

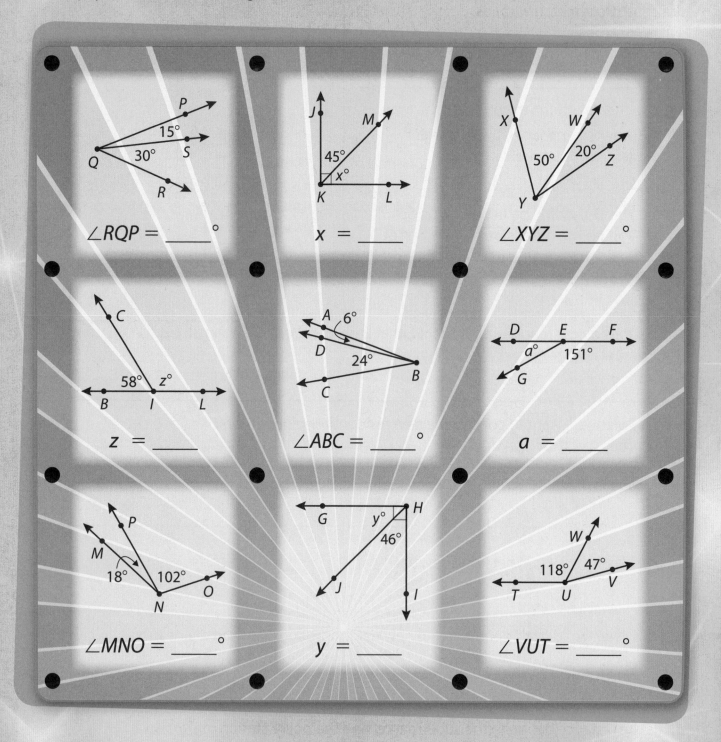

∠RQP = _____ °

x = _____

∠XYZ = _____ °

z = _____

∠ABC = _____ °

a = _____

∠MNO = _____ °

y = _____

∠VUT = _____ °

Name _____

Chapter Practice 13

13.1 Points, Lines, and Rays

Name the figure. Write how to say the name.

1.

•
F

2.
G•
      •H

3.
J   K

Draw and label the figure.

4. $\overrightarrow{LM}$

5. $\overleftrightarrow{NO}$

6. $\overline{PQ}$

Use the figure.

7. Name a line segment.

_____

8. Name two different rays.

_____

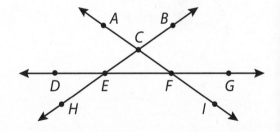

13.2 Identify and Draw Angles

9. Write a name for the angle and classify it.

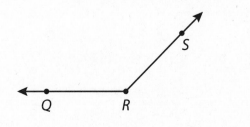

10. ∠TUV is a right angle. Draw and label the angle.

© Big Ideas Learning, LLC

13.3 Identify Parallel and Perpendicular Lines

Draw and label the lines with the given description.

11. $\overleftrightarrow{MN} \parallel \overleftrightarrow{OP}$

12. $\overleftrightarrow{AB} \perp \overleftrightarrow{CD}$
$\overleftrightarrow{AB}$ and $\overleftrightarrow{CD}$ intersect at point E.

13.4 Understand Degrees

Find the measure of each angle.

13.

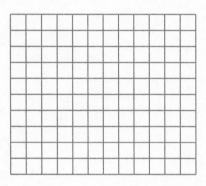

$\dfrac{115}{360}$

14.

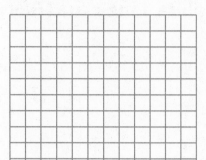

$\dfrac{1}{5}$

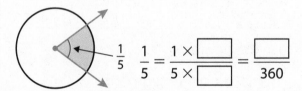
$$\frac{1}{5} = \frac{1 \times \boxed{}}{5 \times \boxed{}} = \frac{\boxed{}}{360}$$

15.

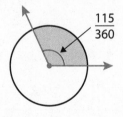

$\dfrac{1}{4}$

16. A circle is divided into 12 equal parts. What is the measure of the angle that turns through 2 parts?

17. Which One Doesn't Belong? Which angle measure does *not* belong with the other three?

$\dfrac{1}{6}$ of a circle $\dfrac{60}{360}$ of a circle $60°$ $\dfrac{1}{8}$ of a circle

(13.5) Find Angle Measures

Use pattern blocks to find the measure of the angle.

18.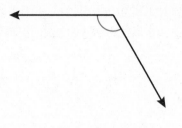

19.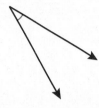

20.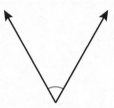

21.

(13.6) Measure and Draw Angles

22. Find the measure of the angle. Then classify it.

A •

B

C

23. Use a protractor to draw a 45° angle.

24. Modeling Real Life On a map, two straight railroad tracks intersect. One of the angles formed by the intersection is 30°. What are the three other angle measures?

13.7 **Add Angle Measures**

25. Write an equation to find the measure of ∠EFG.

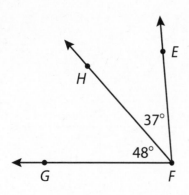

26. Use a protractor to find the measure of each angle in the circle. Use the angle measures to write an equation.

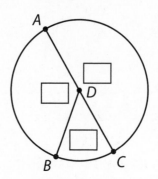

13.8 **Find Unknown Angle Measures**

Write and solve an equation to find the measure of the angle.

27. ∠ABD

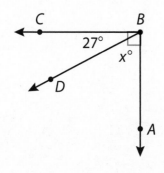

28. ∠HFG

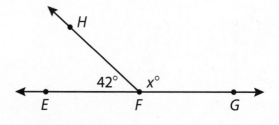

29. ∠MKL

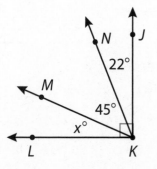

30. ∠SPR

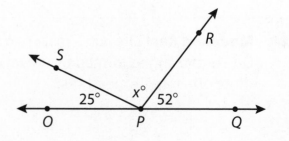

Identify Symmetry and Two-Dimensional Shapes

Chapter Learning Target:
Understand symmetry and two-dimensional shapes.

Chapter Success Criteria:
- I can define symmetry.
- I can describe two-dimensional shapes.
- I can compare angles and shapes.
- I can draw different angles and shapes.

- Where might you see triangles used in construction?
- How can you use side lengths to classify a triangle?

14 Vocabulary

Name _____

Review Words

hexagons
octagons
quadrilaterals
triangles

Organize It

Use the review words to complete the graphic organizer.

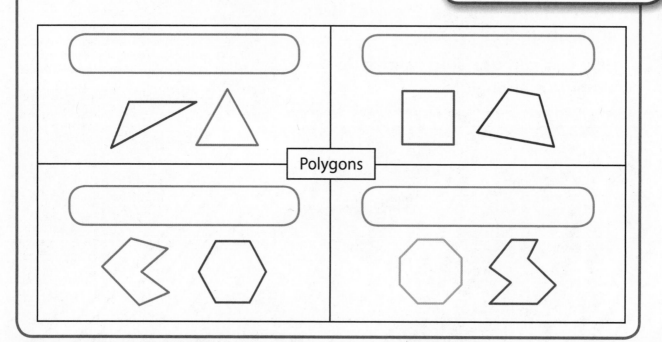

Polygons

Define It

Use your vocabulary cards to match the word to a shape.

1. equilateral
triangle

2. isosceles
triangle

3. right
triangle

4. scalene
triangle

Chapter 14 Vocabulary Cards

acute triangle

equiangular triangle

equilateral triangle

isosceles triangle

line of symmetry

line symmetry

obtuse triangle

parallelogram

© Big Ideas Learning, LLC

A triangle that has three angles with the same measure

A triangle that has three acute angles

A triangle that has two sides with the same length

A triangle that has three sides with the same length

The symmetry that a shape has when it can be folded on a line so that two parts match exactly

A fold line that divides a shape into two parts that match exactly

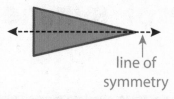

line of symmetry

A quadrilateral that has two pairs of parallel sides

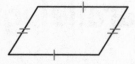

A triangle that has one obtuse angle

Chapter 14 Vocabulary Cards

rectangle

rhombus

right triangle

scalene triangle

square

trapezoid

A parallelogram that has four sides with the same length

A parallelogram that has four right angles

A triangle that has no sides with the same length

A triangle that has one right angle

A quadrilateral that has exactly one pair of parallel sides

A parallelogram that has four right angles and four sides with the same length

Learning Target: Identify shapes that have line symmetry.

Success Criteria:
- I can determine whether a shape has line symmetry.
- I can identify how many lines of symmetry a shape has.
- I can draw each line of symmetry a shape has.

 Explore and Grow

How many ways can you fold the Letter X so that the two parts match exactly? Draw models to support your answer.

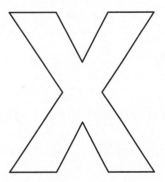

 Structure What other letters can you fold so that the two parts match exactly? Draw models to support your answer. Compare your models with a partner.

Think and Grow: Identify Line Symmetry

A shape has **line symmetry** when it can be folded on a line so that two parts match exactly. The fold line is called a **line of symmetry**.

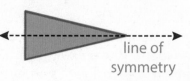

line of symmetry

Example Determine whether the shape has line symmetry.

The shape can be folded so that two parts match exactly.

The shape has _____ lines of symmetry.

So, the shape _____ line symmetry.

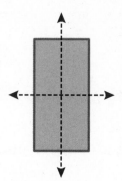

A line of symmetry divides a shape into two parts that are mirror images of each other.

Example Determine whether the shape has line symmetry.

The shape cannot be folded so that two parts match exactly.

The shape has _____ lines of symmetry.

So, the shape _____ line symmetry.

Show and Grow   I can do it!

Determine whether the line is a line of symmetry.

1.
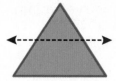

2.

3.
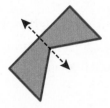

Determine whether the shape has line symmetry. Draw each line of symmetry.

4.

5.

6.

Name _____

✓ Apply and Grow: Practice

Determine whether the shape has line symmetry. Draw each line of symmetry.

7.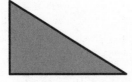

8.

9.

10.

11.

12.

13. **MP Structure** Create a three-digit number that has a line of symmetry.

0 1 2 3 4 5 6 7 8 9

14. **Writing** How can you tell when a line is *not* a line of symmetry?

15. **DIG DEEPER!** Draw four lines of symmetry for the circle. Can you draw more lines of symmetry? Explain.

© Big Ideas Learning, LLC

Think and Grow: Modeling Real Life

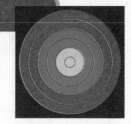

Example   Divide the archery target into multiple sections using each of its lines of symmetry. An archer gets 2 arrows in each section. How many arrows does the archer get on the target?

Draw each line of symmetry on the target.

The target has _____ lines of symmetry.

Count the sections.

The lines of symmetry divide the target

into _____ sections.

The archer gets 2 arrows in each section, so multiply the number of sections by 2.

_____ × 2 = _____

So, the archer gets _____ arrows on the target.

Show and Grow   I can think deeper!

16. Divide the soccer field into multiple sections using each of its lines of symmetry. At the start of the game, there are 3 players in each section. How many players are on the field?

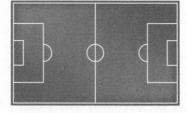

17. **DIG DEEPER!**   Your friend folds a rectangular sheet of paper in half horizontally, and then in half again vertically. She then draws the shape shown on the folded paper, cuts it out, and then unfolds it. How many lines of symmetry does your friend's cutout have? Explain.

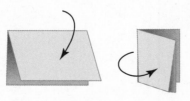

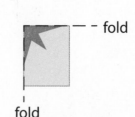

fold

fold

Learning Target: Identify shapes that have line symmetry.

Example Determine whether the shape has line symmetry.

The shape can be folded so that two parts match exactly.

The shape has __1__ line of symmetry.

So, the shape _has_ line symmetry.

Determine whether the line is a line of symmetry.

1.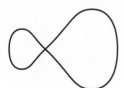

2.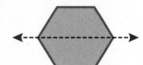

3.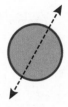

Determine whether the shape has line symmetry. Draw each line of symmetry.

4.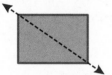

5.

6.

7.

8. **N**

9.

10. **MP Precision** Which figure correctly shows all the lines of symmetry of a square?

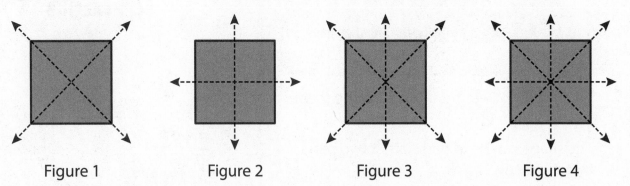

Figure 1   Figure 2   Figure 3   Figure 4

11. **YOU BE THE TEACHER** Your friend says the shape has exactly three lines of symmetry. Is your friend correct? Explain.

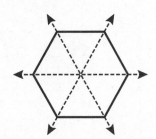

12. **Modeling Real Life** Divide the tennis court into multiple sections using each of its lines of symmetry. There are 4 players on the court with an equal number of players in each section. How many players are in each section?

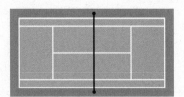

13. **DIG DEEPER!** In art class, you are making a black and white art piece. Your teacher says it has to have exactly 1 line of diagonal symmetry. Shade the square below to show what the art piece could look like.

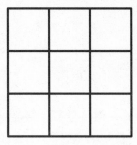

Write the fraction as a multiple of a unit fraction.

14. $\dfrac{8}{12}$

15. $\dfrac{5}{100}$

Learning Target: Draw symmetric shapes.
Success Criteria:
- I can draw a symmetric shape given one half of the shape and a line of symmetry.
- I can draw a symmetric shape given one half of the shape.

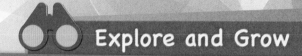

You want to create a mask that has at least 1 line of symmetry. Does either mask meet your requirement? Explain.

Complete the mask below so that it has 1 line of symmetry.

MP **Reasoning** When given one half of a figure and a line of symmetry, how can you draw the other half of the figure? Explain.

If a shape has line symmetry, then it is *symmetric*.

Example One half of a symmetric shape is shown. Draw the rest of the shape.

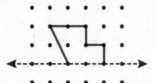

One Way: Draw a line of symmetry.

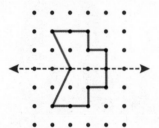

Draw the other half of the shape on the opposite side of the line of symmetry.

Another Way: Draw a different line of symmetry.

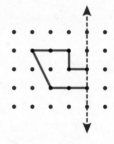

Draw the other half of the shape on the opposite side of the line of symmetry.

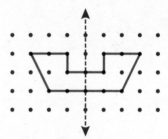

Show and Grow   I can do it!

1. One half of a shape and a line of symmetry are shown. Draw the rest of the shape.

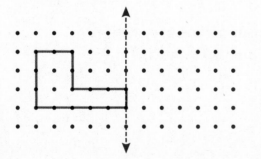

2. One half of a symmetric shape is shown. Draw the rest of the shape.

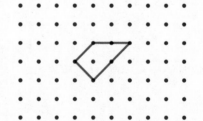

Apply and Grow: Practice

One half of a symmetric shape is shown. Draw the rest of the shape.

3.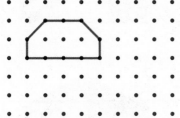

4.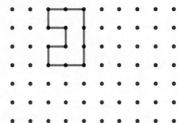

5.

6.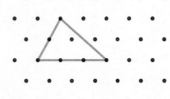

7. (MP) **Reasoning** Draw a shape that has exactly one line of symmetry. Draw the line of symmetry.

8. **YOU BE THE TEACHER** Your friend draws the other half of the shape on the opposite side of the line of symmetry. Is your friend correct? Explain.

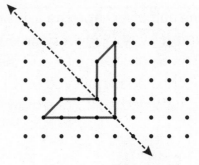

Think and Grow: Modeling Real Life

Example A *rokkaku* is a six-sided Japanese kite. One half of a symmetric rokkaku and a line of symmetry are shown. Draw the rest of the kite. Then draw each additional line of symmetry, if any.

Draw the other half of the rokkaku on the opposite side of the line of symmetry.

The rokkaku can also be folded in half vertically so that two parts match exactly. So, draw a vertical line of symmetry.

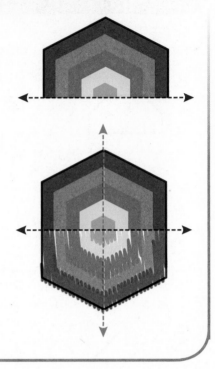

Show and Grow   I can think deeper!

9. The Jamaican flag is symmetric. One half of the flag and a line of symmetry are shown. Draw the rest of the flag. Then draw each additional line of symmetry, if any.

10. **DIG DEEPER!** A symmetric quilt is folded in half horizontally, and then in half again vertically. The folded quilt and fold lines are shown. Draw the unfolded quilt. Then draw each line of symmetry.

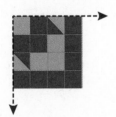

Name _____

Learning Target: Draw symmetric shapes.

Example One half of a symmetric shape is shown. Draw the rest of the shape.

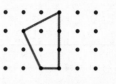

One Way: Draw a line of symmetry.

Draw the other half of the shape on the opposite side of the line of symmetry.

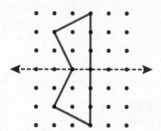

Another Way: Draw a different line of symmetry.

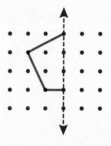

Draw the other half of the shape on the opposite side of the line of symmetry.

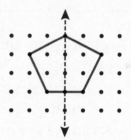

1. One half of a shape and a line of symmetry are shown. Draw the rest of the shape.

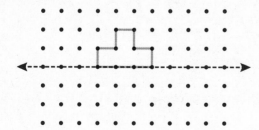

2. One half of a symmetric shape is shown. Draw the rest of the shape.

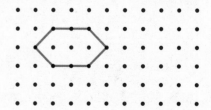

© Big Ideas Learning, LLC

One half of a symmetric shape is shown. Draw the rest of the shape.

3.

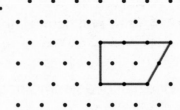

4.

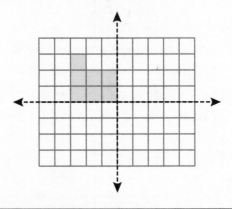

5. **MP Structure** Draw a shape that has 5 sides and exactly 1 line of symmetry.

6. **MP Structure** One fourth of a shape and two lines of symmetry are shown. Draw the rest of the shape.

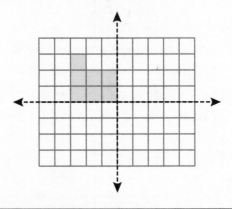

7. **Modeling Real Life** The flag of the Bahamas is symmetric. One half of the flag and a line of symmetry are shown. Draw the rest of the flag. Then draw each additional line of symmetry, if any.

8. **DIG DEEPER!** Snowflakes are symmetric. One half of a snowflake and a line of symmetry are shown. Draw the rest of the snowflake. Then draw each additional line of symmetry, if any.

Review & Refresh

Find the equivalent weight.

9. 2 T = _____ lb

10. 15 lb = _____ oz

Name _____

Learning Target: Classify triangles by their sides.
Success Criteria:
• I can identify sides of a triangle with the same length.
• I can identify sides of a triangle with different lengths.
• I can use sides to classify a triangle.

Sort the triangles into two or more groups using their side lengths. Explain how you sorted the triangles.

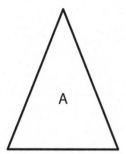

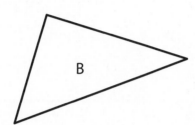

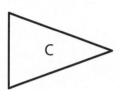

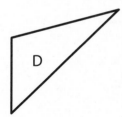

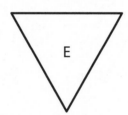

 Structure Can you draw a triangle that does *not* belong in any of your groups above? Explain.

Think and Grow: Classify Triangles by Sides

The red tick marks mean that the sides of the figure have the same length.

Triangles can be classified by their sides.

An **equilateral triangle** has three sides with the same length.

An **isosceles triangle** has two sides with the same length.

A **scalene triangle** has no sides with the same length.

Example Classify the triangle by its sides.

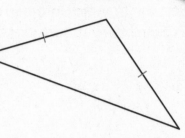

The triangle has _____ sides with the same length.

So, it is an _____ triangle.

Show and Grow I can do it!

Classify the triangle by its sides.

1.

2.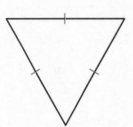

3.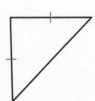

4. Use the triangular grid to draw any triangle. Classify the triangle by its sides.

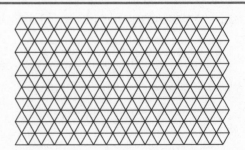

Name _____

Classify the triangle by its sides.

5.

6.

7.

8.

9.

10.

11. Draw a triangle that has three lines of symmetry. Classify the triangle by its sides.

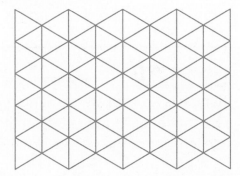

12. Draw a triangle that has no sides with the same length. Classify the triangle by its sides.

13. **MP Reasoning** How many lines of symmetry does a scalene triangle have? Explain.

14. **DIG DEEPER!** Write an addition equation and a multiplication equation for the perimeter, P, of the triangle.

s

Example   Classify the yield sign by its sides. Then find the perimeter of the sign.

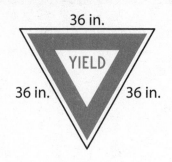

The yield sign is a triangle that has 3 sides with the same length.

So, it is an _____ triangle.

To find the perimeter of the yield sign, find the sum of all of its side lengths.

$36 + 36 + 36 =$ _____

So, the perimeter of the yield sign is _____ inches.

Show and Grow   I can think deeper!

15. Classify the sports pennant by its sides. Then find the perimeter of the pennant.

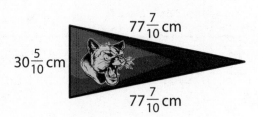

16. **DIG DEEPER!** The perimeter of the canoe sail is 29.75 feet. Find the unknown side length. Then classify the sail by its sides.

17. **DIG DEEPER!** An emergency warning triangle is an equilateral triangle. It has a perimeter of 51 inches. What are the side lengths of the warning triangle?

Name _____

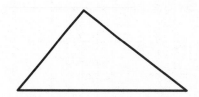

Learning Target: Classify triangles by their sides.

Example Classify the triangle by its sides.

The triangle has __no__ sides with the same length.

So, it is a ___scalene___ triangle.

Classify the triangle by its sides.

1.

2.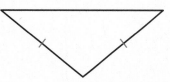

3.

4.

5.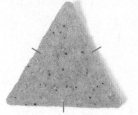

6.

7. Draw a triangle that has exactly 2 sides with the same length. Classify the triangle by its sides.

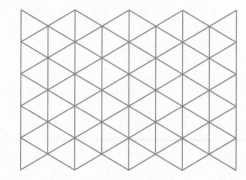

8. Draw a triangle that has exactly 1 line of symmetry. Classify the triangle by its sides.

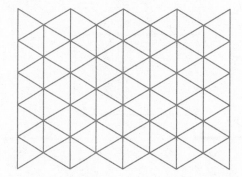

9. Draw a triangle that has no lines of symmetry. Classify the triangle by its sides.

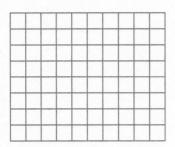

10. **Structure** Classify the triangle pattern block by its sides.

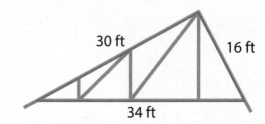

11. **MP Reasoning** Can the triangle have 3 lines of symmetry? Explain.

12. **MP Reasoning** Your friend draws a triangle with side lengths of 25.3 centimeters, 15.2 centimeters, and 12.6 centimeters. Classify your friend's triangle.

13. **Modeling Real Life** Classify the roof truss by its sides. Then find the perimeter of the roof truss.

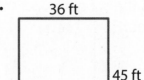

30 ft   16 ft

34 ft

Review & Refresh

Find the perimeter of the rectangle.

14.

32 yd

20 yd

15.

36 ft

45 ft

Learning Target: Classify triangles by their angles.
Success Criteria:
• I can identify an angle as right, acute, or obtuse.
• I can use angles to classify a triangle.
• I can use angles and sides to classify a triangle.

Explore and Grow

Sort the triangles into two or more groups using their angle measures.
Explain how you sorted the triangles.

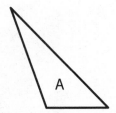

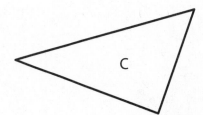

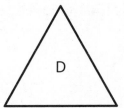

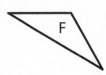

MP **Construct Arguments** Your friend says a triangle that has three
angles with the same measure also has three sides with the same
length. Is your friend correct? Explain.

Triangles can be classified by their angles.

An **acute triangle** has three acute angles.

An **obtuse triangle** has one obtuse angle.

A **right triangle** has one right angle.

Equiangular triangles are also acute and equilateral.

An **equiangular triangle** has three angles with the same measure.

The red arcs mean that the angles of the figure have the same measure.

Example Classify the triangle by its angles.

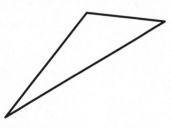

The triangle has one _____ angle.

So, it is an _____ triangle.

Example Classify the triangle by its angles and its sides.

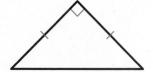

The triangle has one _____ angle.

and _____ sides with the same length.

So, it is an _____ _____ triangle.

Show and Grow   *I can do it!*

1. Classify the triangle by its angles.

2. Classify the triangle by its angles and its sides.

Apply and Grow: Practice

Classify the triangle by its angles.

3.

4.

5.

Classify the triangle by its angles and its sides.

6.

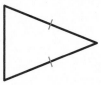

7.

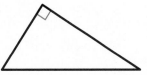

8.

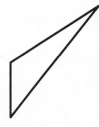

9.

10.

11.

12. (MP) **Precision** Draw an acute scalene triangle.

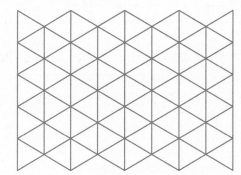

13. **DIG DEEPER!** Can an obtuse triangle also be an equilateral triangle? Explain.

Think and Grow: Modeling Real Life

Example Classify the large triangle on the shuffleboard court by its angles. Verify your answer by finding the measure of each angle.

The triangle does not have a right angle or an obtuse angle.

So, it is an _____ triangle.

Verify: Use a protractor to find the measure of each angle.

The measure of ∠ABC is _____.

The measure of ∠BCA is _____.

The measure of ∠CAB is _____.

Because each angle measure is less than 90°, you can conclude

that the triangle is a _____ triangle.

Show and Grow   I can think deeper!

14. Classify the triangle in the clothes hanger by its angles. Verify your answer by finding the measure of each angle.

15. **DIG DEEPER!** In the picture, the tree is perpendicular to the ground. Draw the triangle formed by the tree, the wire, and the ground. Classify the triangle by its angles. Explain.

Name _____

Learning Target: Classify triangles by their angles.

Example Classify the triangle by its angles.

The triangle has three

___acute___ angles.

So, it is an ___acute___ triangle.

Example Classify the triangle by its angles and its sides.

The triangle has one __obtuse__ angle and

__no__ sides with the same length.

So, it is an __obtuse__ __scalene__ triangle.

Classify the triangle by its angles.

1.

2.

3.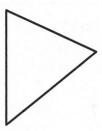

Classify the triangle by its angles and its sides.

4.

5.

6.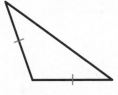

7.

8.

9.

10. **Precision** Draw a right isosceles triangle.

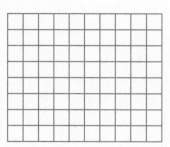

11. **Reasoning** Can a triangle have more than one right angle? Explain.

---

12. **Which One Doesn't Belong?** Which triangle does *not* belong with the other three?

  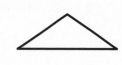

13. **DIG DEEPER!** Draw $\overline{BD}$. Then classify each triangle by its angles and its sides.

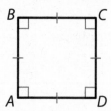

---

14. **Modeling Real Life** Classify the face of the bird house by its angles. Verify your answer by finding the measure of each angle.

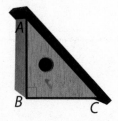

15. **Modeling Real Life** A construction worker measures a triangle formed by the supports on a bridge. The angle measures are 120°, 36°, and 24°. The side lengths are 12.65 meters, 8.61 meters, and 5.91 meters. Classify the triangle by its angles and its sides.

Review & Refresh

Add.

16. $2\frac{2}{6} + 4\frac{3}{6} = $ _____

17. $10\frac{1}{5} + 8\frac{4}{5} = $ _____

18. $3\frac{5}{10} + 6\frac{3}{10} + \frac{6}{10} = $ _____

Learning Target: Classify quadrilaterals.
Success Criteria:
- I can identify parallel sides and sides with the same length in a quadrilateral.
- I can identify right angles of a quadrilateral.
- I can use angles and sides to classify a quadrilateral.

Explore and Grow

Sort the quadrilaterals into two or more groups. Explain how you sorted the quadrilaterals.

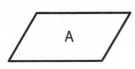
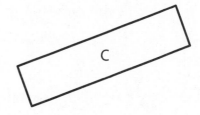

MP **Precision** You draw a quadrilateral with four right angles. Your friend draws a quadrilateral with two pairs of parallel sides. Did you and your friend draw the same type of quadrilateral? Explain.

Quadrilaterals can be classified by their angles and sides.

A **trapezoid** is a quadrilateral that has exactly one pair of parallel sides.

A **parallelogram** is a quadrilateral that has two pairs of parallel sides. Opposite sides have the same length.

A **rectangle** is a parallelogram that has four right angles.

A **rhombus** is a parallelogram that has four sides with the same length.

A **square** is a parallelogram that has four right angles and four sides with the same length.

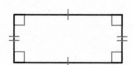 

A square is also a rectangle and a rhombus.

Example Classify the quadrilateral in as many ways as possible.

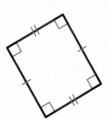

The quadrilateral has _____ right angles,

_____ pairs of parallel sides, and

_____ pairs of opposite sides with the same length.

So, it is a _____ and a _____.

Show and Grow   I can do it!

Classify the quadrilateral in as many ways as possible.

1.

2.

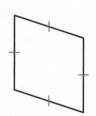

Name _____

Classify the quadrilateral in as many ways as possible.

3.

4.
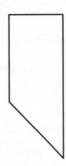

5.

6.

7. **MP Structure** The formula for the perimeter of a square with side lengths of s is $P = 4 \times s$. Can you use this formula to find the perimeter of any other type of quadrilateral? If so, name the type of quadrilateral.

8. **MP Structure** How many lines of symmetry can a parallelogram have?

9. **DIG DEEPER!** Write *All*, *Some*, or *No* for each statement.

_____ parallelograms are rectangles.

_____ squares are rectangles.

_____ trapezoids are parallelograms.

_____ rectangles are squares.

_____ trapezoids have four sides with the same length.

Think and Grow: Modeling Real Life

Example Two artists each want to paint an identical half of a painting, like the one shown. Classify the shape of the painting in as many ways as possible. Then identify and show how many different ways the artists can divide the painting, if any.

Classify the shape of the painting in as many ways as possible.

The painting has _____ sides,

_____ pairs of parallel sides,

_____ right angles, and

_____ sides with the same length.

So, it is a _____, a _____, and a _____.

Determine whether the painting has line symmetry. If so, find how many different ways the artists can divide the painting.

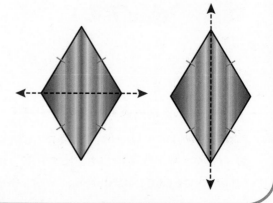

The rhombus-shaped painting has _____ lines of symmetry.

So, the artists can divide the painting _____ different ways.

Show and Grow   I can think deeper!

10. You and your friend each want to share an identical half of the tabletop. Classify the shape of the tabletop in as many ways as possible. Then identify and show how many different ways you and your friend can divide the tabletop, if any.

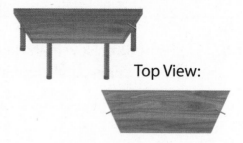

Top View:

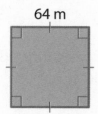

64 m

11. **DIG DEEPER!** A horse needs at least 4,046 square meters of pasture. Classify the shape of the pasture in as many ways as possible. Is the pasture large enough for the horse? Explain.

Name _____

Learning Target: Classify quadrilaterals.

Example Classify the quadrilateral in as many ways as possible.

The quadrilateral has __2__ pairs of parallel sides

and __4__ sides with the same length.

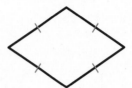

So, it is a _parallelogram_ and ___rhombus___ .

Classify the quadrilateral in as many ways as possible.

1.

2.

3.

4.

5.

6.

7.  **Structure** Your friend sorts the shapes into two different groups. How do you think she sorted? Where does the shape below belong? Explain.

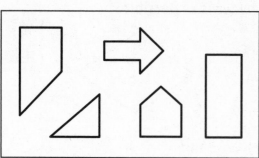

8. **Reasoning** All of the sides of an equilateral triangle have the same length. Is an equilateral triangle a rhombus? Explain.

9. **DIG DEEPER!** Within the star, trace at least two different examples of trapezoids and parallelograms. Explain how you found each quadrilateral.

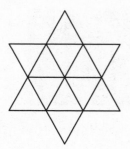

10. **Modeling Real Life** You and your friend each want to share an identical half of the whiteboard shown. Classify the shape of the whiteboard in as many ways as possible. Then identify and show how many different ways you and your friend can divide the whiteboard, if any.

11. Write $\frac{7}{10}$ as hundredths in fraction form and decimal form.

12. Write $\frac{50}{100}$ as tenths in fraction form and decimal form.

© Big Ideas Learning, LLC

Performance Task 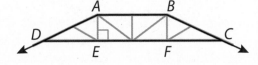 **14**

Roof trusses are wooden structures that support the roof of a building. They come in many different shapes and sizes.

1. The truss has exactly one pair of parallel sides.
   a. What polygon describes the shape of the truss?

....

   b. Does the truss have line symmetry? Explain.

....

   c. Name an acute angle, a right angle, and an obtuse angle.

....

   d. Name a ray.

_____

2. Most trusses are built in the shape of a triangle.
   a. Classify each triangle by its sides. Identify any lines of symmetry.

   _____   _____   _____   _____

....

   b. Why do you think roof trusses come in different shapes and sizes?

_____

3. You see a truss in the shape of an obtuse isosceles triangle. The perimeter of the triangle is 36 feet. The length of the side opposite the obtuse angle is 16 feet. What are the lengths of the other two sides?

_____

4. Draw a triangular roof truss that has line symmetry. Include a few support lines inside the truss. Classify your triangle by its sides. What types of angles are on the inside of the truss?

Pyramid Climb and Slide

Directions:

1. Players take turns spinning the spinner.
2. On your turn, move your counter to the next triangle that best matches your spin.
3. If you land at the bottom of a ladder, climb to the top of the ladder. If you land at the top of a slide, slide down to the bottom of the slide.
4. The first player to reach the top of the pyramid wins!

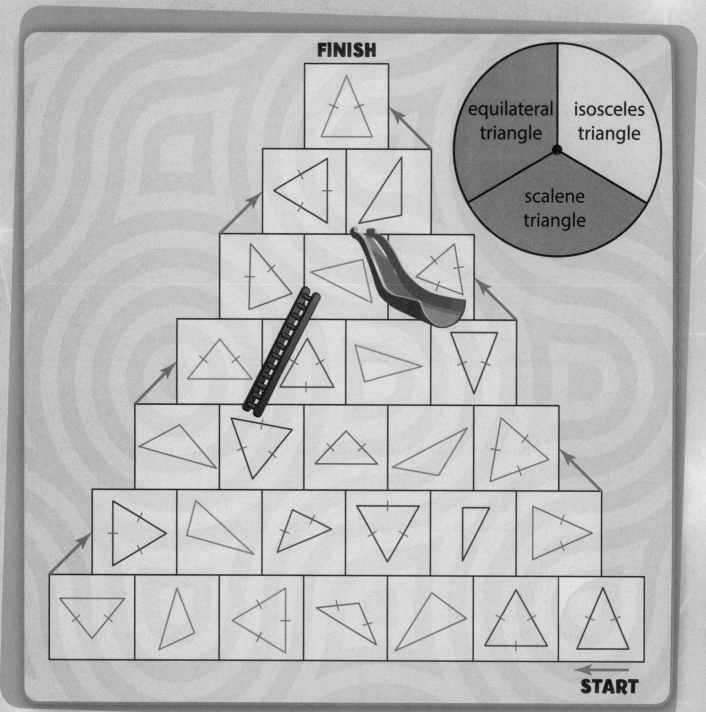

Name _____

Chapter Practice 14

14.1 Line Symmetry

Determine whether the line is a line of symmetry.

1.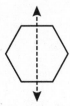

2.

3.

Determine whether the shape has line symmetry. Draw each line of symmetry.

4. **B**

5.

6.

7. **Modeling Real Life** Divide the parking lot shown into multiple sections using each of its lines of symmetry. When there are 4 cars in each section, how many cars are in the parking lot?

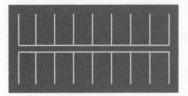

14.2 Draw Symmetric Shapes

8. One half of a shape and a line of symmetry are shown. Draw the rest of the shape.

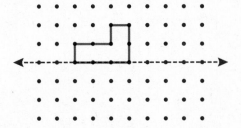

9. One half of a symmetric shape is shown. Draw the rest of the shape.

© Big Ideas Learning, LLC

Chapter 14

681

Classify Triangles by Sides

Classify the triangles by its sides.

10.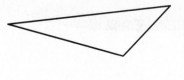

11.

12.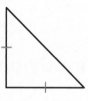

 **Classify Triangles by Angles**

Classify the triangle by its angles and its sides.

13.

14.

15.

16. Which One Doesn't Belong? Which triangle does *not* belong with the other three? Explain.

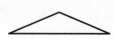

 Classify Quadrilaterals

Classify the quadrilateral in as many ways as possible.

17.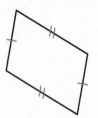

18.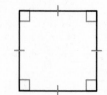

Cumulative Practice 1-14

1. What is the difference of 10 and $4\frac{7}{8}$?

Ⓐ $6\frac{7}{8}$　　　Ⓑ $14\frac{7}{8}$　　　Ⓒ $5\frac{1}{8}$　　　Ⓓ $7\frac{3}{8}$

---

2. Which letters have at least one line of symmetry?

☐ A　　　　☐ X　　　　☐ N

☐ W　　　　☐ Z　　　　☐ H

---

3. The table shows the amount of rain that falls in each city in 1 day. Which city has more rainfall than Detroit and less rainfall than Seattle?

Ⓐ Orlando　　　Ⓑ Chicago

Ⓒ Boston　　　Ⓓ None of the cities

City	Amount of Rain (centimeters)
Detroit	0.45
Chicago	0.72
Boston	1.55
Seattle	0.85
Orlando	0.96

---

4. Which shapes have four sides with the same length?

☐ rhombus　　　　　　☐ trapezoid

☐ square　　　　　　☐ equilateral triangle

---

5. A movie starts at 2:55 P.M. and ends at 4:45 P.M. How long was the movie?

Ⓐ 2 hours 30 minutes　　　Ⓑ 1 hour 50 minutes

Ⓒ 7 hours　　　　　　　　Ⓓ 1 hour 45 minutes

6. Which are equivalent to $3 \times \dfrac{5}{6}$?

☐ $\dfrac{5}{6} + \dfrac{5}{6} + \dfrac{5}{6}$ ☐ $(3 \times 5) \times \dfrac{1}{6}$

☐ $\dfrac{8}{6}$ ☐ $\dfrac{15}{6}$

---

7. The rectangle has a perimeter of 48 centimeters. What is the width of the rectangle?

(A) 33 cm   (B) 720 cm

(C) 18 cm   (D) 9 cm

w cm

15 cm

---

8. Which two lines appear to be parallel?

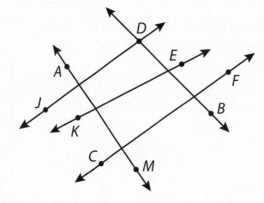

(A) $\overleftrightarrow{JD}$ and $\overleftrightarrow{CF}$ (B) $\overleftrightarrow{JD}$ and $\overleftrightarrow{AM}$

(C) $\overleftrightarrow{JD}$ and $\overleftrightarrow{KE}$ (D) $\overleftrightarrow{DB}$ and $\overleftrightarrow{AM}$

---

9. Your friend draws a triangle with side lengths of 10 centimeters, 12 centimeters, and 10 centimeters. What type of triangle did your friend draw?

(A) scalene   (B) equilateral

(C) isosceles   (D) equiangular

10. What is the quotient of 846 and 3?

    Ⓐ 282   Ⓑ 280

    Ⓒ 28   Ⓓ 2,538

---

11. Which rectangular dimensions have an area of 3,600 square miles?

    ☐ 72 miles long and 50 miles wide   ☐ 1,000 miles long and 800 miles wide

    ☐ 75 miles long and 48 miles wide   ☐ 80 miles long and 45 miles wide

---

12. The angle measures of a triangle are 57°, 60°, and 63°. How can you classify the triangle?

    Ⓐ right   Ⓑ obtuse

    Ⓒ equiangular   Ⓓ acute

---

13. Newton is walking on Path X that continues straight ahead. He turns onto Path Y.

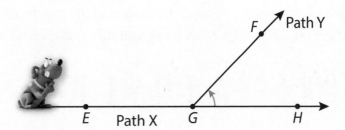

Using a protractor, which statement is true about ∠*FGH?*

    Ⓐ The angle is 45°, and is acute.   Ⓑ The angle is 45°, and is obtuse.

    Ⓒ The angle is 135°, and is obtuse.   Ⓓ The angle is 135°, and is acute.

14. You jump $3\frac{1}{2}$ feet. How far do you jump in inches?

---

15. Which of the following shows $\overrightarrow{DE}$?

Ⓐ
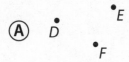

Ⓑ

Ⓒ
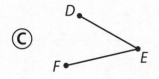

Ⓓ

---

16. A rectangular backyard has a perimeter of 280 feet. The length of the backyard is 75 feet. What is the area of the backyard?

Ⓐ 4,875 square feet

Ⓑ 825 square feet

Ⓒ 65 square feet

Ⓓ 140 square feet

---

17. Your friend makes a banner by taping the edges of 10 pieces of paper together. Each piece of paper is 28 centimeters long and 22 centimeters wide.

Think
Solve
Explain

CONGRATULATIONS!

Part A What is the length of the entire banner? Explain.

Part B Your friend wants to place ribbon along the outside of the entire banner. How much ribbon will she need?

In computer graphic design, polygons are connected at the vertices and edges to create a two-dimensional image that appears three-dimensional. This is called *polygon mesh*.

1. The elephant graphic is made from different polygons. Do the polygons have the same number of sides? Why do you think that is?

_____

2. Use the quadrilateral shown from the elephant graphic.

   a. Exactly one pair of sides are parallel. Classify the quadrilateral.

   ....

   b. Which two lines are parallel?

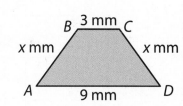

   ....

   c. Which angles are acute?

   ....

   d. The perimeter is 22 millimeters. Find the missing side lengths.

_____

3. There are many different triangles in the elephant graphic. Use the side lengths and angle measures to classify two of the triangles. Trace your triangles in the elephant graphic.

4. In a polygon mesh, each polygon is shaded differently to make the object appear more three-dimensional. In the drawing, two polygons still need to be shaded. Which one should be darker, the triangle or the quadrilateral? Why?

5. Triangle mesh is when a three-dimensional design is created using only triangles. The triangle mesh design below has line symmetry.

   a. Use the line of symmetry to finish the design.

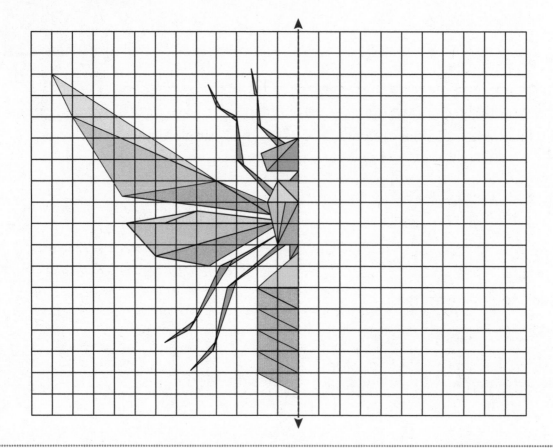

   b. Name two types of triangles you see in the design. Trace your triangles above. Explain.

6. Use the Internet or some other resource to find out more about polygon mesh and how it is used in graphic design. Write one thing that you learn.

Glossary

A

acute angle　[ángulo agudo]

An angle that is open less than a right angle

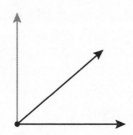

acute triangle　[triángulo acutángulo]

A triangle that has three acute angles

adjacent angles　[ángulos adyacentes]

Two angles that share a common side and a common vertex, but have no other points in common

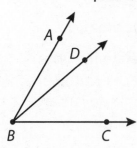

∠ABD and ∠DBC are adjacent angles.

angle　[ángulo]

Two rays or line segments that have a common endpoint

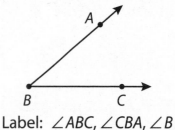

Label: ∠ABC, ∠CBA, ∠B

area　[área]

The amount of surface a figure covers

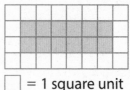

□ = 1 square unit

The area of the rectangle is 12 square units.

B

benchmark　[punto de referencia]

A commonly used number that you can use to compare other numbers

Examples: $\frac{1}{2}$, 1

common factor [factor común]

A factor that is shared by two or more given numbers

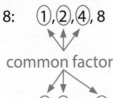

Factors of 8: ①, ②, ④, 8

common factors

Factors of 12: ①, ②, 3, ④, 6, 12

compatible numbers
[números compatibles]

Numbers that are easy to multiply and are close to the actual numbers

$$24 \times 31$$
$$\downarrow \qquad \downarrow$$
$$25 \times 30$$

complementary angles
[ángulos complementarios]

Two angles whose measures have a sum of 90°

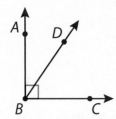

∠ABD and ∠DBC are complementary angles.

composite number
[número compuesto]

A whole number greater than 1 with more than two factors

27

The factors of 27 are 1, 3, 9, and 27.

---

cup (c) [taza (tz)]

A customary unit used to measure capacity

The capacity of the measuring cup is 1 cup.

decimal [decimal]

A number with one or more digits to the right of the decimal point

0.3

0.04

0.59

decimal fraction [fracción decimal]

A fraction with a denominator of 10 or 100

$$\frac{26}{100}$$

$$\frac{9}{10}$$

$$\frac{60}{100}$$

decimal point [punto decimal]

A symbol used to separate the ones place and the tenths place in numbers, and to separate the whole dollars and the cents in money

0.1 $5.06

decimal point

degree (°)   [grado (°)]

The unit used to measure angles

$$1° = \frac{1}{360} \text{ of a circle}$$

Distributive Property
[propiedad distributiva]

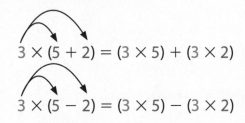

$$3 \times (5 + 2) = (3 \times 5) + (3 \times 2)$$

$$3 \times (5 - 2) = (3 \times 5) - (3 \times 2)$$

divisible   [divisible]

A number is divisible by another number when the quotient is a whole number and the remainder is 0.

$$48 \div 4 = 12 \text{ R0}$$

So, 48 is divisible by 4.

E

endpoints   [puntos extremos]

Points that represent the ends of a line segment or ray

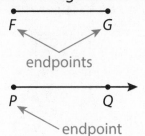

equiangular triangle
[triángulo equiángulo]

A triangle that has three angles with the same measure

equilateral triangle
[triángulo equilátero]

A triangle that has three sides with the same length

equivalent   [equivalente]

Having the same value

$$\frac{8}{8} = 1$$

$$3 = \frac{3}{1}$$

$$2 = \frac{4}{2} = \frac{6}{3}$$

equivalent decimals
[decimales equivalente]

Two or more decimals that have the same value

$$0.40 = 0.4$$

equivalent fractions
[fracciones equivalentes]

Two or more fractions that name
the same part of a whole

$$\frac{2}{3} = \frac{4}{6}$$

estimate   [estimación]

A number that is close to an exact number

$$8{,}195 + 9{,}726 = ?$$

Exact Sum: 17,921

Estimate: 18,000

 F

factor pair   [par de factores]

Two factors that, when multiplied,
result in a given product

factor pair

$$2 \times 4 = 8$$

factor   factor

2 and 4 are a factor pair for 8.

formula   [fórmula]

An equation that uses letters and numbers
to show how quantities are related

$$P = (2 \times \ell) + (2 \times w)$$

$$A = \ell \times w$$

 G

gallon (gal)   [galón (gal)]

A customary unit used to
measure capacity
There are 4 quarts in 1 gallon.

The capacity of the jug is 1 gallon.

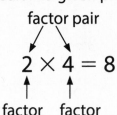 **H**

hundredth   [centésimo]

1 of 100 equal parts of a whole

one hundredth →

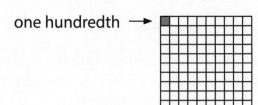

hundredths place
[posición de los centésimos]

The second place to the right of the
decimal point

0.01
↑
hundredths
place

I

intersecting lines [líneas secantes]

Lines that cross at exactly one point

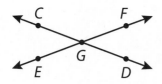

isosceles triangle [triángulo isósceles]

A triangle that has two sides with the same length

K

kilometer (km) [kilómetro (km)]

A metric unit used to measure length There are 1,000 meters in 1 kilometer.

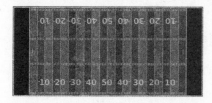

1 kilometer is about the length of 10 football fields including the end zones.

L

line [línea]

A straight path of points that goes on without end in both directions

Label: $\overleftrightarrow{CD}, \overleftrightarrow{DC}$

line of symmetry [línea de simetría]

A fold line that divides a shape into two parts that match exactly

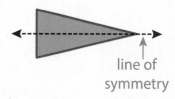

line of symmetry

line segment [segmento lineal]

A part of a line that includes two endpoints and all of the points between them

Label: $\overline{FG}, \overline{GF}$

line symmetry [simetría lineal]

The symmetry that a shape has when it can be folded on a line so that two parts match exactly

mile (mi)   [milla (mi)]

A customary unit used to measure length
There are 1,760 yards in 1 mile.

When walking briskly, you can walk
1 mile in about 20 minutes.

millimeter (mm)   [milímetro (mm)]

A metric unit used to measure length

1 millimeter

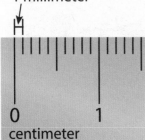

There are
10 millimeters in
1 centimeter.

centimeter

mixed number   [número mixto]

Represents the sum of a whole number
and a fraction less than 1

Examples: $2\frac{1}{3}, 1\frac{4}{5}, 5\frac{3}{10}$

multiple   [múltiplo]

The product of a number and any other
counting number

$1 \times 4 = 4$
$2 \times 4 = 8$
$3 \times 4 = 12$
$4 \times 4 = 16$

↑
multiples of 4

obtuse angle   [ángulo obtuso]

An angle that is open more than a right
angle and less than a straight angle

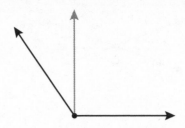

obtuse triangle
[tríangulo obtusángulo]

A triangle that has one obtuse angle

ones period   [período de las unidades]

The first period in a number

Thousands Period			Ones Period		
Hundreds	Tens	Ones	Hundreds	Tens	Ones
8	1	5,	7	9	6

ounce (oz)   [onza (oz)]

A customary unit used to measure weight

A slice of bread weighs about 1 ounce.

P

parallel lines [líneas paralelas]

Lines that never intersect

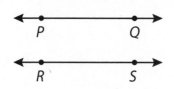

Label: $\overleftrightarrow{PQ} \parallel \overleftrightarrow{RS}$

parallelogram [paralelogramo]

A quadrilateral that has two pairs of parallel sides

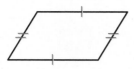

partial products [productos parciales]

The products found by breaking apart a factor into ones, tens, hundreds, and so on, and multiplying each of these by the other factor

$$\begin{array}{r} 39 \\ \times 7 \\ \hline \end{array}$$

partial products $\Big\langle$ $\boxed{63}$ 7×9

$+ \boxed{210}$ 7×30

$\overline{273}$

partial quotients [cocientes parciales]

A division strategy in which quotients are found in parts until the remainder is less than the divisor

partial quotients

$$\begin{array}{r} 6)\overline{84} \\ -60 = 6 \times \boxed{10} \quad 10 \\ \hline 24 \\ -24 = 6 \times \boxed{4} \quad +4 \\ \hline 0 \qquad\qquad 14 \end{array}$$

perimeter [perímetro]

The distance around a figure

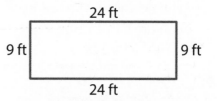

The perimeter is 66 feet.

period [período]

Each group of three digits separated by commas in a multi-digit number

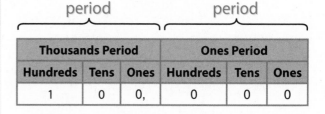

period			period		
Thousands Period			Ones Period		
Hundreds	Tens	Ones	Hundreds	Tens	Ones
1	0	0,	0	0	0

perpendicular lines [líneas perpendiculares]

Lines that intersect to form four right angles

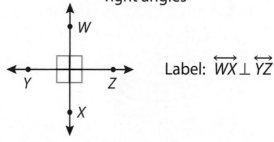

Label: $\overleftrightarrow{WX} \perp \overleftrightarrow{YZ}$

pint (pt) [pinta (pt)]

A customary unit used to measure capacity
There are 2 cups in 1 pint.

The capacity of the carton is 1 pint.

A7

place value chart
[gráfico de valor posicional]

A chart that shows the value of
each digit in a number

Thousands Period			Ones Period		
Hundreds	Tens	Ones	Hundreds	Tens	Ones
2	8	5,	7	4	3

---

point   **[punto]**

An exact location in space

A
●

Label: point *A*

---

pound (lb)   **[libra (lb)]**

A customary unit used to measure weight
There are 16 ounces in 1 pound.

A loaf of bread weighs about 1 pound.

---

prime number   **[número primo]**

A number greater than 1 with exactly
two factors, 1 and itself

11
The factors of 11 are 1 and 11.

---

protractor   **[transportador]**

A tool for measuring and drawing angles

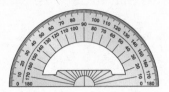

Q

quart (qt)   **[cuarto de galón (qt)]**

A customary unit used to
measure capacity
There are 2 pints in 1 quart.

The capacity of the carton is 1 quart.

R

ray   **[semirrecta]**

A part of a line that has one endpoint and
goes on without end in one direction

P   *Q*

Label: $\overrightarrow{PQ}$

---

rectangle   **[rectángulo]**

A parallelogram that has four right angles

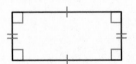

remainder [resto]

The amount left over when a number cannot be divided evenly

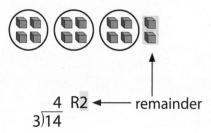

$$3\overline{)14}$$ = 4 R2 ← remainder

rhombus [rombo]

A parallelogram that has four sides with the same length

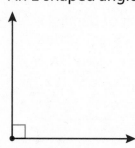

right angle [ángulo recto]

An L-shaped angle

right triangle
[triángulo rectángulo]

A triangle that has one right angle

rule [regla]

Tells how numbers or shapes in a pattern are related

Rule: Add 3.
3, 6, 9, 12, 15, 18, 21, 24, . . .

Rule: triangle, hexagon, square, rhombus

S

scalene triangle [triángulo escaleno]

A triangle that has no sides with the same length

second (sec) [segundo (seg)]

A unit of time

1 second

There are 60 seconds in 1 minute.

square [cuadrado]

A parallelogram that has four right angles and four sides with the same length

straight angle   [ángulo llano]

An angle that forms a straight line

---

supplementary angles
[ángulos suplementarios]

Two angles whose measures
have a sum of 180°

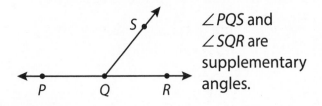

∠PQS and
∠SQR are
supplementary
angles.

---

tenth   [décimo]

1 of 10 equal parts of a whole

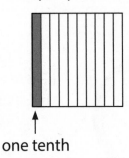

one tenth

---

tenths place
[posición de los décimos]

The first place to the right of the
decimal point

0.1

tenths
place

---

thousands period
[período de las milésimas]

The period after the ones period
in a number

Thousands Period			Ones Period		
Hundreds	Tens	Ones	Hundreds	Tens	Ones
8	1	5,	7	9	6

---

ton (T)   [tonelada (T)]

A customary unit used to measure weight
There are 2,000 pounds in 1 ton.

A small compact car weighs about 1 ton.

---

trapezoid   [trapecio]

A quadrilateral that has exactly one
pair of parallel sides

---

unit fraction   [fracción unitaria]

Represents one equal part of a whole

Examples:

$\dfrac{1}{2}$ $\dfrac{1}{5}$

A10

vertex   [vértice]

The endpoint at which two rays or line segments of an angle meet

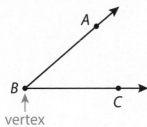

vertex

Index

using models to find, 261–266

generating equivalent fractions using, 317–322

using models to find quotients and remainders in, 211–216

of money amounts, 481–486

of multi-digit numbers, by one-digit numbers, 235–240

by one-digit numbers, 241–246

    multi-digit numbers, 235–240

    tens, hundreds, or thousands, 199–204

    two-digit numbers, 229–234

using partial quotients, 217–222

    with remainders, 223–228

patterns in, 286–290

using place value

    in dividing by one-digit numbers, 241–246

    multi-digit numbers by one-digit numbers, 235–240

    tens, hundreds, and thousands, 199–204

    two-digit numbers by one-digit numbers, 229–234

of prime numbers, 279–284

of two-digit numbers, by one-digit numbers, 229–234

word problems solved using, 247–252

Division facts

to divide by tens, hundreds, or thousands, 200

to estimate quotients, 205–210

Dollar(s)

amounts in fractions and decimals, 475–480

operations with, 481–486

Dollar sign, 476

Drawing

angles, 599–604, 623–628

intersecting, parallel, and perpendicular lines, 605–610

points, lines, and rays, 593–598

symmetric shapes, 655–660

E

Elapsed time

measuring on number line, 538, 540

solving word problems involving, 537–542

ELL Support, *In every lesson. For example, see:* T-2, T-87, T-173, T-260, T-323, T-445, T-587, T-679

Endpoints

definition of, 594

vertices as, 600

Equal groups, remainders in division into, 211–216

Equiangular triangles

classifying, 668–672

definition of, 668

Equilateral triangles

classifying, 662–666, 668

definition of, 662

Equivalent, definition of, 306

Equivalent decimals

comparing, 464

definition of, 458

Equivalent fractions

adding decimal fractions and decimals using, 469–474

adding mixed numbers using, 383–388

comparing fractions using, 329–334

definition of, 306

generating

    by dividing, 317–322

    by multiplying, 311–316

modeling and writing, 305–310

on number line, 306–310, 312, 319, 321

writing tenths and hundredths as, 457–462

Equivalent measurements

capacity

    in customary units, 519–524

    in metric units, 501–506

Index

Index

for finding quotients and remainders, 211–216

for subtracting fractions, 365–370

Modeling

of Distributive Property, 87–92

of equivalent fractions, 305–310

of fractions and mixed numbers, 377–382

Modeling Real Life, *In every lesson. For example, see:* 8, 38, 74, 148, 204, 266, 310, 352, 414, 450

Money

amounts in fractions and decimals, 475–480

operations with, 481–486

Months

definition of, 532

equivalent time in, 532–536

in mixed measures, 545

More, how many (comparison), 69–74

Multi-digit numbers

adding, 39–44

strategies for, 51–56

comparing, 15–20

dividing by one-digit numbers, 235–240

identifying values of digits in, 3–8

multiplying by one-digit numbers, 111–116

reading and writing, 9–14

rounding, using place value, 21–26

standard, word, and expanded forms of, 10–14

subtracting, 45–49

strategies for, 51–56

Multiple Representations, *Throughout. For example, see:* 4, 52, 144, 162, 180, 330, 356, 659

Multiples

of 10, multiplication by, 143–148

using number line, 144

using place value, 75–80, 143–148

using properties, 143–148

definition of, 274

relationship between factors and, 273–278

of unit fractions

on number line, 410, 413, 417

writing fractions as, 409–414

writing multiples of fractions as, 415–420

Multiplication

in area formula, 569–574

using area models

Distributive Property and, 87–98, 161–166

expanded form and, 93–98

place value and, 99

two-digit numbers, 155–166, 179, 180

Associative Property of, 117–122

definition of, 118

multiples of fractions and, 416, 418

multiplying by tens using, 143–148

multiplying fractions by whole numbers using, 422, 425

multiplying two-digit numbers using, 179, 183

Commutative Property of, 70, 117–122

comparing numbers using, 69–74

Distributive Property of, 87–92, 117–122

area models with, 87–98, 161–166

definition of, 88, 118

expanded form and, 93–98

finding perimeter with, 568

multiplying two-digit numbers with, 161–166, 179, 183

multiplying whole numbers and mixed numbers using, 427–432

estimating products in, 149–154

choosing expression for, 149

using compatible numbers, 149–154

using rounding, 81–86, 149–154

of fractions

fractions and whole numbers, 421–426

whole numbers and mixed numbers, 427–432

generating equivalent fractions using, 311–316

letters representing unknown numbers
in, 123–128, 185–190
of money amounts, 481–486
of multi-digit numbers, by one-digit
numbers, 111–116
by multiples of 10, 143–148
using number line, 144
using place value, 75–80, 143–148
using properties, 143–148
on number line, by multiples of 10, 144
using partial products, 99–104
with area models, 155–166, 179, 180
multi-digit numbers by one-digit
numbers, 111–116
two-digit numbers, 167–172, 179, 180
two-digit numbers by one-digit
numbers, 105–110
patterns in, 286–290
in perimeter formula, 563–568
using place value
by multiples of 10, 75–80, 143–148
with partial products, 99–104
by tens, hundreds, or thousands,
75–80
two-digit numbers, 167–172, 179, 180
using properties, 117–122
of two-digit numbers, 173–178
using area models, 155–166, 179, 180
using Associative Property, 179, 183
using Distributive Property, 161–166,
179, 183
estimating products of, 149–154
by multiples of 10, 143–148
by one-digit numbers, 105–110
using partial products, 167–172,
179, 180
using place value, 167–172, 179, 180
practicing strategies of, 179–184
using regrouping, 174, 177–180
word problems solved using, 185–190
word problems solved using
comparisons, 69–74
multi-step, 123–128, 185–190
with two-digit numbers, 185–190

Naming
angles, 599–604
lines, line segments, and rays, 593–598
Number(s), *See specific types of numbers*
Number line
adding on, 53, 55
decimal fractions and decimals, 469
fractions, 348, 351
comparing decimals using, 464–465, 467
comparing fractions using, 324, 327
elapsed time on, 538, 540
finding equivalent fractions using,
306–310, 312, 319, 321
mixed numbers on, 378, 380, 382
multiples of unit fractions on, 410, 413,
417
multiplying on, by multiples of 10, 144,
148
plotting decimals and fractions on, 457,
459, 461
rounding number on, 22, 26
subtracting on, 52
fractions, 366, 369, 372
weight on, 513
Number patterns
creating and describing, 285–290
definition of, 286
Number Sense, *Throughout. For example, see:*
8, 38, 71, 169, 204, 272, 328, 417,
453, 497
Numerators
adding, in fractions with like
denominator, 359–364
in comparing fractions, 329–334
in generating equivalent fractions
by dividing, 317–322
by multiplying, 311–316
multiplying by whole numbers, 421–426
subtracting, in fractions with like
denominator, 371–376

Index

Patterns
number, 285–290
shape, 291–296

Patterns, *Throughout. For example, see:* 76, 80, 184, 287, 322, 417, 474, 500

Pennies, as hundredths, 451, 476

Pentagons, line symmetry/line of symmetry in, 650

Performance Task, *In every chapter. For example, see:* 27, 63, 129, 191, 253, 297, 335, 401, 439, 487

Perimeter
definition of, 564
of rectangles
finding unknown measures from given, 575–580
formula for, 563–568
solving word problems involving, 581–586

Period
definition of, 4
in reading and writing multi-digit numbers, 9–14
in understanding place value, 4–8

Perpendicular lines
definition of, 606
identifying and drawing, 605–610
symbol for, 606, 609

Pints (pt)
definition of, 520
equivalent capacity in, 519–524
in mixed measures, 545, 546, 548

Place value
adding multi-digit numbers using, 39–44
adding partial sums using, 51, 52
comparing numbers using, 15–20
division using
multi-digit numbers by one-digit numbers, 235–240
by one-digit numbers, 241–246
tens, hundreds, and thousands, 199–204
two-digit numbers by one-digit numbers, 229–234

estimating sums and differences using, 33–38
groups (periods) of, 4
lining up addition problem using, 39–44
lining up subtraction problem using, 45–50
multiplication using
by multiples of 10, 75–80, 143–148
with partial products, 99–104
by tens, hundreds, or thousands, 75–80
two-digit numbers, 167–172, 179, 180
reading and writing multi-digit numbers using, 9–14
rounding multi-digit numbers using, 21–26
understanding, 3–8

Place value charts
comparing decimals on, 464, 466, 467
comparing numbers on, 15–20
definition of, 4
extending
to include hundredths, 452, 455
to include tenths, 446, 449
identifying value of digits on, 4–8
using to read and write numbers, 10–14

Platform scale, for weighing, 513

Points
definition of, 594
identifying, drawing, and naming, 593–598

Polygon mesh, 687, 688

Pounds (lb)
definition of, 514
equivalent weight in, 513–518
in mixed measures, 544–547

Precision, *Throughout. For example, see:* 57, 74, 190, 355, 462, 481, 509, 553, 625, 654

Prime numbers
definition of, 280
identifying, 279–284

Problem solving, *See* Word problems

Problem Solving Plan, *Throughout. For example, see:* 58, 124, 186, 248, 396, 434, 538

Products, *See also* Multiplication
    estimating, 149–154
        choosing expression for, 149
        using compatible numbers, 149–154
        using rounding, 81–86, 149–154
    partial (*See* Partial products)
    unknown, letter representing, 123–128, 185–190

Protractor
    definition of, 624
    finding unknown angle measures with, 635–640
    measuring and adding angles with, 629–634
    measuring and drawing angles with, 623–628

Q

Quadrilaterals, classifying, 673–678
Quarts (qt)
    definition of, 520
    equivalent capacity in, 519–524
    in mixed measures, 545–548
Quotients, *See also* Division
    definition of, 218
    estimating, 205–210
    using models to find, 211–216
    partial (*See* Partial quotients)
    writing zero in, 242, 245

R

Rays
    definition of, 594
    identifying, drawing, and naming, 593–598
Reading, *Throughout. For example, see:* T-97, T-215, T-289, T-315, T-523
Reading multi-digit numbers, 9–14
Real World, *See* Modeling Real Life

Reasoning, *Throughout. For example, see:* 8, 33, 74, 145, 205, 272, 305, 364, 409, 457

Rectangles
    area of
        finding unknown measures from given, 575–580
        formula for, 569–574
        solving word problems involving, 581–586
    classifying, 674–678
    definition of, 674
    finding factor pairs using, 261–266
    line symmetry/line of symmetry in, 650, 652, 654
    perimeter of
        finding unknown measures from given, 575–580
        formula for, 563–568
        solving word problems involving, 581–586

Regrouping
    in adding multi-digit numbers, 39–44
    in dividing
        to find quotient and remainder, 212
        multi-digit numbers by one-digit numbers, 236–240
        by one-digit numbers, 241–246
        two-digit numbers by one-digit numbers, 230–234
    in multiplying
        multi-digit numbers by one-digit numbers, 111–116
        by multiples of 10, 144
        two-digit numbers, 174, 177–180
        two-digit numbers by one-digit numbers, 105–110
    in subtracting multi-digit numbers, 45–50
Remainders
    definition of, 212
    in dividing by one-digit numbers, 241–246

in dividing multi-digit numbers by
 one-digit numbers, 235–240
in dividing two-digit numbers by
 one-digit numbers, 229–234
using models to find, 211–216
using partial quotients with, 223–228

Repeated Reasoning, 3, 75, 143, 199, 347,
 365, 617

Response to Intervention, *Throughout. For
 example, see:* T-1B, T-43, T-141B,
 T-227, T-303B, T-443B, T-493B, T-584

Review & Refresh, *In every lesson. For
 example, see:* 8, 38, 178, 204, 266,
 310, 352, 414, 450, 500

Rhombus
classifying, 674–678
definition of, 674
lines of symmetry in, 676
pattern blocks, measuring angles using,
 617, 618

Right angles
classifying quadrilaterals by, 673–678
classifying triangles by, 667–672
complementary angles of, 636–640
definition of, 600
identifying, drawing, and naming,
 600–604
measuring
 using degrees, 612–616
 using pattern blocks, 617–622

Right triangles
classifying, 668–672
definition of, 668

Rokkaku (Japanese kite), symmetry of, 658

Rounding numbers
estimating products with, 81–86, 149–154
estimating sums and differences with,
 33–38
multi-digit, using place value, 21–26

Rule(s)
definition of, 286
divisibility, 268, 274, 280, 283
number pattern, 286–290

S

Scaffolding Instruction, *In every lesson. For
 example, see:* T-5, T-71, T-187, T-287,
 T-331, T-417, T-545, T-631

Scale(s)
of drawing angles, 624
of line plot, 526
for measuring mass, 501
for measuring weight, 513

Scalene triangles
classifying, 662–666
definition of, 662

Seconds (sec)
definition of, 532
equivalent time in, 531–536
measuring elapsed time in, 538, 541, 542
in mixed measures, 545, 547

Shape patterns, creating and describing,
 291–296

Shapes, two-dimensional
classifying quadrilaterals, 673–678
classifying triangles
 by angles, 667–672
 by sides, 661–666, 668
line symmetry in, 649–654, 676
symmetric
 definition of, 656
 drawing, 655–660

Show and Grow, *In every lesson. For example,
 see:* 4, 34, 70, 144, 200, 262, 306,
 348, 410, 446

Side lengths
classifying quadrilaterals by, 673–678
classifying triangles by, 661–666, 668
finding area from, 569–574
finding perimeter from, 563–568
of rectangles, finding unknown, 575–580

Sides, parallel, 674–678

Squares
classifying, 674–678
definition of, 674
line symmetry/lines of symmetry in, 654

Index

© Big Ideas Learning, LLC

multi-step, 123–128, 185–190
with two-digit numbers, 185–190
with perimeter and area, 581–586
Writing, *Throughout. For example, see:* 5, 35,
71, 148, 222, 263, 313, 349, 426, 447

Yards
definition of, 508
equivalent length in, 507–512
finding area in, 570, 572, 573
finding perimeter in, 565–568
in mixed measures, 545, 547

Years
definition of, 532
equivalent time in, 532, 534, 536
in mixed measures, 545
You Be the Teacher, *Throughout. For example,
see:* 5, 41, 83, 145, 201, 266, 307,
352, 423, 456

Zero (0)
patterns, in multiplying by tens, 143–148
writing in quotient, 242, 245

Reference Sheet

Symbols

×	multiply	°	degree(s)	$\overleftrightarrow{AB}$	line AB
÷	divide	⊥	is perpendicular to	$\overrightarrow{AB}$	ray AB
=	equals	∥	is parallel to	$\overline{AB}$	line segment AB
>	greater than	A.	point A	$\angle ABC$	angle ABC
<	less than				

Money

¢ cent or cents

$ dollar or dollars

1 penny = 1¢ or $0.01

1 nickel = 5¢ or $0.05

1 dime = 10¢ or $0.10

1 quarter = 25¢ or $0.25

1 dollar ($) = 100¢ or $1.00

Length

Metric

1 centimeter (cm) = 10 millimeters (mm)

1 meter (m) = 100 centimeters

1 kilometer (km) = 1,000 meters

Customary

1 foot (ft) = 12 inches (in.)

1 yard (yd) = 3 feet

1 mile (mi) = 1,760 yards

Mass

 1 kilogram (kg) = 1,000 grams (g)

Weight

 1 pound (lb) = 16 ounces (oz)

1 ton (T) = 2,000 pounds

Capacity

Metric

 1 liter (L) = 1,000 milliliters (mL)

Customary

 1 pint (pt) = 2 cups (c)

1 quart (qt) = 2 pints

 1 gallon (gal) = 4 quarts

Reference Sheet

Time

1 second

1 minute (min) = 60 seconds (sec)	1 week (wk) = 7 days
1 hour (h) = 60 minutes	1 year (yr) = 12 months (mo)
1 day (d) = 24 hours	1 year = 52 weeks

Area and Perimeter

Area of a rectangle

$$A = \ell \times w$$

Perimeter of a rectangle

$$P = (2 \times \ell) + (2 \times w)$$

length (ℓ)

width (w)

Perimeter of a polygon

$$P = \text{sum of lengths of sides}$$

Angles

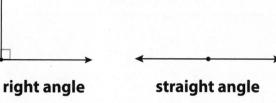

right angle   **straight angle**

acute angle   **obtuse angle**

Triangles

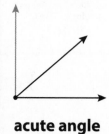

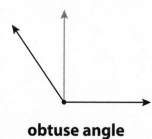

equilateral triangle   **isosceles triangle**   **acute triangle**   **obtuse triangle**

scalene triangle   **right triangle**   **equiangular triangle**

Quadrilaterals

 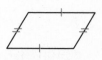 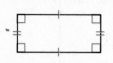

trapezoid   **parallelogram**   **rectangle**   **rhombus**   **square**

A34

Credits

Front matter

i Brazhnykov Andriy /Shutterstock.com; **vii** Steve Debenport/E+/Getty Images

Chapter 1

1 fbxx/iStock/Getty Images Plus; **6** SSSCCC/Shutterstock.com; **8** DanielPrudek/iStock/Getty Images Plus; **11** 3DMI/Shutterstock.com; **12** Lagutkin Alexey/Shutterstock.com; **17** adventtr/iStock/Getty Images Plus; Good Life Studio/E+/Getty Images Plus; **18** Ron_Thomas/E+/Getty Images; **20** ABIDAL/iStock/Getty Images Plus; **24** Rawpixel/iStock/Getty Images Plus; **26** Maren Winter/iStock/Getty Images Plus

Chapter 2

31 SeanPavonePhoto/iStock/Getty Images Plus; **36** *top* grimgram/iStock/Getty Images Plus; Triduza Studio/Shutterstock.com; *bottom* shihina/iStock/Getty Images Plus; **38** ciud/iStock/Getty Images Plus; **41** ET-ARTWORKS/iStock/Getty Images Plus, irin717/iStock/Getty Images Plus; **42** rmbarricarte/iStock/Getty Images Plus; **44** *left* Ann W. Kosche/Shutterstock.com; *right* romakoma/Shutterstock.com; **47** efks/iStock /Getty Images Plus; **48** *left* Rawpixel/iStock/Getty Images Plus; *right* Vladimiroquai/iStock/Getty Images Plus; **50** sndr/E+/Getty Images; **54** *top* vchal/iStock/Getty Images Plus; *Exercise 14* vchal/iStock/Getty Images Plus; *bottom* vchal/iStock/Getty Images Plus; **56** SteffenHuebner/iStock/Getty Images Plus; **59** *top* Brberrys/Shutterstock.com; *bottom* anankkml/iStock/Getty Images Plus; **62** Stubblefield Photography/Shutterstock.com; Todor Rusinov/Shutterstock.com

Chapter 3

67 franckreporter/iStock/Getty Images Plus; **71** Kikkerdirk/iStock/Getty Images Plus; **72** *right* Avesun/iStock/Getty Images Plus; *left* GaryAlvis/E+/Getty Images; **74** *left* catinsyrup/iStock/Getty Images Plus; *right* mphillips007/iStock/Getty Images Plus; **77** malerapaso/E+/Getty Images; **78** *top* k_samurkas/iStock/Getty Images Plus; *bottom* Tempusfugit/iStock/Getty Images Plus; **81** Andy445/E+/Getty Images; Matt Benoit/Shutterstock.com; **83** scanrail/iStock/Getty Images Plus; **84** pictafolio/E+/Getty Images; **90** *right* luminis/iStock/Getty Images Plus; *left* neuson11/iStock/Getty Images Plus; **92** *Exercise 10* AdamParent/iStock/Getty Images Plus; *Exercise 11* cynoclub/iStock/Getty Images Plus; **96** *top* Goddard_Photography/iStock/Getty Images Plus; *bottom* thawats/iStock/Getty Images Plus; **98** *top* CathyKeifer/iStock/Getty Images Plus; *bottom* Steve Collender/Shutterstock.com; **102** *top* lorcel/iStock/Getty Images Plus; *bottom* W6/iStock/Getty Images Plus; **104** *Exercise 12* vencavolrab/iStock/Getty Images Plus; *Exercise 13* adogslifephoto/iStock/Getty Images Plus; **108** *top* Ververidis Vasilis/Shutterstock.com; *bottom left* YinYang/iStock/Getty Images Plus; *bottom right* filrom/iStock/Getty Images Plus, Vereshchagin Dmitry/Shutterstock.com; **110** *Exercise 15* ID1974/Shutterstock.com; *Exercise 16* Nerthuz /Shutterstock.com; **113** paylessimages/iStock/Getty Images Plus; **114** *top right* leksele/iStock/Getty Images Plus; David Osborn/Shutterstock.com; *Exercise 18* itographer/E+/Getty Images; IPGGutenbergUKLtd/iStock/Getty Images Plus; **120** *top* Carso80/iStock Editorial/Getty Images Plus; *center* D3Damon/iStock/Getty Images Plus; *bottom* Iakov Filimonov/Shutterstock.com; 4kodiak/iStock Unreleased/Getty Images Plus; **122** *left* 4kodiak/iStock Unreleased/Getty Images Plus; *right* Aerotoons/DigitalVision Vectors/Getty Images; **123** Mirko Rosenau/Shutterstock.com; **125** *top left* GlobalP/iStock/Getty Images Plus; *top right* Antagain/iStock/Getty Images Plus; *bottom* roberthyrons/iStock/Getty Images Plus; **126** PeopleImages/E+/Getty Images; **128** kropic1/Shutterstock.com, ©iStockphoto.com/Chris Schmidt, ©iStockphoto.com/Jane norton; **129** *top* Maxiphoto/iStock/Getty Images Plus; *bottom* dibrova/iStock/Getty Images Plus; **130** mocoo/iStock/Getty Images Plus; ONYXprj/iStock/Getty Images Plus; Sylphe_7/iStock/Getty Images Plus; **134** magnez2/iStock Unreleased/Getty Images Plus; **136** popovaphoto/iStock/Getty Images Plus; **139** *top* TimBoers/iStock/Getty Images Plus; *bottom* Nielskliim/Shutterstock.com; **140** Wiese_Harald/iStock/Getty Images Plus

Chapter 4

141 Liufuyu/iStock/Getty Images Plus; **145** JuSun/iStock/Getty Images Plus; **146** VStock/Alamy Stock Photo; **148** Steve Collender /Shutterstock.com; **152** GlobalP/iStock/Getty Images Plus; **157** bjdlzx/iStock/Getty Images Plus; **158** *top* spanteldotru/E+/Getty Images; *bottom* AlbertoRoura/iStock Editorial/Getty Images Plus; **160** mipan/iStock/Getty Images Plus; **164** *top* bortonia/DigitalVision Vectors/Getty Images; *bottom* artisteer/iStock/Getty Images Plus, vectorloop/DigitalVision Vectors/Getty Images; **166** Thor Jorgen Udvang /Shutterstock.com; **169** GlobalP/iStock/Getty Images Plus; **170** *top* martinhosmart/iStock/Getty Images Plus; *Exercise 13* ianmcdonnell/E+/Getty Images; **176** *top* ChrisGorgio/iStock/Getty Images Plus; *Exercise 13 right* Konstantin G/Shutterstock.com; *Exercise 13 left* Triduza/iStock/Getty Images Plus; *bottom left* John_Kasawa/iStock/Getty Images Plus; **178** leezsnow/iStock/Getty Images Plus; **182** *top* Isaac74/iStock Editorial/Getty Images Plus; *bottom* breckeni/E+/Getty Images; **184** Jamesmcq24/E+/Getty Images; **185** Blade_kostas/iStock/Getty Images Plus; **186** tanyasharkeyphotography/iStock/Getty Images Plus; **187** *Exercise 4* creatOR76/Shutterstock.com; *Exercise 6* ZU_09/DigitalVision Vectors/Getty Images; **188** THEPALMER/E+/Getty Images; **189** *top* macrovector/iStock/Getty Images Plus; *bottom* RelaxFoto.de/E+/Getty Images; **190** *Exercise 6* filo/DigitalVision Vectors/Getty Images; *bottom* Aun Photographer/Shutterstock.com; **191** vladru/iStock/Getty Images Plus; **196** *Exercise 45* Believe_In_Me/iStock/Getty Images Plus; *Exercise 46* BrianAJackson/iStock/Getty Images Plus

Chapter 5

197 BanksPhotos/iStock/Getty Images Plus; **201** Grigorenko/iStock/Getty Images Plus; **202** *top* skynesher/E+/Getty Images; *bottom* quavondo/iStock/Getty Images Plus; **204** GlobalP/iStock/Getty Images Plus; **207** mar1koff/iStock/Getty Images Plus; **208** *top* Antonio V. Oquias /Shutterstock.com; *bottom* dageldog/iStock/Getty Images Plus; **210** *top* Twoellis/iStock/Getty Images Plus; *Exercise 10 left* ahirao_photo/iStock/Getty Images Plus; *Exercise 10 right* mtruchon/iStock/Getty Images Plus; **214** *top* Peter Hermus/iStock/Getty Images Plus; *bottom* kroach/iStock/Getty Images Plus; **216** duckycards/E+/Getty Images; **220** *top* Valerie Loiseleux/iStock/Getty Images Plus; *bottom* kali9/Vetta/Getty Images; **222** cynoclub/iStock/Getty Images Plus; **225** FatCamera/E+/Getty Images; **226** *top* FatCamera/E+/Getty Images; *Exercise 18* ONYXprj/iStock/Getty Images Plus; **228** Mathisa_s/iStock/Getty Images Plus; **232** *top* Voren1/iStock/Getty Images Plus; *Exercise 18* Goce Risteski/Hemera/Getty Images; **234** *top* sarent/iStock/Getty Images Plus; *Exercise 13* tashka2000/iStock/Getty Images Plus; **237** ziherMP/iStock/Getty Images Plus; **238** *top* CTRPhotos/iStock Editorial/Getty Images Plus; *bottom* sudok1/iStock/Getty Images Plus; **240** *top* Cgissemann/iStock/Getty Images Plus; *Exercise 15* WildDoc/iStock Unreleased/Getty Images; **243** humonia/iStock/Getty Images Plus; **244** McIninch/iStock/Getty Images Plus; **246** aluxum/iStock/Getty Images Plus; **247** kaanates/iStock/Getty Images Plus; **248** artplay711/iStock/Getty Images Plus; **249** *top* Monkeybusinessimages/iStock/Getty Images Plus; *bottom* Onandter_sean/iStock/Getty Images Plus; **250** AdamRadosavljevic/iStock/Getty Images Plus; **251** *left* AndreaAstes/iStock/Getty Images Plus; *right* OlegAlbinsky/iStock/Getty Images Plus; **252** *top* EdnaM/iStock/Getty Images Plus; *bottom* USO/iStock/Getty Images Plus; **253** Werner Otto/Alamy Stock Photo; **256** vladimir_n/iStock/Getty Images Plus; **258** shark_749/iStock/Getty Images Plus

Chapter 6

259 monkeybusinessimages/iStock/Getty Images Plus; **264** *top right* crossbrain66/E+/Getty Images, karandaev/iStock/Getty Images Plus; *Exercise 15* SeaHorseTwo/iStock/Getty Images Plus; **266** mipan/iStock/Getty Images Plus; **270** ivanmateev/iStock/Getty Images Plus; **272** Diana Taliun/iStock./Getty Images Plus; **276** *top* Balkonsky/Shutterstock.com; *bottom* pagadesign/E+/Getty Images; **282** *top* BruceBlock/iStock/Getty Images Plus; *bottom* brozova/iStock/Getty Images Plus; **284** kutaytanir/E+/Getty Images; **288** *top* nojustice/E+/Getty Images; *bottom* myistock88/iStock/Getty Images Plus; **290** Evgeny555/iStock/Getty Images Plus; **297** *top* leezsnow/iStock/Getty Images Plus; *center* elinedesignservices/iStock/Getty Images Plus; *bottom* stevezmina1/DigitalVision Vectors/Getty Images; **301** labsas/iStock/Getty images Plus; 172969371/E+/Getty Images; ar-chi/iStock/Getty Images Plus

Chapter 7

303 kali9/iStock/Getty Images Plus; **307** stockcam/iStock/Getty Images Plus; **308** *top* Zolotaosen/iStock/Getty Images Plus; *center* repinanatoly/iStock/Getty Images Plus; *bottom* wavebreakmedia/Shutterstock.com; **310** AYImages/E+/Getty Images; **314** *top* sarahdoow/iStock/Getty Images Plus; *bottom* France68/iStock/Getty Images Plus; **316** Elnur Amikishiyev/Hemera/Getty Images Plus; stuartbur/iStock/Getty Images Plus; **320** Nikada/iStock/Getty Images Plus; **322** *left* Eyematrix/iStock/Getty Images Plus; *right* RimDream/iStock/Getty Images Plus; **325** Remus86/iStock/Getty Images Plus; **326** JoKMedia/iStock/Getty Images Plus; **328** dem10/iStock/Getty Images Plus; Dixi_/iStock/Getty Images Plus; **332** *top* suksao999/iStock/Getty Images Plus; *bottom* Krasyuk/iStock/Getty Images Plus; **334** mgkaya/iStock/Getty Images Plus; **337** AlexStar/iStock/Getty Images Plus; valery121283/iStock/Getty Images Plus; **339** pressureUA/iStock /Getty Images Plus, Rawpixel/iStock /Getty Images Plus; **340** OLEG525/iStock/Getty Images Plus; **342** kali9/E+/Getty Images; **343** GCShutter/E+/Getty Images

Chapter 8

345 FatCamera/E+/Getty Images; **350** *top* fstop123/E+/Getty Images; *bottom 15* Cheng Wei/Shutterstock.com; **356** *top* JodiJacobson/iStock/Getty Images Plus; *bottom;* Emevil/iStock/Getty Images Plus; **358** flas100/iStock/Getty Images Plus; **362** *top* Lonely__/iStock/Getty Images Plus; *bottom* etvulc/iStock/Getty Images Plus; **368** *top* pr2is/iStock/Getty Images Plus; *bottom* RonBailey/iStock/Getty Images Plus; **370** rossandgaffney/iStock/Getty Images Plus; **373** chictype/E+/Getty Images; **374** sharply_done/E+/Getty Images; **380** Quality-illustrations/iStock/Getty Images Plus; **386** Alter_photo/iStock/Getty Images Plus; **388** filo/E+/Getty Images; **392** *left* AndreaAstes/iStock/Getty Images Plus; *right* Lawrence Manning/Corbis/Getty Images; **395** *top* mazzzur/iStock/Getty Images Plus; *bottom* Taalvi/iStock/Getty Images Plus; **396** solarseven/iStock/Getty Images Plus; **397** *top* ana belen prego alvarez/iStock/Getty Images Plus; *bottom* MR1805/iStock/Getty Images Plus; **398** *top* onurdongel/iStock/Getty Images Plus; *bottom* bluestocking/E+/Getty Images; **400** PIKSEL/iStock/Getty Images Plus

Chapter 9

407 georgeclerk/E+/Getty Images; **412** *top* timsa/iStock/Getty Images Plus; *bottom* EHStock/iStock/Getty Images Plus; **414** *top* anna1311/iStock/Getty Images Plus; *bottom* AbbieImages/iStock/Getty Images Plus; **418** *top* cris180/iStock/Getty Images Plus; *bottom* StockPhotosArt/iStock/Getty Images Plus; **420** Scientifics Direct/www.ScientificsOnline.com; **424** *top* Jupiterimages/PHOTOS.com>>/Getty Images Plus; *bottom* mbbirdy/iStock Unreleased / Getty Images Plus; **430** *top* atosan/iStock/Getty Images Plus; *bottom* wickedpix/iStock/Getty Images Plus; **432** Scrambled/iStock/Getty Images Plus; **433** filo/DigitalVision Vectors/Getty Images; **434** eriksvoboda/iStock/Getty Images Plus; **435** fcafotodigital/E+/Getty Images; **436** Elenathewise/iStock/Getty Images Plus; **437** margouillatphotos/iStock/Getty Images Plus; **438** FernandoAH/E+/Getty Images; **439** mm88/iStock/Getty Images Plus

Chapter 10

443 StephanieFrey/iStock/Getty Images Plus; **444** TokenPhoto/E+/Getty Images; **447** berean/iStock/Getty Images Plus; **448** *top* Juanmonino/iStock/Getty Images Plus; *bottom* JamesBrey/E+/Getty Images; **450** *Exercise 14* master1305/iStock/Getty Images Plus; *Exercise 16* nicolamargaret/E+/Getty Images; **453** *right* sumos/iStock/Getty Images Plus; *left* OSTILL/iStock/Getty Images Plus; **454** *top* DmitriyKazitsyn/iStock/Getty Images Plus; *bottom* skegbydave/iStock/Getty Images Plus; **456** *top left* mrPliskin/E+/Getty Images; *top right* kyoshino/E+/Getty Images; *Exercise 21* Nearbirds/iStock/Getty Images Plus, dosrayitas/DigitalVision Vectors/Getty Image; **460** *top* Coprid/iStock/Getty Images Plus; *bottom* banprik/iStock/Getty Images Plus; **462** *left* Donald Miralle/DigitalVision/Getty Images; *right* FatCamera/iStock/Getty Images Plus; **466** nidwlw/iStock/Getty Images Plus **472** *top* ET1972/iStock/Getty Images Plus; *bottom* Imgorthand/E+/Getty Images; **474** *top* GlobalP/iStock/Getty Images Plus; *bottom* Chris Mattison / Alamy Stock Photo; **478** *right* Oakozhan/iStock/Getty Images Plus; *left* FuzzMartin/iStock/Getty Images Plus; **480** esanbanhao/iStock/Getty Images Plus; **483** popovaphoto/iStock/Getty Images Plus; **484** ChrisGorgio/iStock/Getty Images Plus; kbeis/DigitalVision Vectors/Getty Images; **485** ryasick/iStock/Getty Images Plus; **486** *Exercise 5* ryasick/iStock/Getty Images Plus; *Exercise 7 left* Africa Studio/Shutterstock.com; *Exercise 7 right* AlexLMX/iStock/Getty Images Plus; **487** *right* SednevaAnna/iStock/Getty Images Plus; *left* eduardrobert/iStock/Getty Images Plus; **489** DebbiSmirnoff/iStock/Getty Images Plus; **492** *left* phantq/iStock/Getty Images Plus; *right* esseffe/iStock/Getty Images Plus

Chapter 11

493 kali9/E+/Getty Images; **494** *left* PLAINVIEW/E+/Getty Images; *center* cmannphoto/iStock/Getty Images Plus; *right* wwing/iStock/Getty Images Plus; **494b** *From left to right* Ryan McVay/Photodisc; sarahdoow/iStock/Getty Images Plus; SerrNovik/iStock/Getty Images Plus; antpkr/iStock/Getty Images Plus; Canadapanda/iStock/Getty Images Plus; whitewish/iStock/Getty Images Plus; Hemera Technologies/PhotoObjects.net/Getty Images Plus; youngID/DigitalVision Vectors/Getty Images; **498** *top* FatCamera/iStock/Getty Images Plus; *Exercise 18 left* Rvo233/iStock/Getty Images Plus; *Exercise 18 right* Onfokus/E+/Getty Images; *bottom* TonyTaylorStock iStock Editorial/Getty Images Plus; **500** DougBennett/E+/Getty Images; **502** ikitano/iStock/Getty Images Plus; **503** Marakit_Atinat/iStock/Getty Images Plus; **504** PicturePartners/iStock/Getty Images Plus; **510** *left* amattel/iStock/Getty Images Plus; *right* cellistka/iStock/Getty Images Plus; **514** Blade_kostas/iStock/Getty Images Plus; **516** *top* Cloudtail_the_Snow_Leopard/iStock/Getty Images Plus; *bottom* DarthArt/iStock/Getty Images Plus; **518** GlobalP/iStock/Getty Images Plus; **522** Elenathewise/iStock/Getty Images Plus; **524** Photogrape/iStock/Getty Images Plus; **525** sam74100/iStock/Getty Images Plus; **527** Farinosa/iStock/Getty Images Plus; **529** Hreni/iStock/Getty Images Plus; **530** Turnervisual/iStock/Getty Images Plus; **534** JackF/iStock/Getty Images Plus; **539** Madmaxer/iStock/Getty Images Plus; **541** kali9/E+/Getty Images; **542** JonathanCohen/E+/Getty Images; **545** skaljac/Shutterstock.com; **546** jdwfoto/iStock Unreleased/Getty Images Plus; **548** Erdosain/iStock/Getty Images Plus; **549** Rich Vintage/Vetta/Getty Images; **551** mbongorus/iStock/Getty Images Plus; **552** Mastervision/Bi-Silque; **553** scubaluna/iStock/Getty Images Plus; **554** samards/iStock/Getty Images Plus; **558** Colin_Davis/iStock/Getty Images Plus; **559** Krasyuk/iStock/Getty Images Plus; **560** Pixsooz/iStock/Getty Images Plus

Chapter 12

561 dsabo/iStock/Getty Images Plus; **566** *left* finevector/iStock/Getty Images Plus; *right* ensieh1/iStock/Getty Images Plus; **568** iconogenic/iStock/Getty Images Plus; **572** *top* Eyematrix/iStock/Getty Images Plus; *bottom* GrafVishenka/iStock/Getty Images Plus; **574** denisik11/iStock/Getty Images Plus; **578** *Exercise 11* nonnie192/iStock/Getty Images Plus; *Exercise 12* Krimzoya/iStock/Getty Images Plus; **581** ismagilov/iStock/Getty Images Plus; **583** *Exercise 5* marekuliasz/iStock/Getty Images Plus; *bottom* VvoeVale/iStock/Getty Images Plus; **584** kpalimski/iStock/Getty Images Plus; **587** stocknshares/E+/Getty Images, paci77/E+/Getty Images; **590** elinedesignservices/iStock/Getty Images Plus

Chapter 13

591 JaysonPhotography/iStock/Getty Images Plus; **610** elinedesignservices/iStock/Getty Images Plus; **614** *top* Vitalliy/iStock/Getty Images Plus; *center* MicrovOne/iStock/Getty Images Plus; *bottom* szefei/iStock/Getty Images Plus; **616** Orla/iStock/Getty Images Plus; **620** *top* AnatolyM/iStock/Getty Images Plus; *center* marimo_3d/iStock/Getty Images Plus; *bottom* olgna/iStock/Getty Images Plus; **622** jonathansloane/E+/Getty Images, OLEKSANDR PEREPELYTSIA/iStock/Getty Images Plus; **634** iZonda/iStock/Getty Images Plus; **638** pialhovik/iStock/Getty Images Plus

Chapter 14

647 suebee65/iStock/Getty Images Plus; **655** adekvat/iStock/Getty Images Plus; VectorPocket/iStock/Getty Images Plus; **664** marekuliasz/iStock/Getty Images Plus; **665** *Exercise 4* Carol_Anne/iStock/Getty Images Plus; *Exercise 6* StockImages_AT/iStock/Getty Images Plus; **669** *Exercise 9* lucielang/iStock/Getty Images Plus; *Exercise 10* blue64/E+/Getty Images; *Exercise 11* Marje4/E+/Getty Images; **670** photovideostock/E+/Getty Images; **671** *Exercise 7* SlidePix/iStock/Getty Images Plus; *Exercise 8* ibooo7/iStock/Getty Images Plus; *Exercise 6* Casey Botticello/iStock/Getty Images Plus; *Exercise 5* stevezmina1/DigitalVision Vectors/Getty Images; **677** antpkr/iStock/Getty Images Plus; **681** egal/iStock/Getty Images Plus; **687** Vladimir/iStock/Getty Images Plus; **688** *top* snowpeace19/iStock/Getty Images Plus; *bottom* Vladimir/iStock/Getty Images Plus

Cartoon Illustrations: MoreFrames Animation
Design Elements: oksanika/Shutterstock.com; icolourful/Shutterstock.com; Valdis Torms